NAMES OF PLACES
Essays in Toponymy

by

Leonard R. N. Ashley

ISBN: 0-7596-9098-7 (e-book)
ISBN: 0-7596-9099-5 (Paperback)

This book is printed on acid free paper.

1st Books - rev. 3/17/03

In real life, unlike in Shakespeare, the sweetness of the rose depends upon the name it bears. Things are not only what they are. They are, in a very important respect, what they seem to be.

–Hubert Horatio Humphrey, Speech, 26 March, 1966

In Memoriam

George R. Stewart

whose *Names on the Land* **began a new era**
in the American study of placenames

TABLE OF CONTENT

PREFACE

I get to say something about my book here. I begin with mentioning V. S. Naipaul's *Letters between a Father and His Son.* There the fictional Mr. Biswas starts out as a sign painter, becomes a newspaperman, and has ambitions to be a serious writer. He writes off to the Ideal School of Journalism in London. Its address in the Edgeware Road is intended to alert you to the unglamorous status of this correspondence school. The school advises him to write about "the Romance of Place-Names". It advises "your vicar is likely to prove a mine of colourful information". Books such as Frank K. Gallant's *A Place Called Peculiar* (1997) and uncounted others, plus newspaper columns, make this clear.

You hold in your hand evidence of my fascination with "the Romance of Place-Names" and with the colorful information they preserve for us about many things, from the intentions of explorers or the enthusiasms of namers of new features to the hopes of settlers to the evocative and even sentimental use of placenames in literature. Placenames occur in fact and fiction and even tell us of ancient trade routes and of settlement patterns. They enshrine history. They have inspired adventure, sparked imaginative literature, and sent people off on adventures to the far corners of the earth.

Written for various audiences over a period of years, my placename essays varied in intent, style, and probably in usefulness to the reader. I believe, however, that each one revised to appear here has something in it worth saving, even something to inspire you with "the Romance of Place-Names." Whereas most placename scholars specialize in the names of a single settlement, a county or township, a state, or a country, or the names of natural features and such, I speak of Canada, of Mexico, of the United States, of New York; Connecticut, Vermont, Kansas and Iowa, of California, of English names, French names, Spanish names, of Amerindian names, of names of England, Cornwall, and Wales. I treat neighborhood names in New York City and names of New Orleans' French Quarter in terms of local history. I speak of house names and slang names and names in verse and catch phrases, and much more. You do not have all that I can say about placenames but you do have here examples of most of the sub-fields of placename study in which I am interested, from folklore and fun to sociodynamics. I hope you will be interested in them, as I am.

There may be some repetition still in evidence, because these articles were conceived for different audiences at different times, but making a good point more than once is no crime. After all, it has been said that professors never say anything just once—especially those who are anxious for students to retain information presented to them—and I am a professor still, though an *emeritus* one, who does not have to worry about preparing candidates for examinations and can communicate for the pleasure of readers. I have written here not academic lectures but, I hope, communicate in a conversational style. There can be no class discussions, though I would be pleased to think that as they read my readers will pause to turn over in their minds the points I bring out and to connect my facts and opinions with their own experience and ideas. I have not hesitated to be personal; you be personal, too. Conduct your own dialogue with the author as you read.

I leave the matters of least interest, such as terms for geographical features and etymologies, for others to write about elsewhere. These are subjects that are of lesser concern to non-specialists, important as these subjects are to geographers and linguists. I spare you the scholars' debate over the word I render always as *placename*, and, tempted though I am to tell you how we got some of our English generics from other languages, or how the British used to mock us for words such as *bluff*, I generally steer clear of terms of toponymy (the study of geographical names). I do sneak in a few such terms (and explain them for you in ordinary language). Such technical terms are basically, however, for linguists and geographers and such. Actually, I wish more geographers were interested in names the way I look at placenames, but perhaps even geographers will pick up this book.

As always, I have to defend myself in name study for the *lists* to which you will be subjected. I am of the same mind as David Hume. He wrote in *Of Simplicity and Refinement of Writing* that "no criticism can be instructive which descends not to particulars and is not full of examples and illustrations." I attempt to keep my writing here simple, even refined, entertaining enough for the general reader and authoritative enough for the specialist, and to give lots of examples. I trust you will find patterns in the particulars, mind in the minutiae.

Some of the work here, as I said above, is published for the first time. The essays that have previously been published have been entirely rewritten for this volume; the alterations have been made the better to appeal to the general reader. The editors of these pieces that appeared in scholarly journals, especially Prof. Kelsie B. Harder and Prof. Conrad Rothrauf and Prof. Edward Callary, all over the years editors of *Names*, and Prof. Ronald L. Baker of *Midwestern Folkore*, are not responsible for any errors that may have slipped into my revisions and expansions. Specialists might have welcomed elaborate footnoting of everything or an index larger than the text, but I give you what I think you may need as guides to further reading. I supply what you might possibly be interested in looking up. But I do not clutter my text, nor can I undertake to provide a complete index. (Those lists make that impractical!) If you will look at the Table of Contents you will know where to look for what you want. If you are a scholar seeking one particular name (such as your own!), then you must read the article on the subject—which is no bad thing.

For all the various approaches to placename study that I have presented, I omitted as not very useful in this collection certain other topics, as I have said.

One, for instance, is the study of placenames in wine (where *Napa Valley,* for instance, does not mean that all the wine in the bottle comes from there, any more than that Philadelphia Cream Cheese comes from Philadelphia or New York cut steak must come from New York). I am something of an expert on tradenames and product naming, an art that often involves not just placing a product but relating to placenames, but I do not go into that here. I cannot undertake to cover all the ways placenames enter our lives. Placenames are used in naming not only persons but even racehorses and commercial products. I hope only to have interested the reader in a topic which, in one way or another, has engaged some of the best scholars in America.

Once, on one of the two occasions when I was president of The American Name Society (1979, 1987), I had the honor of introducing at a banquet of the society the guest of honor, an eminent scholar to whom I dedicate this collection, Prof. George R. Stewart. Or, rather, I was scheduled to have that honor, but the service at the restaurant in San Francisco was glacially slow. Prof. Stewart was old and he tired and had to leave. There were no remarks made by him and no presidential address delivered by me. Later I published one. I made it an appreciation of the career of Prof. Stewart, dean of American toponymists. Now I offer to his memory this collection of placename studies he was instrumental in inspiring. He was a hero of mine in scholarship and, I am sure, of many other name scholars both in America and abroad, where placename scholarship has a longer history but few writers who could make the subject as appealing as he did.

I make some reference to placenames in satire and in other kinds of literature, in popular culture, etc., in other books. The book on satire, which I call *Art Attack,* has had to be the briefest of the lot: "There is no possibility," asserted Lady Sneerwell, "of being witty without a little ill nature"—and a little ill nature goes a long, long way. A really big book of it would be depressing. The books on names in literature and names in popular culture are much larger. Look them up if you are interested in names in those areas.

Placenames, especially derogatory nicknames for places, can exhibit ill nature (and wit) but there are better things that placenames can do. We can regard placenames as communicating the saddest memories of bloody battles or we can play with them. We can even work in the same spirit, say, that informed the camp *Ballets Trocadero de Monte Carlo,* wherein burlesque went for the jugular of Mr. B, the master choreographer, in the hilarious *Go for Barocco,* with what dance critic Tobi Tobias in 1983 called parody of "ultra-neoclassical Balanchine (the strangulating daisy chains...)". As we study names of any kind, placenames included, we must keep our sense of humor as well as our sense of history. I have therefore attempted to present in this collection of essays whatever I think the general reader may find informative and I have tried to be entertaining without becoming too flip. What I have to say here is always couched in a tone that is deliberately light. I hope you do not find it excessively light, because even

xi

Balanchine's career warns us of the dangers of crossing the line between a "fine excess" and "singularity" and descending into the unconsciously hilarious or the utterly ridiculous. In presenting loads of information here I want to avoid the pedantic. Mr. B created 425 choreographies and today only 75 are ever staged, which has reminded me to be highly selective in presenting representative examples of the work in placenames that I have done over the decades. I hope I have chosen well and offer a useful variety. The study of names is more than placenames, though placenames often came first in the work of researchers. I hope you may go beyond placenames in time and look into the ways of personal naming (revelatory of individual and societal preferences and penchants) and even into such amusing, if less important, matters as the use of names in name-calling and in poetry and satire. There is much accomplished by even the slightest jibe as this:

My name is George Nathaniel Curzon.

I am a most superior person.

That is about enough for now. On to the essays. I hope you will enjoy them—and not find them too long. I have had no such discipline as Pres. Millard Fillmore showed when he wrote his autobiography (in 15 pages). The literary essay in journals is now almost defunct. In this book I go on as long as I think there is more you need to or will like to know. I trust you will come to share my enthusiasm for placenames. You can always stop and rest—ideally, stop and think—when reading.

You might also think of how placenames have led to words such as a*ngora, baloney, calico, dumdum, English, frankfurter, ghetto, hack, italics, jodpurs, Kentish fire, limerick, magnesia, naugahyde, ottoman, pandemonium, quonset, rugby, serendipity, tariff, utopia, vaudeville, worsted, xanadu, yorker* and *Zion.* Placenames are everywhere!

I address American, Canadian, and Mexican placenames here especially but in every choice I have kept in mind the need of illustrative examples; one cannot cover all placenames of even one country in one book, but one can use various kinds of placename approaches to underline matters all over the world. There are many books on the US (as from George R. Stewart), Canada (as from Alan Rayburn), and Mexico already in print. The Mexican ones include the numerous guidebooks (Lonely Planet, Eyewitness, Let's Go, People's Guide, etc.) and there are specialist books (such as David Stuart & Stephen Houston's *Classic Maya Place Names,* 1994), but no book attempts as much as I do with the names. Many older books, such as *Indian Place-Names in Mexico and Central America* (1964) are no longer available—and the general reader wants wide scope.

The study of placenames is older if perhaps not quite as revealing of man the naming animal as the study of trends in personal names and the inventions in fiction, but we must not, because it has been called scientific where other onomastic science has not, allow placenames be taken *overly* seriously.

Geography can be rather dull, but placenames, studied in connection with the psychology of ordinary people and the sensitivity of the poets, never. .

And now I am pleased to turn over the rest of this introductory piece to the most impressive placename expert I have ever had the good fortune to know: Prof. Kelsie B. Harder. Most of the rest of the Preface is by him (and I thank him for the kind words which I trust will gain me your confidence so that I can show you what I find in placenames). The preface to my *Names in Popular Culture*, by Arthur Berliner, was more "autobiographical" than the preface here (but Mr. Berliner's personal love of names was worth stressing, and naturally I could not alter it anyway). Prof. Harder writes less of himself, but he, too, has had a very active life in the study of names. After his introductory remarks I shall put in a few acknowledgements, for a book such as this owes a lot to a lot of people. Now, Prof. Harder:

*

The study of placenames as clues to ancient languages both living and dead was an early interest of philologists. That gave to onomastics (the study of names in general) the reputation of a science, especially after the German philologists of the nineteenth century published elaborately and extensively on toponymy (placenames). By the end of that century, the United States government created the United States Board on Geographical Names. It still functions under the Geological Survey in the Department of the Interior to regularize our US placenames.

The present book by Leonard R. N. Ashley illustrates the interest that scholars have had in matters of both government and non-government concern. Government wants to name all geographical features and inhabited places with official names, to establish the names of post offices, and so on, but scholars are also interested in names in terms of linguistics and literature and folklore and culture in general. Ashley writes of all these kinds of interests.

He writes of the earliest American placenames and the names that replaced the aboriginal ones as the European explorers arrived and of the names the new settlers gave. He writes of more modern placenames, official and unofficial, and of the place of placenames in prose and poetry and in everyday life. He leaves aside the debates over whether it should be place name, place-name, or placename, or Cape Canaveral or Cape Kennedy, Frenchman's Creek or Frenchmans Creek, Nigger Creek or something else. What he wants to do is to be sound enough for the scholars but to address the general reader who can be interested in the British names in Connecticut or the house names in South Carolina, the evocative names in verse, the colorful names in slang. He wants to emphasize the importance of placenames in all of our lives. He even discusses the placenames of Mexico (in terms of the clash of cultures), the Spanish names of California (with reference to how they sometimes got bungled), the ancient names of Turkey (and how and why the Turks changed them), the placenames of Cornwall (in a dead language which the Cornish have been for some time trying to revive), names in humor, placenames in almost any way you can think of. He discusses the origins of placenames and their sometimes attractive stories and he is unfailingly entertaining as well as full of facts. There is a great deal of fun as well as fact in his *Names of Places.*

This will give the book appeal for the general reader. Placenames already have a wide appeal to geographers, literary critics, historians of high culture and of popular culture, sociologists, psychologists, lexicographers, linguists, and many other specialists. This book will be of interest to politicians concerned with language problems and policies in California and Florida, and to many others. Ashley's knowledge of names is broad and deep. He has a great ability to transcend the rather artificial boundaries that scholars have erected around their academic disciplines. He makes incisive interdisciplinary and cross-cultural comments. He sees the whole multicultural picture and how the various parts relate to each other. This guarantees that his book will be authoritative enough for any specialist and at the same time give a reliable overview and be readable by anyone who picks it up.

As with any book by Ashley—and he is the author of many—the combination of scholarship and style will capture your attention and reward your reading. Dipping into the book anywhere, a reader will find something intriguing and will be encouraged to go on and read the whole book for entertainment and enlightenment. Those who begin by sampling will stay to enjoy a book unique in its scope but also in its vigor and verve.

I once wrote: "A study of names is a study of humans in all their humanness, uniqueness, and physical, intellectual, or emotional action." I also wrote, when Ashley finished his book *What's in a Name?*:

> Dr. Ashley is indeed the foremost authority in the study of names. His *What's in a Name?* reflects the depth and width of his knowledge and also his ability to write in a cheerful and scholarly style about a subject that affects us all. We know much more about the way we identify ourselves and other persons and objects now that we have Ashley's survey before us.

Here is *Names of Places.* It consists of a lot of brand new material as well as total revisions of articles which Ashley has published over a long career as student of names. Everything is very readable by both expert and general reader. I reiterate my praise of Ashley and add that after reading these articles of his in *Names in Place* anyone will know a great deal more about the important subject of placenames.

Kelsie B. Harder, Ph.D.
Distinguished Professor, *Emeritus*
The State University College at Potsdam, New York

*

First in acknowledgments, my thanks to Prof. Harder and to the American Name Society in which we have both served. The essays collected here, excepting a few created especially for this book, were first published in various places. Versions appeared in *Names* (the journal of the American Name Society); in journals of the regional associations of the American Name Society such as *Connecticut Onomastic Review* of the Connecticut Place Name Symposium at Eastern Connecticut State University, and *Names, Northeast: Adirondack Names* of the Northeast Regional Names Institute, the Center for Adirondack Studies of North Country Community College; in *Midwestern Folklore* (the journal of the Hoosier Folklore Society); in **Onomastica Canadiana** (the journal of the Canadian Society for the Study of Names/*Société canadienne pour l'étude des noms*); in **450 Ans de noms de lieux français en Amérique du nord** (Papers of the first International Congress on French Toponymy of North America, 1964); or they were delivered at onomastic meetings of the American Name Society or the International Congress of Onomastic Sciences and now first published. I am grateful to the editors and the members of these organizations, and also to the *Omni Gazetteer of the United States* and other reference books for which I have been invited to write on placename topics, and to Genealogical Publishers (Baltimore, MD) who published my general survey of names, *What's in a Name?*, in both original and revised editions. I have tried not to repeat information on placenames that occurs in *What's in a Name?* As a general survey it does something to integrate placenames with other kinds of names, providing a larger context.

There are so many interesting uses of placenames, from names of actual places to names such as the fictional theme park called Christland in George Saunders' satires and the inventive names of the Harry Potter stories, that I cannot by any means undertake to cover all aspects. I do strive here to approach the study of placenames from a number of different angles. I believe the reader will not find placenames treated in so many ways in any other book, not even in onomastic encyclopedias (to which I have contributed).

One of the pleasures of placename study for me is to have had the opportunity to go outside my own discipline of literature and linguistics and to meet scholars in a number of other humanities and sciences. To list all the distinguished placename scholars I have been privileged to know in the American Name Society over the years is impossible, but I must mention just a few in connection with placename study: Prof. George R. Stewart, Prof. Allen Walker Read, Prof. Kelsie B. Harder, Prof. André Lapierre of Ontario, Lewis L. McArthur of Oregon (in the distinguished tradition of his father, Lewis A. McArthur), Prof. W. H. F. Nicolaisen of Aberdeen, Prof. William Bright, Prof. Wilbur Zelinsky, Dr. Donald Orth and Dr. Roger Payne of the United States

Board on Geographical Names, Pierre L. Sales the great expert on African placenames, Robert M. Rennick of Kentucky, the former secretary of the Canadian secretariat for names Alan J. Rayburn, and other Canadian authorities, as well as Dr. Peter Raper in South Africa, Ola J. Holten in Sweden, Prof. Ernst Eichler in Germany and Leslie A. Dunkling in Britain. There are many others I have not space to mention. Each has contributed immensely to the study of placenames and each has been an inspiration to myself and to everyone who loves names and has brought to the scholars and general public information on the value of the study.

Leonard R. N. Ashley

AMERINDIAN PLACENAMES OF MASSACHUSETTS

**Not that the Red Indian will ever possess
the broad lands of America. At least I
presume not. But his ghost will.**

—D. H. Lawrence, *Studies in Classic American
Literature*

It seems fitting to begin with the Amerindian. I prefer that term to Red Indian
or Indian or even to the now popular Native American. (All persons of whatever
race born in the United States are native Americans, in my estimation.) I start
with Massachusetts, *massa-ad-chu-es-et*, Algonkian (or Algonquian, if you like)
for "at the big hill." The reference is to a feature of the Blue Hills near Boston—
and *Boston* gives you a clue to what was going to be the fate of the names the
Pilgrim Fathers encountered after they landed on what they soon called Plymouth
Rock. Typically, the Winthrops further cleared away Poquannock (Cleared Land)
and gave the place the name of their estate back in England, Groton. This was
more than nostalgia; it was asserting dominion, claiming.

Of the approximately 800 Amerindian names on the official maps of
Massachusetts over the centuries, many have no adequate explanation, whether
they are in Algonkian, Delaware, Ojibway, or in some other aboriginal language.
John C. Hutten's classic *The Indian Place Names of New England* (1962) leaves
a great many names unexplained, and no wonder: these names have been so
corrupted in some cases that it is difficult or impossible to know what language
they were in, in the first place, let alone how to translate them.

One thing is immediately obvious: the white man was determined to get a
foothold and then an empire, to put his mark on everything he could grab, and to
a striking extent only the geographical features that the white man could not take
over did he leave with their aboriginal names. So French and Dutch and English
and other European names were put on the land. The old names were largely
scrapped, so that when we find one, such as Agwam, we may not know what to
think. Whether Agwam means a resort for fish of passage or ground overflowed
with water or a place where fish were dried, who knows? However, the
Kennedys (with Hyannisport and that infamous bridge), and many others, have
made the Amerindian placenames of Massachusetts familiar to us all, as familiar
as Boston and Cambridge. What is not so commonly known is what the non-
English names mean, or what the native name cover in the area looked like in the
past or looks like now.

1

Hyannis came from the lands of Iyanough or Quyanough or Hianna or Yanno—early spelling was erratic. These Puritans knew the biblical names and the names of places they themselves came from. They were not so conversant with the names they came upon among the "savages," whom they generally considered to be devils, the spawn of Satan. Our friend Yanno was a *sachem* (chief) whom the Puritans encountered in 1621. Chappaquiddick means "separated island," which explains that bridge.

First let us recall some of the people who, though they would never have memorialized themselves in placenames—considering that they just passed through this earthly realm and did not own it—are remembered in placenames. I shall cite just a few. Abrams Creek and Abrams Point are named for Abram Quarry (d. 1854), the last Amerindian who lived there. Alum Pond is named for Allumps, *sachem* of the Quinebaug—unless it is named for a dog. (The pond is also given the name of a tribe, Pookookapoug, variously spelled.) *Sachem* and such names recall a person by title but not by name. Quanapowitt takes its name from the brother of the *sachem* whose land was purchased for Wakefield (1641); the colonists called him Runnymarsh, maybe recalling Runnymead or Romney Marsh in England. Camp Squanto is from Squantum, a chief who befriended the Pilgrims. Chickatawbut Hill recalls a chief whose name we translated as House Afire. Miscoe is from George Miscoe, whose Amerindian name meant Pebbles.

Some other personal names we replaced with Christian names and surnames or even nicknames: think of King Philip's War. "King Philip" has a lookout named for him now, but his name was Metacom, Pometacom, maybe Metacomet, if indeed that was not a placename used as a kind of title. All we are really sure of is that he died in 1676 and at that time Amerindian tribal life in southern New England pretty much came to a halt. After that the erasing of Amerindian names was even easier.

John Konkapot (1774) was a *sachem* of the Mahicans (or however you want to spell it) and has a brook and a river named for him. Sassaquin may be Tispaquin (Black Sachem). Whites knew Spotsa as Daniel Spotsor (says Godfrey, 1882), Wauwinet of Nantucket (also noted by Godfrey) is recalled. So was Wampatuck (who has a hill named for him, whoever he was). There was some Waban (who has a hill and other features to his credit). The US Board on Geographical Names has him down as East Wing; his name means East Wind. Then there is *Uncas*, but that's a title, not a name.

Keyup Brook is said to have been "named for an Indian," but I have no more information. Hobomuck seems to come from either the Wamesit evil spirit or a chief who died in the seventeenth century (from which time we still have some placenames such as Monohasset and Nashomis and—still unresolved—Narragansett). Wamesit had a name meaning Devil. Was that given by his people, or by enemies?

Often Amerindian names we use were given by enemies or strangers to the tribes. The French named the Nez Percé, the Huron, the Iroquois, the Sioux, etc. The English named the Blackfeet, the Creek, the so-called Civilized Tribes, etc. The Spaniards named the Pueblos and the Zuñi (or you can omit the accent) and called the big river Río Grande, but the Amerindians called it Pajo, Paslapane, Posoge, and by other names. Each Amerindian group in its own language called itself something like The People or The Men, never by the names the strangers or enemies used (the Zuñi called their enemies simply Apache, which means "enemy"). The Hopi called themselves Hopi, meaning Peaceful Tribe. Some Amerindians were nomadic and some settled, even arranging for the settlements sometimes to be governed for six months of the year by one group, six months by another (whence Winter People and Summer People). The "oldest city" in what is now the US is not what you think! It is Old Oraibi on a mesa in Arizona: the Hopis have lived there for the last 800 or 900 years.

No place in Massachusetts is as old as the pueblos of the Southwest, and maybe not as old as the great mounds of the pre-historic Middle West, but even with fairly modern sites named for families, Pegan and Pimn(e)ys Point and such, sometimes it is impossible to say whether these were white or red people. Nason (1874) alleges that Wampum was "named for an Indian family," but most people would recognize that this was the word for the equivalent of money, which came as "black string" and "white string," the latter being the more valuable. It served the way gold does as a store of value.

An "Indian" name may be as misleading as Adam and as complicated as the famous non-personal (maybe somewhat faked) name of the lake Chaubunagungamaug, said to have been a boundary: "you fish on your side, I fish on my side, nobody fishes in the middle."

We appear to have given up on Amerindian names to a great extent. Our red men (which is where we got *Oklahoma*) have to try to preserve as much of their culture as they can, while white men either squirrel away "Indian relics" in museums or plough them under and forget them. Before the Armenians and the Jews there were genocide attempts, more than we usually think of, more than we like to think about.

It is only fair to say that while Massachusetts must be called pioneering in the misunderstanding of the redmen, and their languages, the Commonwealth is not alone in mishandling the legacy. Maine (for instance) even ravaged French (*Ciel Trappe* to Seal Trap, D'Orvilles as Devil's Head, Burnt Coat Island is from the French for "burnt coast," Lumadoo from *L'Homme de Dieu*, Socks from Jacques). Not surprisingly, Maine gave local Abnaki names a beating (Quahog to Hog, Quaquajo "boundary mountain" to Quaggy Joe, etc.). The Abnaki for Island Rocks first became Ragged Ass in Maine, was cleaned up to Raggertask, and now is just Ragged Island. In Maine, locals (who dropped the *r* in English's Larkin to make Lakin, Marsh to make Mash, etc.) changed Pongookwahcock

3

"place of woodpeckers" to Haymock. They likewise changed Aboljackarnegassic "bare of trees" to Abol Mountain. On the other hand, Maine created some "Injun" names: Mackamp (from Mac's Camp), Pocomoonshine, etc. The same sort of thing could be found by anyone who wants to look closely at the placenames of any state in the Union. Massachussetts and Maine are not isolated cases.

The relations (or history) of the early colonists in Massachusetts are better than the early records of some other states. The Puritans give us some native names, but in the whole of our history we have tended to translate Quanah to Parker and call a man whose Amerindian name was the equivalent of Red Deer, Crispus Attucks. Attucks was the first man to fall in American rebellion against Britain. Attucks is a man now claimed to be Negro rather than Amerindian. Amerindian origin has been largely erased in the case of Attucks and is hidden in such names in our larger history as those of Joseph Brant of the Mohawks, William McIntosh of the Lower Creeks, William Weatherford (Red Eagle of the Creeks), George A. Thomas (*royaner* or "fire keeper" of the Onondagas), Robert Smallboy (Cree), George Nelson (Powhattan Confederation), Captain Jacob (Delaware), Captain Jack (Kintapuash of the Modocs). Our most famous Indians are often just Black Hawk, Red Cloud of the Lakota, Crowfoot (son of Sitting Bull), and Roman Nose (who prophesied his own death in 1868). Those names sound typically "Injun" to Americans. In Canada, where the First Nations are more honored and where the descendants of the aborigines have been given a sort of sovereignty over the huge area of Nunavut, Amerindian names have hung on better, especially in the less inhabited areas of the frozen north. Almost half of the more than 300,000 Canadian-Amerindians speak one of about 50 a native language at home. Canada has 15 or 16 Amerindian languages spoken also in the US today and more than 20 spoken only in Canada. These and native languages now dead produced many placenames. Here are a dozen of the many Amerindian placenames in Canada: Athabasca, Chicoutimi, Kamloops, Kapuskaising, Medicine Hat, Nipigon, Ottawa, Rimouski, Slave, Toronto, Ungava, and Winnipegosis. Some such names appear also in the US (such as Ontario). Probably the most famous Amerindian name of Canada was that of a half-breed, Louis Riél, who led a nineteenth-century rebellion. For Amerindian placenames see excellent books by Virgil Vogel and William Bright (US) and Alan Rayburn (Canada). Throughout my book, which will have no bilbliography at the back, I give you enough information (author's name, or title, sometimes both) to get you started on a library or on-line search if you are interested.

Here are some names of famous Amerindians: Lone Wolf of the Kiowa, American Horse and Little Big Man of the Oglala, Little Crow of the Santee, Red Horn of the Piegan, Red Jacket of the Seneca, Standing Bear of the Ponca, Lean Bear and Two Moons and Dull Knife of the Cheyenne, Dragging Canoe of the Cherokee, Little Turtle of the Miami, and Handsome Lake (Gan-Yo-Die-Yo of the Seneca). We make fun of such names in joke names such as Rain in the Face and Running Water (with three sons: Hot, Cold, and Luke) and silly and syllabified names. But we find some romance in the names as well. A white man of romantic temper passed himself off as Grey Wolf.

In Spanish-speaking areas, Amerindians might be called Geromimo or Vitorio (after baptism) or Mangas Coloradas. In English-speaking areas, there was (as mentioned) King Philip of the Wampanoag and an associate called Alderman who was a traitor. There was also Chief Joseph of the Nez Percé, Sagamore John of the Nipmuck, Pope of the Tewas, Hendrick of the Mohawks, Cornstalk of the Shawnees, Willie Boy of the Piute, Old Charlie (Tsali of the Cheyenne), Jumper of the Seminoles, Blackfish of the Shawnee, Chief Seattle…. When you see a name such as Yokum, think not about Mammy Yokum in *L'il Abner* but of *Joachim.* Some Amerindian of that adopted name may account for Massachusetts' Yokum. Not all the names I cite here are from Massachusetts, of course.

All these men fought with or against the white man and all hoped to be able somehow to retain their traditional hunting grounds and sacred lands in the face of European incursion and expansion. The warring Delawares were promised that they could form the fourteenth state. Actually, it was not until 1937 that the US government recognized them as a tribe (if not a nation). It was only in the twentieth century that Amerindians were given US citizenship. The names that the Amerindians left on the land have sometimes outlived the peoples who gave them. They may be all that is living of languages whose last native speakers are long gone.

Most of the historical personal names of Massachusetts are in the history books and most of the Amerindian placenames of the Massachusetts area are typical descriptors and refer to fishing places, mountains, rivers, parallel features, and the like; but we do find an occasional Attitash (Huckleberry), Hackmetack (Tamarack, tree), Mahkeenac and Camp Mah-Kee-Nac (*michimackinac* = "large turtle"), Ashumet (spring), and Cataumet (a tribal name). There are questions about whether Large Turtle or the like might be a personal name put on the land by some white men and there are some names that look like English but undoubtedly are simply corruptions (Horseneck is Hausmak, Hummock is Nanunhumak, Teaticket is *titicut* "big river", and Choate may be Coatue). Or they may look English and are not (Wakeby is "pond bends around").

We always see Amerindian names with variant spellings. Masscuppic or Massuppick or what? Maybe that does not seem important, but Assonet was Assonate in 1656—which could be significant. Assawomsett Pond has a name that refers to stone, either a white stone or a stone in the middle, but who knows which? Charnock Hill, Caruth Brook, and some other names we are assured are Amerindian may make us wish to doubt the experts. Anbencotants Island is too far off the mark for even experts to guess at what it was originally called. Is

Aberjona (for a pond and a river) a reference to cattails or to enemies? Cape Higgon was once *cappigon*, Algonkian for "enclosed." Could Little Asnebumskit Hill be *mushamugget* "at the great fishing-place"?

When we don't know the languages with which we are dealing we can create placenames such as Sahara Desert, Mount Fujiyama, and, in Massachusetts, Manwhaug Plain. When the Amerindians were calling it *manwhauge* it was to them just "the plain," not what we might technically call a placename at all. Sometimes the Amerindians definitely avoided giving direct names; the Inuit still call the musk ox "the bearded one". (That is what I heard Cubans in Havana calling Dr. Castro.) Amerindian "names" then were picked up as our placenames. Sample examples when we do know the language (more or less): Mashpee or Massapoag (Large Pond), Mattapan ("resting place," usually on a portage), Mattawa ("the rivers join"), Merrimack ("sound of the falls" or maybe "sturgeon"), Miacomet ("at the meeting place"), Minnechoag ("berry land"), Monatiquot (Lookout), Mushquashcut (Red Cedars), Monponsett ("at the deep pond" or "many nets" or "many ponds" or "ponds with short connecting channel"). From another part of the alphabet, for variety, I offer these: Sagamore (a kind of *sachem*), Sasquatucket ("at the mouth of the tidal water"), Sasquitch ("plenty of clams"), Saugus (""extended" or "small outlet"), Shumatuscacant ("spring meadow"), Shawmee ("neck of land"), Skug ("black river"), Squannacook ("salmon-fishing place"), Squibnocket ("sliding" or "steep slope"), and so on. Some are hard to say (Scituate, "nearly-closed estuary") and some have a romantic sound (Housatonic, "beyond the mountain", Winnecunnet, "boundary" or "beautiful place of pine trees," Willimansett, from *wollamon* = "red ochre") or amusing (Tuckernuck, "loaf of bread", or Touisett, "at or about the old fields").

Some Amerindian names I may or may not spell as you know them. The US Board on Geographical Names is particular about how any US placename should be spelled—bureaucrats want things settled—but neither the general public nor the occasional expert always goes along with them. I shall attempt to spell Amerindian names the best way I can and usually this will be the same way the USBGN spells them. However, my piece on California (coming up later) will suggest to you that when it comes to mistakes the USBGN is not ready to correct the official names unless and until there is pressure from the public to do so. When and if that pressure comes, they can even change names and scrap history or ratify error. With Amerindian names and with all sorts of placenames, in fact, we are often back in the old days when everyone could spell "according to his own conscience."

We are told by the USBGN that not just Teaticket and Wakeby are Amerindian in origin but that Amerindian also are Moose Brook, Mugget Hill, Mystic, Nunket's Pond, Onset Bay and Onset Island, Pasque Island, Petee Pond, Seapit River, Wyer's Pond, and (incredibly, since no evidence is offered)

Somerset. One can with some difficulty see Mugget Hill related to *mashamugget*, Onset to *ontset*, Mystic to the Amerindian for "large tidal river," but one wonders why such names as Wabash and Winona, known to non-Commonwealth sources, are not called Amerindian by the US Board on Geographical Names in MA. The fact is that one cannot get from them—or anyone—a list of "all the Amerindian names of Massachusetts" which can be said to be completely reliable. The whole placename picture of the US, even the corpus of the official names that have appeared on maps and is stored in a vast computer system, is a vast work in progress. Considerable advances have been made over the last century by USBGN, particularly since computers came into play. But there is a very long way to go.

Year by year, the Amerindian experts grow fewer. Virgil Vogel and others I knew have passed on. The early missionaries took a great interest in the native languages. They had to, to convert the natives. The missionaries created grammars and dictionaries, having first to create a writing system for the unwritten languages. The modern linguists take far less interest. They seldom study the old books. Moreover, experts are jealous of each other, so Amerindian scholars bicker and some native speakers of dying languages even refuse to speak to each other!

Here is what Massachusetts has: There are many interesting Amerindian names, largely hydronyms (water names). The placenames give one a fairly good idea of the lay of the land and recall many of the comparatively small number of natives known to history. Here is what Massachusetts does not have: Explantions for most of the Amerindian names, adequate, documented, and correct. Many placenames no one has even tried to translate, and many who have tried have come up with answers that look very dubious. Considering that Unquity Brook– the same as Unkety Brook— involves one in *Oukote, Uncataquisset, Unquityquisset*, and worse, one can see their point.

The most famous Massachusetts name (Boston) is not Amerindian, of course, and neither is the famous Lexington. The same year that "the shot heard round the world" was fired at Lexington, Massachusetts (1775), the placename appeared in Tennessee. Then it appeared in Missouri, Arkansas, Texas, New York, Pennsylvania, Ohio, Indiana, Illinois, Michigan, Iowa, and, as Prof. Allen Walker Read says, "many others until it reached the Pacific Coast in Oregon." No Massachusetts name of aboriginal origin could compete with that, not even the famous Nantucket (the sole Amerindian county name in the state).

There is no possibility that we shall (as Stephen Vincent Benét put it in "The Devil and Daniel Webster") "give the country back to the Indians." We shall probably never honor the treaties long since made with them. We really ought, however, to regard as our inheritance as well as theirs whatever scraps of Amerindian culture—including the placenames—we can salvage. They are, as Benét puts it in another of his works, where he speaks or books and not names, a part of man's memory and his aspiration, The link between his present and his past, the tools he builds with. We turn now to another state with an Amerindian name, Connecticut. Connecticut is a place where the Amerindian names have almost completely been wiped off the map, except for rivers and other features that are not white man's real estate.

Across the US you will find Amerindian names. Mohican—and variants such as Mahican and Mohegan also are to be found—is on the map in Alaska and New Jersey, on Mohican School in Louisiana, in Maryland there is a Mohican Hills, in Michigan a Mohican Lake, in Montana a Mohican Creek, in New York a Camp Mohican, a Mohican Canyon, a Mohican Island, two Mohican Lakes (one a settlement, one water). In North Carolina there's a Mohican Trail, in Ohio a Mohican River, a Mohican Church, a Mohicanville, a Mohican State Forest.... But in Connecticut you will find that the traces of the red man have been far more studiously obliterated. Ever hear of a Mohegan casino?

Still, Kentucky has even fewer Amerindian names on the land than Connecticut does. This is as you might expect, if you know that what we now call Kentucky was once an area that various tribes passed through but considered holy ground, not suitable for regular residence. So Kentucky may have the fewest Amerindian names of any state. Of course it makes up for that with some of the strangest US placenames, as Robert M. Rennick tells us: Breeding (for Charles Breeding), Davella (for Dave and Ella Delong), Galdie (it was supposed to be for Goldie Brown, but the post office officials got it wrong), Kayjay (Kentucky-Jellico Coal Co.), Natlee (for Nathaniel Lee), Rabbit Hash (a staple food of the locals), and Zag (both Zig and Zag were submitted and the post office officials chose). Even Ono (from I *Chronicles* 8: 12) has the story attached that when any name was suggested in the public meeting to choose one, someone would always cry "O no!"

Stories about how this or that Amerindian name, real or ersatz, was created are an interesting subject, and Massachusetts has its share of good stories. But we shall ignore them and move on to Connecticut now. Massachusetts has nothing as silly as the folklore that Huntingdon (West Virginia) was named for Amerindians coming back shouting "Hunting done! Hunting done!" That whopper only underlines two facts: we like to make every name mean something, even the odd-sounding Amerindian ones, and the habit of inventing stories to explain *Narraganset* or the like can get out of hand! I keep telling that story in book after book, There will be some repetition in this book of material found in others, because I hope you will read the "set" but I cannot be sure you will.

With the names Connecticut borrowed from Britain, we have a different story.

NEW ENGLAND LOOKS LIKE OLDE ENGLAND IN THE PLACENAMES OF CONNECTICUT

Qui transtulit sustinet.— Motto of Connecticut

You are going to be confronted with this Ashley, the author, now and then throughout this book, which, though it is not an autobiography (my life in onomastics) is certainly not going to be written without an admitted, even featured, aspect of the subjective. That, if nothing else, will underline the fact that even in the so-called scientific study of toponymy (placenames) a certain amount of the subjective inevitably is involved. Here is another Ashley: the first Ashley to settle in Connecticut was forenamed Samuel. He arrived in Willimantic in April of 1717. By the end of that century we had completed our revolution and our new form of government convinced our Founding Fathers (mothers were not at that time considered) that we needed to know how to apportion our legislature, so in 1790 we had our first census. Looking up the Ashleys recorded in the first census of the United States, I noted that the Connecticut heads of families in 1790 all bore biblical names: Abner, Abraham, David, Joseph, Rachel, and Jonathan. The Old Testament influence was great, of course, especially on the Puritans. It was striking also that in 1790 the 45 Ashleys living in Connecticut resided in counties called Windham, Litchfield, Hampton, and Pomfret. The English heritage—and that's what this section is about: the English heritage in placenames in Connecticut, a state that Alexis de Tocqueville (1805 – 1859) called a "little yellow spot on the map" that "makes the clock-peddler, the schoolmaster and the senator." In his Fourth of July address, delivered in Paris after he had returned from America, Tocqueville, author of *Democracy in America* and the man who was the most perceptive visitor ever to describe our country, added:

> The first gives you the time; the second tells you what to do with it;
> and the third makes your law and civilization.

The poet Bliss Carmen once used Connecticut as the measure of Heaven itself:

> Heaven is no larger than Connecticut;
> No larger than Fairfield County.

You could compare the estimate of Heaven's size that St. Augustine gave, remembering that Connecticut holds both the elect and the non-elect. Less ambitiously I only undertake to use Connecticut here as a measure of the mark that English placenames brought by English people such as the Ashleys (and people much more famous in early American history) have made upon the United States in one part of New England.

The New Englanders came in for a charge of lack of imagination, according to H. L. Mencken in the revised edition (1962) of his *The American Language*:

> The original English settlers, it would appear, displayed little imagination in naming the new settlements and natural features of the land they came to. Their almost invariable tendency at the start was to make use of names familiar at home, or to invent banal compounds. *Plymouth Rock* at the North and *Jamestown* at the South are examples of their poverty of fancy; they filled the narrow tract along the coast with new *Bostons, Cambridges, Bristols,* and *Londons,* and often used the adjective as a prefix.

That is nonsense, despite the fact that it is stated with Mencken's characteristic cocksureness. The settlers were not lacking in imagination. They were full of nostalgia for the Old World they had left and they had also the determination to create a New London, if not a New Jerusalem, in the New World. "Names familiar at home" would, here, make their homes more pleasant. Placenames like Providence expressed their faith. And Mencken ignores the fact that the settlers also took up Amerindian names: look at Massachusetts and Connecticut, for instance. Settlers retained aboriginal names on the land even when as strange as Naugatuck. That was from an Algonquian language, from some important single tree (*nau-ga-tungh*) or perhaps from a bend in the river (*noggue tookoke*), though the latter seems far-fetched to me. The settlers retained it even if they did not know exactly what it meant. If they did not like a name they changed it: the Sqontuk (or something that sounded pretty much like that to the Englishmen) became the Fulling Mill River and Nawbesetuck became Mansfield, while nearby Willimantic remained. Helen Earle Sellers in *Connecticut Town Origins* (which reached a second edition in 1973) says Willimantic's name translates as "a good lookout where (the river) winds around a bold hill or cedar swamp," still another of those open-ended and perhaps not very convincing explanations of an Amerindian name.

Placenames take a lot of care. It has been alleged that Rutland (Vermont) is copied from Rutland in England. Very possibly so. But it has also often been said that Rutland in England comes from the red earth there. Not so. A British placename expert, Adrian Room, wrote to the *Times Literary Supplement* (14 April 2000. P. 21) to say authoritatively:

The Anglo-Saxons did not name Rutland for its ruddy earth any more than they named Oakham after its oaks....The name means "Rota's land," after the owner of the well-defined estate here. His own name means "glad," "cheerful"....

The settlers in New England probably did not care much about the etymologies of the English names they imported and they knew very little and cared perhaps even less about the origins of the Amerindian names they might displace. This was their land now to name as they pleased and to make comfortable for themselves by means of those names.

The settlers were in a New Canaan, a land of milk and honey, and the savages were to be driven off so that a new nation, shining like a beacon on a hill, could be built here. So the whites killed or drove off the Sons of Satan and they created Bethany, Bethel, Bethlehem, Bozrah (later changed to Bath by the General Assembly), Goshen (whose inhabitants wanted to call it New Bantam), Hebron, Lebanon (the first town to get a biblical name in Connecticut, 1705), Salem (because its founder, Col. Browne, had formerly lived in Salem in the Massachusetts Colony), Sharon, and so on. Such biblical names were to be expected among the religious people who baptized an Indian Stream as the Jordan River and argued that Mystic was "in memory of that victory God was pleased to give His people of Connecticut over the Pequot Indians." (In fact it is from Mistuket, says the *Mobil Travel Guide*.) They thought not only of the Old Testament but also of the Old Country: there was a New Canaan and a New Britain (originally New Briton, 1754, and for a while after our Revolution it was Berlin to honor our Prussian allies). They also thought of business, with Yankee shrewdness. New Britain (a city from 1870) became "The Hardware City," and produced sleigh bells and locks, later selling lots of hardware and machinery. The era came in which an American president announced that "the business of America is business." That was a far cry from the Puritans, but they, too, thought that if you got rich it was proof positive that God loved you. In time "the bible" came to mean the mail-order catalogue in Connecticut!

Naturally there was also farming. The "fair fields of Uncoway" (actually Unquowa or Ongkoe) produced a New Fairfield, recalling some Fairfield of Derbyshire or Lincolnshire. That was 1667. Since 1728 there has been a Fairfield County in the area previously called Powntucktuck (Anglicized as Potateuk or Potatuck) inhabited by the Amerindians "near the falls." Suckiage became Hartford after being just a New Towne. It was named for Hertford (pronounced as spelled in Connecticut), principal town of Hertfordshire, origin of the Rev. Samuel Stone, one of the three men of God who arrived at the Massachusetts Colony aboard *The Griffin* on 4 September 1633. The Rev. Cotton Mather (1663 – 1728) later remarked, playing on the names of the three ministers, that God "had supplied them with…their three great Necessities, Cotton, for their Cloathing, Hooker for the fishing and Stone for their Building."

Also arrived (1637) the Puritan divine John Davenport (from the parish of Old Jewry in London) and by the next year Davenport and Theophilus Easton were dickering with the chief Momaquin at Quinnipock (in early documents spelled Quillipeague and Quinipiocke) for the purchase of lands now in Connecticut. A letter now in the British Library written by Davenport 28 September 1639 at Quinnipock says: "The sight of ye harbour did so please ye Captain of the Ship and all the passengers that he called it Fayre Haven." Fair Haven as a name, like Quinnipac (long water country) soon disappeared. The General Court held in Fair Haven 1 July 1640 declared: "This town is now named New Haven."

Other settlers who did not tarry in Quinnipac settled more or less nearby. One William Fowler built a mill, so the settlement became Milford, recalling Milfords in England. It had been called Wepawaug (meaning it was at the narrows). Another town in the Weantinoque (whirlpool, or where the water whirls as it sweeps around an obstruction, a good place for a *willimantic* or place to observe river traffic) or New Purchase arose when John Noble of Westfield (Massachusetts) started New Milford in 1712.

Among the new towns, at least one of which was named for the New Town in the Massachusetts Colony, was New London. The "ancientest book" speaks of a settlement on that site called in 1646 Naneeug (fishing place). A town meeting of 1649 debated the adoption of a better (more pronounceable?) name and "the inhabitants did consent and desire that the plantation"—the people had been "planted" there said John Winthrop "to be a curb to the Indians"—"may be called London." Mrs. Sellers (already mentioned) writes: "This name came into colloquial use soon to be generally known in the abbreviated style of the times as 'Lon'on Town' or "new Lon'on." I do not see an abbreviation there, only a name still farther movement from old King Lud's town name. The General Court wanted to call New London "Faire Harbour," maybe with the same public-relations intent as is obvious in a name such as Greenland. The citizens refused and called it Naneage. The debate raged until March 1657/8 (the years then began in March) when the "Plantation at Pequet" was "named by this Court, New London." This deepwater port on the convenient river the Dutch had called Frisius and later it was on the Little Fresh River and then the Great River (though it had increased not a whit in the interval) and then The Thames. So a New London arose on a new Thames and there was to be "a preamble inserted in the same [Court record] which is inserted in the closure of ye Acts of this Session." Because of its interest, I insert it, too:

Whereas it hath bene a commendable practise of ye inhabitants of all the Collonies of these parts, that as this Countrey hath its denomination from our deare native Countrey of England, and thence it is called New England, soe the planters, in their first settling of most new Plantations, have given those names to those Plantations of some Citties and Towenes in England, thereby intending to keep up and leave to posterity the memoriall of several places of note there, as Boston, Hartford, Windsor, York, Ipswitch, Bra[i]ntree, Exetter; This Court considering that there hath yet noe place in any of the Collonies bene named in memory of ye Citty of London, there being a new plantation within this Jurisdiction of Connecticut setled upon ye faire River of Monhegan, in ye Pequot Countrey, it being an excellent harbour and a fit and convenient place for future trade, it being alsoe the only place which ye English of these parts have possessed by conquest and yt [that] by a very iust war upon yt great and warlike people, ye Pequots, that therefore they might leave to posterity the memory of yt renowned citty of London, from whence we had our transportation, have thought fit, in honour of that famous Citty to cal ye said Plantation, London.

So much for Mencken's mistaken notion about lack of imagination. Rather the settlers who sailed from London—"transportation" here does not mean what it did in the case of Australia—wanted to celebrate their victory against the Pequots (1637) and were even suggesting that history needed to have a London in the New World so the London of the Old World would live in memory! They did not despise the land they had left. They simply expected to do better in the new land and they remained loyal Englishmen. There was no lack of wit here, no problem with foreign tongues, but a philosophical or political or religious sentiment, or all three. William Blake may have wished to build a New Jerusalem "In England's green and pleasant land" after the eighteenth century, but the American colonists of the seventeenth century wanted to build it on this side of the Atlantic. They looked to a perfected England in a new land. Now *there's* imagination for you! That is what they had in mind with English names transferred to New England. That went for New names and Old. Old Saybrook and Old Lyme are relevant, too.

William Fiennes (1582 – 1662), heir to the barony of Saye and Sele (made a viscounty in 1624), helped to set up a company of adventurers for the organization of what was to be called Providence Island. By 1632 he had acquired a patent for land along the Connecticut River. Sir Robert Rich (1587 – 1658), Earl of Warwick, granted to a Puritan group associated with Saye and Sele and Robert Greville (1608 – 1643), Baron Brooke, who was involved in the Providence Island and Henrietta Islands schemes (God and royalty both got named), "that part of New England in America which lies and extends itself from a River there called Narragansett…Forty Leagues upon a straight line…towards Virginia…and also all and singular the Lands…North and South…from the Western Ocean to the South Sea."

Sounds like a great deal! In the end it came down to an expanse of some ten square miles: Saybrooke, Old Saybrook, Westbrook, Essex, Chester and parts of Old Lyme and Lyme. The company appointed John Winthrop the Younger "Governor of the River Connecticut" and dispatched about 20 men to the area. There they established Saybrook "for gentlemen of quality" to live in, and they successfully turned away a Dutch sloop sent by the governor of New Amsterdam (New York to be), Wouter van Twiller. The Dutch thought they had better build a fort near Pattaquassett (the mouth of the Connecticut River) at what we now call Saybrook Point and what they called Kievet Hook (after the pewit bird common in the vicinity).

A letter from Lion Gardiner, an engineer retained by the Company to draw up plans for the English settlement and its defenses, was sent to Governor Winthrop headed "Saybrook, 6 Nov. 1636." So by then Saybrook was a name (from Saye and Lord Brooke, having nothing to do with a brook) in use. In 1852, Saybrook and Old Saybrook were separated, so the original Saybrook is now Old Saybrook. Some records have SeaBrook, which would have been even more confusing.

In 1648 the "outlands" of Saybrook were divided into "quarters" (three of them, by the way, but Americans speak of "three alternatives," so do not be surprised). The three areas were called Oyster River (obviously oysters there, the way there was a puddling furnace in 1847 at Puddletown, or an applewood flute factory at Fluteville in the 1830's), Eight Miles Meadow (also known as Potopauge), and East Side of the River (what an odd name!). In 1854, Old Saybrook (which until 1716 had been the site of Yale) was broken up. It then became part of Essex (after Essex County in Massachusetts, named from an English county from which many early settlers of Connecticut originated, which explains why we see the likes of Colchester "in the countie of Newlondon").

One of the early settlers was Fitz-John Winthrop. He had lived in Groton in that English shire of Essex which John Norden had described in 1694 as "most fatt, fruitful, and full of profitable things exceding (as far as I can find) anie other shire for the general commodities and plenty." The Essex men brought this pride to America. Their Colchester recalled the River Colne at home and Col[ne]chester, the Roman camp on that river, once the Roman settlement called Camulodunium. Camelodunium was where the British queen Boadicea (or Bonducca, if you like) terrified the legions of Claudius with scythes on the wheels of chariots driven right into the masses of Roman troops. Her success was recalled when the defenders of the American Revolution held the old Siege House of our Colchester against the British.

Essex men brought to Connecticut the ways and names of Danbury (with its views over the Blackwater), Dedham (of later Constable fame) in Massachusetts, and familiar names such as Waltham, near Great Waltham. In Essex are great country seats such as Hyde Hall and Langleys and the ruins of the castle that was once that of the Lords High Constable of England. There were also Hadley (British Hadleigh), Hampstead (whose greatest native sons were William Harvey, rediscoverer of the circulation of the blood, and Dick Turpin, the notorious highwayman), Maldon (where was fought in AD 993 the battle against the Danes, the subject of a great Anglo-Saxon epic), Newport (still boasting one superb old street), and more. Some wonderful Essex names did not get imported, to our sorrow and loss. Consider Wimbish, Great Leighs, Steeple Bumstead, and Audley's End. Great Leighs has a tenth-century church but the name might not have fared well in American mouths.

Lyme (which means "forest") was a Dorset name that came to Connecticut. Lyme Regis (a resort that boasts that a king enjoyed it, as does Bognor Regis— "Oh, bugger Bognor," exclaimed one monarch) was the origin. Of course we dropped the Regis. On land belonging to the original Saybrook, Lyme was settled about 1664 and in 1647 the General Court at Hartford declared that the Amerindian name should be dropped. Nehantic was that name, given by the tribe that lived between the Nehantic and Connecticut rivers. The Court decreed that "ye Plantation on ye East side of ye River over against Saye-brooke for ye future be named Lyme." This was probably at the request of the Hill and Humphrey families, who came from Dorset. When East Lyme appeared (1839), Lyme became Old Lyme. In time a new Lyme appeared. Then all the Lymes and part of East Haddam were collectively known as East Saybrook.

The settlers from Dorset may have thought that the Connecticut River as it enters the channel at the point of their settlement looked like the area of Dorset's Lyme. The town was first called Hadham, then Haddum (1668), then Haddam replaced the Amerindian name Higganompos (rock for tomahawks) or Cockaponset (shortened by the whites to Punset). Haddam came from Hertfordshire, an English "home county" dating from AD 1000. In time Old Lyme seemed the right name for the picturesque charm of a town filled with the mansions of sea captains (more of them, perhaps, than anywhere else along this stretch of coast). Growing populations and suburban snobbery have created more reasons for distinctions, and so Old Lyme and Lyme, not Lyme and New Lyme, are on the map.

You have been subjected to a good deal of history thus far. Many of the present inhabitants know little and care less about the history. Many do not share the English background. They will tell you about citrus fruit and Lyme—but that is a scurvy idea. There are no limes involved, any more than the elsewhere the Oranges are about oranges. There is a Connecticut Orange, on land bought for trinkets from the *sachem* Ansantawae (1639). A town came into being there soon

15

after another Milford was laid out in 1687. In 1688, the so-called Glorious Revolution broke out in England. James II, who had lost his pension from Louis XIV in 1685 by maintaining good relations with the *Statholder* of The Netherlands, saw those good relations collapse as William of Orange landed in England in the early days of 1688 to press claims on the throne. His wife Mary [Stuart] had a claim on the English throne. She was the leading Protestant heiress and the monarch by then had to be Protestant. William refused her permission to take the crown unless he ruled jointly. So the English Protestants welcomed him as William III. English Protestants in Connecticut, many of them from the West Country of England where William landed and received support, named Orange in his honor. Elsewhere, Princeton University (starting as The College of New Jersey) and its town were named for William of Orange (whence Nassau Street, Nassau Hall, the orange-and-black Tigers, and all the rest), thanks to the royal governor of New Jersey. They were going to name it all after him, but his surname was Belcher, so it was fortunate he insisted that he preferred they honor "the great prince of Orange"!

History does have some amusing tales to tell. It is a shame to join Henry Ford in his view that "history is bunk." Moreover, much of history depends upon people who made a name for themselves and much is explained by the names they put on the land where they lived. Names are not trivia. Names are evidence of significant human behavior.

Andover was a name borrowed from England via another American place: Andover (Massachusetts) was from Andover (Hampshire) and replaced Pomakuck in Connecticut. Wabbasquassett (where rushes for weaving are found) in Massachusetts became David Jacob's Scituate in Massachusetts and then a Connecticut New Scituate, later Ashford in honor of the place in Kent. In the Nod Divisions (from Amerindian *noate*, pronounced "node," meaning "distant") an Old Farmington settlement grew into Avon (incorporated 1830), from the river in Shakespeare's Warwickshire. That seems preferable to Stratford, for now we have to distinguish between the Canadian one and the Connecticut one. We have a Shakespeare Industry here like that of Stratford-upon-Avon in England. Stratford (CT) was a modern version of the entrepreneurial (and often dishonest) Yankee-ness that caused Connecticut to be termed "The Nutmeg State." Yankees sold carved wooden fake nutmegs to the unsuspecting. Now they offer plays for tourists.

In 1959 the state legislature declared that Connecticut was "The Constitution State," on the grounds that the Fundamental Orders of Connecticut were tantamount to the first written constitution in America. The honor perhaps ought to go to the state first to sign the US Constitution, but Yankees are enterprising and bold.

Back to the names derived not from the Dutch (like Yankee) but from England. Barkhampstead (1732, since 1795 spelled without the *p*) recalled

Berkhamstead (Hertfordshire, which the British abbreviate as Hants.). Bolton (house town) was in 1718 "the plantation on the mountain east of Hartford," and it was for a while called Hanover (for the connections of the British royal family). It became Bolton (1720) well before any independence movement in America. Branford, breaking off from New Haven in 1685, was the closest the colonials came to Brentford, the name of a town in Kent at the Brent River. Some "fforty acors of meddow Land lying att the place we commonly call Poland" in time became connected with Bristol (founded 1785). Sebastian Cabot sailed for America from Bristol in 1497. From the same place many later persons sailed for America. There has even been a suggestion in Bristol that a merchant there gave his name to America, but few non-Bristol people will ever credit that. Brooklyn in Connecticut came from the Dutch who named part of what is now New York City, Breukelen, Brooklyn. Quinnebag (long pond) gave way to Abbington, probably after Abingdon in Berkshire, but later (1752) it was renamed Brookline. Burlington is likewise from England; Sellers wants to trace it to Bridlington in Yorkshire, but there is an English Burlington. Canada was not from the "collection of huts" of our neighbor to the north but from one David "Canaday," who was really a Kennedy, from Salem, Massachusetts. Canterbury was on the Kent Plantation of Maj. James Fitch, Jr. (1697). Cheshire was originally New Cheshire and there was a Chester in the Pattaquonk (round place) part of Saybrook. Colebrook (1732) was from a place in Devon or another Colebrook. Cornwall was named in 1740. Wangumbaug (crooked pond) became Coventry. Danbury (from the original, where the invading Danes were buried, of course) was first Paquiage, then Beantown (the land was said to have been bought for a sack of beans), but Boston took "Beantown" as a nickname. Paugaset (the river widens) became Derby, perhaps because of sheep imported to launch a wool industry. Coginchaug (long swamp) became Durham after the cathedral town which sent many settlers to America after 1650. The Three Mile Division (1673) became East Hampton—but not directly from England. It was, in fact, named for Eastham in Barnstaple County, Massachusetts, from which settlers reached Connecticut in 1716. It was first named Chatham (which replaced Pocotopaug, "divided pond") but on 4 May 1915 it was once again named East Hampton.

Hampton itself was Appaquag (where rushes grow), a name also for what we called the Little River. Wabbauassett is said to be another name for such a place where rushes were collected, to make baskets. Was that a name, really? Rushton would be a name. But what about "the place I always go in the summer"? "Where we go fishing" is a designation, not a name. I contend that what we call Amerindian "names," such as Connecticut, was for them just a descriptor. To some Amerindians, any tidal river was a Connecticut. Early English settlers spoke of Windham Village, for it was near the "Hither Place" called Windham (after Wymonham, Norfolk, where Kett's Rebellion broke out, from which families later to be seen in America, such as the Ripleys and the Lincolns, lived).

17

In 1786 it was unusual for an American place to be named for a royal palace (Hampton Court, built for Cardinal Wolsey, who lost it to Henry VIII). Maybe it was named because there was a "wilderness" in both places. The Connecticut "Wilderness" was really wild. It is also possible that Connecticut honored one of two English politicians surnamed Hampden. The elder John Hampden (1594 – 1643) was one of the leaders of the Long Parliament when the Civil War broke out. Like Oliver Cromwell himself, this Hampden once considered beginning life anew, in America. But he fell at Chalgrove Hill in a skirmish with Prince Rupert's forces and was buried in a church at Great Hampden in Buckinghamshire. The younger Hampden (1656? – 1696), like his father Richard Hampden and his grandfather John (just mentioned), represented Wendover in Parliament. The grandfather was impeached and condemned to death for high treason, but he bribed the judge (George, Baron Jeffries and Petre), was pardoned, and starred in the Covention Parliament. He lived until 1696 (when he committed suicide). Both Hampdens as Roundheads, opposing the Cavaliers of the king, would have been considered heroes by Puritan America. So, there, we are finally arrived at an explanation of how this particular person came, perhaps, to be remembered in a placename so far from home. Every commemorative name has a lot of similar baggage. Also named in the Connecticut Wilderness in 1786 was a Hamden, formerly called Mount Carmel (from *Isaiah* 25:2) and even before that known as Blue Hills and by an Amerindian name.

Going back in the alphabet with these examples (which I hope inform interestingly and do not overwhelm, but, I realize, are numerous), there is Ellington, named for some town in Hampshire, Northumberland, or Yorkshire. Enfield may derive from the "duck field" of Middlesex (which produced Cowper, Keats, Lamb, Leigh Hunt, Walter Pater, Capt. Frederick Marryat, and the famous Enfield rifle from the Royal Small Arms Factory there). The "Plantation called Tuxnis" of 1645 became Farmington. That may or may not have involved a nod to England. Glastonbury (a Celtic name) and Granby (with East Granby) were certainly imported. So was Greenwich—New York's Greenwich Village has a redundant name, for *–wich* is "village"—hard for Americans because we forget the *w* is silent (as in Harwich, which Sir W. S. Gilbert rhymed with "carriage"). Guildford came from the cathedral town where "Lewis Carroll" was born. Hartland (1761) is not "heartland" and may be from a town in Devon. Harwinton is from one in Worcestershire (where Harington is pronounced "Hawinton"). But some say Harwinton in Connecticut combines elements of Hartford (where the Dutch had a "slight forte" whose name translated Good Hope) and Windsor (after the place in England and the Massachusetts place called Windsor but earlier Dorchester). Harwinton in any case was in the "Western Lands" and was originally Waramaug (fishing place).

The Saltonstall family, which gave Connecticut an early governor, also put some English names on the state. Their Yorkshire seat had been Killanslie; in

Connecticut they created Killingly (1708). Mashamoquet (big fishing place) became their Yorkshire's "broken bridge," Pomfret (from *Pontefract*). As with many American names, spelling is affected by either local or Old Country pronunciation. We still retain many pronunciations from England and may even spell that way (Worcester, Wooster). We still retain (though you may not have noticed it) French pronunciations of some Amerindian names such as Chicago and Arkansas. We can simply spell to suit pronunciation: Marlborough in Connecticut has become Marlboro in the land of *thru, lite,* and *nite.*

Matatuck (land not wooded) became Litchfield (graveyard, one of those English names we never stop to analyze) from the Staffordshire seat of the Boylstons. Settlers of a lower class recalled their native Manchester. Meridien was also of English origin, a corruption of Marldon Parish (Compton, Devon) and named by the family of one "Johnathan Gilbord" (Jonathan Gilbert). But Middlebury, which sounds English, is not; it was Middlefield (1644) between Woodbury, Southbury, Waterbury (no one buried in places like that—a corruption of *burg*). Also named for its position was Middletown, formerly Mattabesett or Mattabesick (big brook).

Pyquag (land naturally clear) became Newington for the Oxfordshire home of Ensign Richard Boardman, "a prominent member of this 'westwardmost' Society of Wethersfield," a town itself first called after Massachusetts' Watertown, from which the early settlers went to Connecticut. Potatuck (Mohegan for "around the falls") became Newton, from the place in Massachusetts. Norfolk (1758) is named for the shire, not the city.

English and more than one Amerindian language competed in the area. Algongkian or Algonquin is more common a language than Mohegan. The Algonquins gave the Mohegans their name (meaning "Wolf"). When the Quinnetuquet area was first invaded by the white man (the Dutch as early as 1614, the Puritans out of Massachusetts in the 1630's) there were some 7000 Algonquian speakers in the area, the most powerful tribe being the Pequots (or you can spell it with a *d*, the way Melville spells the name of the ship in *Moby Dick*). Over time, genocide, Manifest Destiny, war or whatever, has caused most Amerindians to disappear from the area—except for a few such as those in Bridgeport (chiefly African-American by now) who want their territory back.

North Branford was first Northford and later the northern part (of course) of Branford, comparable to North Haven and New Haven.

Norwalk sounds English. It isn't. The Norwake River and the Amerindians who lived near it are remembered, though no one seems to notice. Unfortunately, Norwalk looks like "a North walk," while Nyack in New York is clearly not English (it's Algonquin *nayaug, noyank, nyack* – we rendered it variously, as we did *Connecticut*). You know the song?

> Let's take a kayak
> To Quincy or Nyack,
> Let's get away from it all.

I suppose we must get away from all these Connecticut name explanations soon, but if you can hold on for a page or two more, the end is in sight, and you may still be looking for a placename of particular interest to you. That possibility sustains us all throughout.

Norwich (pronounced here with the *w* now, but at first sometimes spelled and said *Norridge* in Connecticut) put an English placename at the junction of the Yantic and Shetucket rivers. Rivers and mountains often retained their Amerindian names; farms and towns one wanted to put one's own name on, to own, but the rivers were everyone's. Plymouth (first called Northbury) and Roxbury came from England via Massachusetts. Portland had quarries and put men from the West Country in mind of quarries in Dorset. Preston recalled the Lancashire home of Thomas Parks. It is worth noting this naming of places with personal connections but not personal names (which happens with the plantation houses of the South, too): Connecticut has remarkably few examples of the sort of Smithown, Jonesville, or Grover's Corners. It does not specialize in the towns and post offices of the rest of the country so frequently given women's forenames in the nineteenth century. When eighteenth-century Isaac Magoon (McGowan? MacKeon?) named a town he named it for his birthplace, not himself. Puritan humility? Something else? At this point it is impossible to say, but we can note that Connecticut places were named before postmistresses of the middle-western states began to be honored in places.

English placenames rather than British surnames abound in Connecticut. It is not certain that Clinton is for the great DeWitt Clinton. Connecticut has few if any places given the forename of someone who is unidentifiable because the surname unknown, but (say) Jack's Creek or names like that were common in our nineteenth-century pioneer areas. In the West, Americans were less likely to give fancy foreign names. They would call a place Boot Hill or Sam's Mountain or Death Valley, something direct and simple.

Weatogue (Wigwams) became Salisbury. Windsor, Wapping (later South Windsor), Wilton, Woodstock, like Stafford, Stanford, Stratford—fords were always important in the old days in England—are all imported names. Wellesley is for the surname of the great duke of Wellington, very English. (Actually he was born in Ireland, but was embarrassed by it. He resented being called an Irishman. He demanded to know if, had he been born like Christ in a stable, he would have been described as an ass.)

Naturally the likes of these are all English: Easton, Weston, Westport, Prospect, Rocky Hill, Stonington (from the Stoney River), Plainfield, Ridgefield, Riverton, Southington, Hopeville—though the last marks the adoption, after the

Revolution, of the French suffix for "town" rather than the English one. Th   ۔s an all-French name: Montville.

Brace yourself for a necessary passage on Connecticut placenames derived from the names of people, mostly British. There are Georgetown and Hanover (British royalty), Ansonia (Anson G. Phelps of Phelps, Dodge & Co., 1889—unusually the forename), Chaplin (Benjamin Chaplin, 1756), Columbia (for Columbus if not from the poetic name of the United States), Cromwell (for Oliver Cromwell—the English pronounce it "Crummel"), Franklin (Benjamin Franklin), Griswold (Gov. Matthew Griswold, 1815), Hamden and Hampton (discussed above), Ledyard (Col. William Ledyard, killed defending Ft.Griswold when Gen. Benedict Arnold burned New London, 1781), Madison (James Madison), Mansfield (Maj. Moses Mansfield of the Indian Wars), Monroe (James Monroe), Morris (Maj. James Morris, 1752 – 1820, and his Morris Academy), Putnam (Gen. Israel Putnam), Redding (Col. John Reading—in England Reading is pronounced as if spelled Redding), Seymour (Gov. Thomas B. Seymour), Shelton (Edward N. Shelton, 1919), Sherman (Roger Sherman, 1802), Simsbury (maybe someone named Sims or Syms, but most likely from Symondsbury, Dorset), Somers (John Somers, Lord Chancellor, friend of Dr. Benjamin Turnbull, Washington's "Brother Jonathan"). Gov. Turnbull, of the same family, had Nichols Farms renamed for him (1797). There are also Sprague (William Sprague, 1856), Sterling (Dr. John Sterling, 1794), Thomaston (for famous clockmaker Seth Thomas, 1785 – 1859), Thompson (Maj. Robert Thompson, 1785), Tolland (a surname or the town in Somerset?), Torrington (a person, or Torringford in Devon?), Vernon (Admiral Vernon, "Old Grog," 1808—not Mount Vernon, Washington's estate), Warren (Gen. Joseph Warren, who fell at the Battle of Bunker Hill—which was not fought on Bunker Hill but on Breed's Hill). There is also a Washington. He is everywhere honored as "The Father of His Country," but Connecticut named for him the very first town incorporated there after the Declaration of Independence was signed. There are Wolcott (Gov. Oliver Wolcott, 1796), Woodbridge (Benjamin Woodbridge, first pastor of the town—and a big relief from all these politicians and soldiers), etc.

The ethnic composition of the state in its early days, and the mindset that determined who would be honored in placenames, what Continental places would be recalled (Berlin, Darien, Lisbon, Poland, etc.) are in Connecticut (as is the case everywhere) evident in the names. Placenames tell us of history and psychology as well as of geography.

But we must be careful. We must look at documents. Samuel Sewell's diary for 18 March 1690 explains why New Roxbury was renamed Woodstock "because of its nearness to Oxford" and his anti-Catholicism—Elizabeth I was imprisoned there by her sister Mary. We must dig deep. Read Benjamin Trumbull's *Complete History of Connecticut from 1630 to 1764* (1804 – 1818) and later general histories (Andrews, Burpee, Bushman, Calder, Crofut,

Heermance, Lee, Mills, Shepard, Zeichner, *et al.*), search in public archives, the WPA records, gather all the data that can be found. Then we see that when Sen. Francis C. Gilletree (1835) suggested Bloomfield it had no Jewish resonances. What did Hebron as a name trigger when it was applied? Berlin recalls that Frederick the Great supported England and her colonies in the Seven Years War. Darien remembers the Darien captured by British troops in 1739. Lisbon notes trade of the local Perkins family with Portugal. Poland has disappeared. Indeed, the state is overwhelmed with placenames from England, despite the Irish, the Lithuanians, and a host of people of other nationalities who have long been part of it. This raises questions concerning how the English placenames affect those of other ethnicities, and how even now when (rather rarely) something new needs to be named it is more likely to be called Danbury Fair than to recognize the existence of (say) residents who speak Spanish. Those are questions to be answered in some other place.

I hope this has been an interesting study. It is limited in scope but designed to make a few points about placenames and to correct Sellers where I can. I trust it is more gripping than a discussion about what Connecticutters (?) call themselves or how the state's name has been spelled an alarming number of ways or how Connecticut has been made up of many people only some of whom have any connection at all with Old England. Or how there is a Lake Chargoggagoggmanchuauggagoggchaubunagungamaugg. First, that is a sentence (alleged to mean "I fish on my side, you fish on your side, nobody fishes in the middle") not a word. Second, it is more folklore than fact. Third, the locals call it Lake Webster.

In response to the possible charge of arid antiquarianism, all I can say is that in the United States, more perhaps than in other countries, the past must not be forgotten as we rush ahead. We are the only nation left with an eighteenth-century constitution, and we have, in Connecticut and elsewhere (though here I stress the English background), a mixture of ethnic backgrounds that cause special problems that need in the present and future to be solved with a fuller understanding of the past. Tocqueville said we are "animated, because men and things are always changing; but monotonous, because all these changes are alike." It is striking how the new peoples who settled Connecticut failed to make clean breaks with their origins. To me that suggests that Americans have to find a way to deal with the differences between their own pasts and futures as well as the differences between these factors and those inheritances and circumstances which control others. Ideally, this experiment in democracy in North America will reflect the motto of Connecticut with which I began and now end: "He who transplanted still sustains."

Now we move on to an area where not just the British (one of whose names was finally given to the place) but also the Dutch and other nationalities were early on or much later to be prominent. The port of Nieuw Amsterdam may have

22

been Dutch but from the start 17 different languages from Europe were heard in and around the settlement and naturally there were a number of Amerindians who peopled the area before the Europeans arrived. Some of their names were retained on the land. So we turn now to a place with more Amerindian names than Connecticut, which is New York.

Leonard R. N. Ashley

VANISHING AMERICAN NAMES: AMERINDIAN TOPONYMS IN NEW YORK

I have fallen in love with American names,
The sharp names that never get fat,
The snakeskin-titles of mining-claims
The plumed war-bonnet of Medicine Hat....

—Stephen Vincent Benét, "American Names"

When Columbus discovered America—*discovered* is now politically incorrect, but you know I mean the end of the fifteenth century—there were hundreds of American languages in use by more than 400 aboriginal nations, or tribes, here. Whoever came before Columbus, Viking or Welsh prince or Irish monk or whatever, had not called the locals anything we know. Columbus called the lot of them Indians. He had been searching, you know, for a sea passage to India. As for New York, which was not where Columbus arrived on any of his voyages, a Dutch map of 1635 shows the Noord River (which we now call after a Dutch employee, the explorer Henry Hudson) and the area inhabited by Matouwacs, Manahattans, Mohicans, Pequatoos, Quirepeys, Mahicans, Tappaneans, Sequins, Nawacs, and Wecke [*gausegeeks*], among others. I hope I have the spellings right, but I may not; the early explorers didn't get them right, filtering them through Dutch, English of a less than high London standard, etc. Moreover in New England, as elsewhere in the US, Amerindian peoples have moved, been removed, and almost exterminated. We shall come later to the state of Iowa, but here, to stress the point that peoples of some importance were more or less forgotten, let me mention a group that lives now three miles from Tama, a small town in Iowa. These few hundred Amerindians are the Mesquakie. You probably never heard of them, but at one time they were the masters of not only Iowa and Illinois and Missouri areas but, earlier, what we call Wisconsin and Michigan as well. They have been unusually resistant to the white man's ways, and they are very poor, without any of the moneymaking casinos that some other Amerindians enjoy. They have treaties with the government but they cannot make much of them. In 1975 Ronald L. Neff & Jay A. Weinstein were reporting in *Transaction* 12: 2 that one young member of the Mesquakie had hidden away copies of the treaties and lived in fear: "At any time someone might come in and shoot him, either to shut him up or to destroy his copies of the real Mesquakie treaties."

Let us return to more familiar history but keep in mind the problems of the Amerindians then and now. Hudson, an Englishman employed by the Dutch, explored what the locals were calling the Mahican and what the Spanish called

Río de Guamas and Río San Antonio. (Features were named over and over, each explorer rejecting or maybe never having heard the earlier names, a point we shall have to repeat in connection with other areas.) Hudson sailed *The Half Moon* all the way up the river we have named for him to Albany. His great river proved to be still another watery highway that did not connect to a Northwest Passage, so sought, so tempting, so impossible.

What is now the tremendous harbor city of New York City was occupied then by those Mantouwacs, Manahattans, Mohicans, Pequatoos, Quirepeys, Mahicans, Tappaens, Sequins, Nawacs, and the Weckegausgeeck tribes—among others. These are Dutch spellings on the map of *Nieu[w] Nederlandt*, which shows *Nieu Amsterdam, 't Lange Eyland*, etc. The orthography of early Dutch, and early English, maps of the area renders the Amerindian placenames uncertain. Why, for instance, do we have *Mahican, Mohegan, Mohican*, and *Taeppans* and *Tappan Zee*? Each wave of Europeans rendered the Amerindian names differently. Explorers picked up names for nations not used by the nations themselves, accepting names used by neighbors, even enemies: in Florida the *Seminoles* had "fires over there." *Dakota* means "allies," and was never a tribe's or nation's name for itself. The white man often mocked the names he did not understand. The enemies of various groups called those groups by insulting names.

James Kirke Paulding in early America (the man who popularized the name Brother Jonathan for a Yankee) mocked Amerindian names. He wrote of

Currituck, Cummashawo,
Chickamoggaw, Cussewego,
Canawalahole, Karatunck,
Lastly great Kathipakakmunck.

But today we have stopped laughing at words such as *Massachusetts, Connecticut, Manhattan, Chattanooga, Wyoming* (which lost the stress on the first syllable when it moved from New England out west). Now we see nothing at all strange in *Alabama*, or *Oregon*, though we may still raise an eyebrow at *Schenectady, Ypsilanti, Yuma*, or *Caughnawaga, Chiliwack*, or *Chibougamau* in Canada. We may make errors and assume Manhan is a specific name when it means any "island".

More or less reliable information is to be found in books such as Reginald Pelham Bolton's *Indian Paths in the Great Metropolis* (1922), The Manhattan Company's *Manna-hattin* (1929), and the principal Amerindian authorities, of which Henry Schoolcraft is the best, but fallible. So many Amerindian names have been lost. So many names have been changed. Anne Hutchinson (a troublemaker pushed out of a secure colony and massacred by Amerindians in 1643) is recalled by Hutchinson River Parkway (though few who drive it have any idea why it is so named) but Annes Hoek became Annes Hook and then Rodmans Hook and poor Anne was expunged from that page of history. Most of all, as I am prone to repeat, Amerindians did not have the kind of fixed placenames we have, certainly not placenames that memorialized individuals. So a lot of placename history and history in placenames antedating the white man is forever lost, in New York State (where placename study has been vigorous) and everywhere else in the US.

The Omni Gazetteer of the United States (a great work due principally to the organizing genius of Frank Abate) will give you the names of New York State and its environs that have occurred on official maps. The first version of this brief report was prepared before that useful reference book came out. This was designed for the second annual North East Names Institute, organized by Murray Heller of the American Name Society. It began by calling for something other than the computer printout I was using for the state; it looked forward to the large national gazetteer that eventually was produced.

I shall undertake to suggest the extent to which the aboriginal names were obliterated around New York City. Yes, everyone knows of Manhattan—the name even occurs in California—and some may know of the Gowanus Canal in Brooklyn, or the "funny names" of Long Island such as Quogue, Patchogue, and Mineola, and the even "funnier" ones of nearby New Jersey such as Secaucus, Hoboken, Persnippany, and Ho-Ho-Kus. Nonetheless, this area has lost a great many Amerindian names, perhaps more than any area of similar extent in the whole of New York State or in the surrounding states. We know more about totally invented placenames for real places such as Gopher Prairie (Sauk City), Franciania (Louisiana), New Boston (New Haven), Flat Creek (Rikers Ridge), Metropolisville (Cannon City), Black Hawk (Red Cloud), maybe Zenith City (if it is Congressman J. Proctor Knott's "zenith city of the unsalted sea," Duluth, as Prof. Walter Randel suggested) than we do about the average authentic American placename.

For one thing, Manhattan's basic reliance on numbered streets and avenues (and some avenues with mere letters, as in Alphabet City on the former Lower East Side East Village and also in Brooklyn) precludes much opportunity for the use of Amerindian names. But even in other boroughs, part of the City of New York, such as Brooklyn (with numbered streets, streets designated by letters of the alphabet, etc.), Amerindian names are fewer than you might expect. And elsewhere, with a baffling Maine placename such as Katadumcook, folklore is likely to give us a whole yarn about some "dumb cook" with no relationship to the aboriginal. We neither know nor care what Chapel Hill (North Carolina) was called before Christians arrived; we would rather chat about how Tom Wolfe made it Pulpit Hill in a novel, no cleverer than his making Old Fort into Old Stockade. There is far more to look into in the real aboriginal placenames.

27

Leonard R. N. Ashley

In Bronx or The Bronx (named for the Dutch farmer Jonas Bronck), for example, a number of different Amerindian tribes lived. But the best-known Bronx street name today is Charlotte Street, a national symbol of urban decay, a mecca for politicians promising urban renewal. Decades later than the time urban revival was touted, the South Bronx is still something of a wasteland, though not about to return to the wilderness of the old Fox estate that the aboriginals knew. Bronx has a reputation today, justified or not, for savages. Charlotte Street once must have been part of some Amerindian area, with another name. So were areas now covered by major highways named for very minor politicos such as Henry Bruckner (borough president of no distinction except for the length of his term in office, 1918 – 1933) and Major William F. Deegan (a major in the National Guard, not even the Regular Army). Practically nobody today could tell you that Major Deegan was a petty politician, a crony of New York mayor "Gentleman Jimmy" Walker. Deegan was Commissioner of Tenement Housing, 1928. Judge Charles P. Daly had an avenue named Daley because his father-in-law was the last private owner of the area now forming Bronx Park. Councilman Mario Merolo had the name of Eden Terrace changed in 1968. Following the devious example of William Penn (who insisted that he was not worthy of having Pennsylvania named for him, a simple Quaker, and requested it be named for his father, Admiral Penn) our Merolo had Eden Terrace named for *his* father.

John McNamara, author of the valuable if now outdated *History in Asphalt: The Origin of Bronx Street and Place Names* (1978), reviewed by myself in *New York Folklore Society Bulletin* 1979 and by Arthur Berliner in *Names* (1980), tells us that the elder Merolo was a "member of the Bronx Grand Jurors Association and an official [employee?] of the Sinclair Oil Company." There may be some justice in the fact that records give his surname as both Marolo and Merolo. I choose Merolo. It may be wrong.

Politicos and police, veterans' associations and ethnic groups, etc., all lobby for placenames in New York City to be named for their choices. The Native Americans are not organized to press for Amerindian names on the lands taken from them. Who is this bearer of a Jewish name who has had this square named for him (sometimes the "square" is just a crossing), this numbered street in the forties in Manhattan given an unnecessary extra name in honor of an owner of the newspaper that got Times Square renamed, this ramp to the bridge decorated with an unusual name? Where are the Amerindian names among Margaret Sanger Square (no square there), Cole Porter Way (another West Forties numbered street, really), and Avenue of The Americas (which no New Yorker worth his salt would call anything but Sixth Avenue, no matter what the signs say)? Where are the first inhabitants remembered?

Should not there be if not a lot at least more Amerinidian placenames around NYC?

There are "Indian" places in the parks: Indian Island in Pelham Bay Park, Indian Lake in Crotona Park, Indian Trail in Silver Beech Gardens. But the East River and the Hudson have lost their Indian names, and so has Roosevelt Island (formerly Welfare Island), Governor's Island, and the bit of land, battled over by both New York and New Jersey, on which the Statue of Liberty stands. Streets get named for The Finest (the police) and The Bravest (the firefighters) and policemen shot off-duty (Slattery in World War I on active service, Lynch chasing a burglar, etc.), or soldiers who died: Bronx disposes of them economically in pairs: Rosa-O'Boyle Square, Neumann-Goldmann Plaza. Even a boy from Bronx who renounced his US citizenship to become Israeli (and was killed in the Israeli force trying to rescue hostages at Entebbe in 1977) is hailed as an American patriot and produces a very strange name on the landscape in the Bronx area: [Lt.-Col.] Yehonatan Netanyahu Lane. *Netanyahu* is an Israeli surname with which Bronxites and all Americans were to become more familiar at a later date. Now it does not look quite so strange—but maybe it does not belong here.

Sir Winston Churchill's mother, the indomitable Jenny Jerome, characteristically took matters into her own hands: she named a boulevard in defiance of the Board of Aldermen by simply going out and putting up Jerome Avenue signs.

Baseball fans have moved through proper (patronage) channels to get places named for Lou Gehrig, "Babe" Ruth, and Roberto Clemente (who also has a school, etc., named for him). Puerto Ricans had a space at East 138 Street and Willis Avenue—who was Willis? No prizes offered!—designated Plaza Boriqueña (not Boriquena Plaza, by the way). But Native American names have been erased one after the other. When East 138 was so named, seven street names disappeared. One of them was that of the Indian chief Ponus. He sold land to the Dutch in the seventeenth-century. I hope he got a better deal than that which was struck for Manhattan Island. That is said to have gone for $24, but that story is untrue. Also, those who sold Manhattan Island to the Dutch did not get ripped off. Those Indians didn't own it. That was an interesting beginning for the fascinating history of Manhattan real-estate deals.

The names of only two chiefs remain. Seneca Avenue disguises its relation to Red Jacket (*c.* 1758 – 1830), which was the name the British gave to an Amerindian who joined them and wore their scarlet soldier's coat. Red Jacket was of the Seneca nation of the Iroquois Confederacy. Seneca bore no relation to the Roman who went from Spain to be tutor to the Emperor Nero, and who wrote plays too bloody to be staged. Red Jacket became a nationally known figure when he toured 1824 – 1825 with his old colleague from Revolutionary days, Gen. Lafayette. There used to be an Uncas Street in what was then The Bronx, for the character in Cooper's *The Last of The Mohicans,* though Cooper thought it was a name. Anyway, it was corrupted to Ungas and then it disappeared. It was part of what is now 150th Street. There is a Cooper Street in Co-Op City. John Adams' diary mentions an Uncasa River on the old Dater estate, but he probably meant Yonkers.

Minneford Avenue may just possibly be named for a chief whose name was once given to what is now blandly called City Island. There is still a Narragansett Avenue, but it is named for another Narragansett, not for the tribe directly the way Canarsie (in Brooklyn) is named.

McNamara is not sure whether Ryawa Avenue in The Bronx is from *rekawi* (sandy) and *ani* (path) in a local Amerindian language or from *Railway and Water Association*. I can find absolutely no trace of any "Railway and Water Association" but I happen to fear the worst in this case. There used to be a Pocahantas Railroad. It was nicknamed Old Pokey and people said it moved so slowly you could stray from the coaches and pick a few wildflowers and still be able to reboard the trains. Pocahontas was the name we gave to a female actually named Makoata. She was the "playful daughter" of Powhatan, whom Capt. John Smith met in Virginia. She married an Englishman, moved to England, and died there.

John Bartow's will (1725) speaks of "all my land at Scabby Indian" in The Bronx. On the whole, Amerindians were treated in a scabby manner (old dictionaries define *scabby* in one sense as "low, mean, base, scurvy").

Many an "Indian" name, whether for a Boy Scout camp or a street or housing development or town across this nation, is made up. McNamara identifies no Bronx examples. He draws his Amerindian expertise largely from Schoolcraft (whom he mentions, but not in his bibliography), from Reginald Pelham Bolton's quaint *Indian Paths in the Great Metropolis* (1922), from the Manhattan Company of New York's odd *Manna-hattin* (1929), and other sources you already have heard about. McNamara is liable to say that, for example, *Go-Wa-Ha-Su-A-Sing* is (he says in "Tooker and Zeisberger") "place of hedges" without giving any other guide to these "Indian experts."

In what I still feel most comfortable calling the Bronx you will see the names Cayuga, Oneida, Seminole (nation names) and Sagamore (chief). These are Amerindian, but they hardly honor Amerindians. Cayuga Avenue (in Riverdale) is rumored to have been named because the surveyor was a graduate of Cornell University ("Far above Cayuga's waters...."). Oneida Avenue seems to be named not for that nation or the no-sex commune of Upstate New York (still recalled in a commercial name for silverware). Cayuga actually was named after a gunboat: the *Cayuga* was commanded by Commodore (later our first Admiral) Farragut at New Orleans. Pontiac Place was not named for the chief (subject of our first Amerindian tragedy on the stage) nor even the automobile out of Pontiac (Michigan) but for the nineteenth-century Pontiac Democratic Club. Remember the "Indian" names such as that of Tammany Hall? ("Boss" Tweed was a Grand Sachem of Tammany.) Sagamore Street was named for Pres. Teddy Roosevelt's home (Sagamore Hill). Levy & Morris, setting out presidential plans for their Van Nest development, discovered that *Sagamore* was already attached to a brook, a cove, and a rock. James Pinchot, another developer, cutting up Woodmansten (the old Pearsall estate) hit on the use of spa names: Narragansett, Newport, Saratoga, some of which just happened to be Amerindian. Saratoga was later changed "for no apparent treason," says McNamara, to Seminole. I have heard that pronounced Sem-IN-oh-lee but (as you may know) New Yorkers, especially Upstate New Yorkers, have the strangest ways of talking.

God knows what earlier generations thought about names such as Katonah (which used to be a village's plain Second Street) and Yzenga. Did they believe they were "Indian"? Guesses at Yzenga range from Polish Ignatz (famous here only in Krazy Kat cartoons) to some "Hungarian nobleman" who was supposed to have married a Bronx beauty.

There may be Amerindian names behind such obsolete toponyms as Bear and Beaver and Black swamps, Black Eagle and other rocks once famous, Burial Point and Rattlesnake Brook, but even with Indian Cave (associated with Chief Niham and the Stockbridge Indians of 1778) no personal names are commemorated. White landowners are remembered in placenames but red men never claimed to own the land. Bronx Amerindian names are about as scarce as those on Staten Island, in Queens, in Brooklyn, and in Manhattan, the boroughs of the metropolis.

Times and populations change. The Bronx has lost its Coney Island (but there's one in Brooklyn) and its Duck Island, Delancy's pine tree, Nigger Woods, Blood Alley and Dangerville, Fort Independence and Spy Oak. Co-Op City has replaced Freedomland. The Bronx is often thought of as African-American and "Hispanic," often a euphemism for the insensitive term "half-breed," but it is not all so. It certainly is on the whole poor, and poor in Amerindian names, even those of Amerindian "half-breeds." New York City doesn't even have a Squaw name to squabble about.

A band of Siwanoy Indians, beheaded by the Matinicocks of Long Island, is said to haunt Haunted Cedar Knoll. Perhaps their spirits linger, but their old names do not. Acqeegenom (where the path goes over) and Cowangon (boundary road) are gone: Cowangon is now Green Hill Road. Aquahong (high bluffs) is now the Bronx River. Aquehounk (these words are variously spelled, and this may mean "high banks" or even "red cedar"), also called Asumowis and Acqueanoucke, is now noted only for Anne Hutchinson (d. 1643). New York City makes a special effort to give full names to avoid confusion: it is Dr. Martin Luther King, Jr., Boulevard and Adam Clayton Powell, Jr., Boulevard (though white New Yorkers may still use the old avenue names). But other once famous people may have disappeared, like the Amerindians.

Lap-Ha-Wach-King —you know how we make the Amerindians sound so childish by breaking up names of theirs we find hard to say!—is now just Hunter

31

Mountain. Its original name says it was the place where shells were obtained to make wampum (which is not exactly what we would call a name), and it literally is "place of string beads." Maninketsuck (strong flowing brook) contains *suck*, which we don't like, so it is now Roosevelt Brook. Quinnahung (planting rock) is now Hunt's Point, and *Hunt's Point* signals "Market" as *Wall Street* says "Finance" and *Broadway* "Theater" (though there is only one real theater left on Broadway itself, The Winter Garden). Sean-auke-pe-ing (river, land, water—or maybe "peanut place") was a Siwanoy village at Clason's Point. The name was shortened to Snakapins ("pins" being better than "pe-ing") and then disappeared entirely. How Amerindian names in the whole country were "improved" by shortening or other means is the subject on which someone ought to write a long book. It would have important implications for popular culture, taste, and linguistics. Sewanhack (great bay of the island of shells), where wampum came from, shells being used for money, was, last time I looked, a parking lot.

Those Siwanoys lived east of the Bronx River—why did nobody think of "Way Down Upon the Siwanoy River"?—on the western side were the Weckgausgeecks. Their Keskeskech (stony ground) we call Bronx, or more exactly Stony Point, for Gouveneur Morris II had the stony island connected to the mainland by a causeway. The village of Nipinchsen (little pond) has vanished. So has Nuasin (shouldn't that be Nuasen? the land between, in this case between Muscoota or the Harlem, originally Haarlem, River and Mentipathe, called Cromwell's Creek). Kingsbridge was Paparinemo or Paparinemin (when it was an island). Beside the Spuyten Duyvil was Shorakapkock, a "sitting down place". It may have been a place where portagers rested. You can, in fact, cross the United States from east coast to west coast by water, if you are ready for some portage, a French word from the old "runners of the woods." Or maybe Shorakapkock means, "wet ground." One of the most famous placenames of the Bronx, from the Weckgausgeecks, remains; it no longer means "smooth stones" and no longer refers to those in what has come to be called Tibbets Brook, but it is still called Mosholu. Ever heard of Mosholu Parkway? Ever wonder where the name came from? I wonder why it stuck. Chinatown and Little Italy stuck but the Irish Channel did not.

Algonkian was a major language here. The Hudson River was sometimes Mahkanituk and sometimes Cha-ti-e-mac or Shatemuc. Schoolcraft romantically rendered that as "stately swan." Unlikely. Saproughah (land spread out) became Biggarts Canal. The US Board on Geographical names doesn't like the apostrophe we ought to use. It doesn't standardize Amerindian spellings, either. It makes the official name whatever the locals want. It cares chiefly that each place have just one name, whatever it may be.

Thomas Pell (first holder of Pelham Manor) is well recalled but not the Amerindians who dealt with him under the Treaty Oak. There used to be a roadhouse called Pell Tree Inn. Pell seems to have even been recalled in the oak itself. Nobody knows whose residence gave a name to Wigwam Brook in the eighteenth century when the Twelve Farms and the redoubtable Morris family (Mount Morris, Morrisania, etc.) were squabbling over the Debatable Lands, a term I like as much as the Great Dismal Swamp (elsewhere). Nobody knows who were the natives of Indian Steps and Indian Rocks, and now even those names are gone. Tackamack Place (on the old Godwin estate) was named for a political club with an Amerindian name, like Tammany in Manhattan and Montauk in Brooklyn. Tallapoosa Point (now a part of Pelham Bay Park) was also derived from machine politics. The connection of party machines with Amerindian names, fraternal organizations such as the Red Men, etc., are worth a study on their own. This is as important a matter to understand as the fact that, the Amerindians having been more or less rendered pitiful wards of the state, America then began to romanticize them. This was reflected in placenames, too, as I shall have more than one occasion to mention.

No one is certain about such names as Ranachqua (Renaque, Ranaqua), part of Jonas Bronck's purchase, or Sackwrahung (whence Sacrahong Street in The Bronx), Winnemak Street (planned in the nineteenth century but never constructed), or Wi-ki-son (once an island in the East River, Beauchamp's *Aboriginal Place Names of New York* saying it meant "reeds"). I wish the Amerindian name had been preserved instead of East River, which is not nearly grand enough. It should have an Amerindian name, not the real-estate trumpery of Narragansett (later Seymour Avenue), Mohawk (later Garrison Avenue), Niagara (later Neill Avenue), Ononda (gone), Saratoga (later Seminole Avenue), not to say Choctaw Place. Our language seized on Choctaw as a proverbially incomprehensible tongue. But Choctaw Place and Pawnee Place survive. The Seminoles belong in Florida, not New York. The Choctaws were centered in Mississippi (with some dispersed in Alabama, Georgia and Louisiana) until they were bundled off to Oklahoma (then Indian Territory) as one of what we called the Civilized Tribes. The Pawnee (better, Pani) moved from Texas to Nebraska and surrounding areas until they too wound up on Oklahoma reservations. I like the Pawnee subdivision names: Skidi (Wolf), Grand, Republican, and Tapage (Noisy).

Real estate developers have cursed this land with phony Amerindian and pseudo-colonial placenames. A Bronx developer offered Seneca Place (1901). An earlier effort put a Tuxedo Street on the old Pearsall estate (1870), but it was named for Tuxedo Park and so was more dinner jacket than Amerindian, really.

We have always had trouble getting Amerindian names right. They come from so many languages. They are so often strange. At first the white man made fun of them. Later the white man called them sonorous, grand. James Kirke Paulding mocked them; the first Thomas Wolfe and Stephen Vincent Benét rhapsodized over their evocative polysyllables. Always we tended to mangle them. This was only to be expected of the semi-educated who made Darius into

Doris, Minuit into Mennewits, Morrisania into Moriseny, Punnet into Punet, Tetard into Tee Taw, Seabury into Zeabury, and disguised [Hercules] Herring Avenue as Hering Avenue, changed a place honoring [Alphonse] Fteley into a Ft. Ely, and so on. We are the people who made "no name" on a map into Nome, Alaska. Old maps struggle with Dutch (Spuyten Duyvel, Spitton Devil, Spiten Devil, Spouting Devil, Spike & Devil, obviously a Spelling Devil) and even easier European names (hummock became Humack). We made a hash of aboriginal names.

New York State has counties such as Cayuga, Onondaga, Seneca, and Tioga, and many Amerindian placenames in one form or another. There are Adirondack, Amagansett, Ashokan, Canandaigua, Catawba, Chenango, East Setauket, Geneseo, Huron, Kitchawan, Lackawanna (also a famous railroad in its day), Manaroneck, Mohegan Lake, Nyack, Oneonta, Oswego, Poughkeepsie, Ramapo, Saranac, Schenectedy, Ticonderoga, Tonawanda, and Wyoming (which eventually went west across the mountains, as you have been told). Some of the most famous places in New York State (Manhattan, Ossining, Niagara) have names not one person in a million can translate from the aboriginal languages. They are "just names," as the linguistis say "lexically opaque." New York for all its Amerindian names does not have an Amerindian name for the state, unlike Minnesota ("Sky Blue Waters" or "Cloudy Waters," your choice), which also has counties named Yellow Medicine, Dakota, Wabasha, Winona, and Chippewa and Itasca, each of those last two names at one time considered suitable for the state name). New York was named for a brother of a British king (and Minnesota never picked up the suggestion it ought to be named for our rulers Washington or Jackson).

Over the centuries, we have lost the names of many Amerindian chiefs. Some of those had Spanish names (Geronimo, Mangas Coloradas), or British names (nicknames such as King Philip as well as full names like John Brant), or other names, and some we recall have names we seldom translate (Tuscaloosa was the Black Warrior of the Mobile Confederacy and Osceola, or however you wish to spell it, was the Black Drink of the Seminoles) or translate wrongly (Sitting Bull was really a Standing Bull, immoveable). We put the names of others on some cities (Seattle and Buffalo are named for persons), and we mangled others. *Moodus* and *Miscoe* and *Quechee* are only fragments of Amerindian placenames. *Seattle* is a mangled version. It was a name we bought from a chief who later worried that the Great Manitou would punish him for selling his name, which was tantamount to selling his soul or identity, but he was assured by the white man that we spelled it so badly even the Great Manitou would not recognize what Seattle had done. We named Maugus (Massachussetts) for one Magus (a *sachem* of the Wellesley area), and we never think that among the Amerindian names of Massachusetts—Nipmak "fishing place," Quitnesset "home of the fawn," Neponset "he walks in his sleep" which means an easy portage), and so on—Adams is named for an Amerindian, as you heard earlier. "Praying Indians" and converts of all varieties often took white surnames as well as Christian forenames. As with many other ethnic groups, Amerindians altered their names on occasion and blended in with the general "American" population.

We think up some strange stories. Did the Canarsie Indians come from a "place fenced in" or (as the Brooklyn *King's County Courier* for 25 September 1978 repeats) did they really seem to the French to have ducks tattooed on their chests? We encounter some strange facts: the first newspaper printed in Kansas (1844) was in Shawnee. Oswego in Kendall Co. Illinois comes from Oswego (Flowing Out) in New York, the name that both the Onandaga (who were the most numerous and powerful in the Great Peace or Five Nations council of the Iroquois) and the Oneida (Stone People—compare the Mohawks' name for themselves: Kaniengehaga, People of the Place of the Flint, though some have translated *Mohawk* as "man-eater" and accused them of cannibalism, like the Eskimos, now Inuit) gave to what we call now Lake Ontario. *Ontario* is Beautiful Lake in Iroquois, and it has the same meaning in Mohawk: Skanodario. Or we find a fact such as that one third of Afro-Americans have some Amerindian blood, although blacks in the 9 and 10 Cavalry and 24 and 25 Regiments in the west fought the red men and won 14 Medal of Honor citations in the Indian Wars. We do not tend to think of blacks as cowboys or as Indian fighters, but they were. We have similar inaccurate views of the red man, mostly derived from dime novels in the nineteenth century, reports of the Wild West as presented by authors who seldom knew the west at all, and by "White man speak with forked tongue" Indians in twentieth-century movies.

But we do not absolutely have to know our history (some of it unnerving) or even what the Amerindian names mean to appreciate beauty. Anyone can hear *Mattawa, Yosemite,* or *Susquehanna* ring. They are not unsayable (as Paulding tried to argue) and they are not to be thrown away. Amerindians will not get their land back—they have difficulty getting others to drop Red Men, Chiefs, Braves and other unfortunate team names in sports, not to mention demeaning sports mascots (such as Noc-a-homa)— but there is no reason why their very names should perish. The person that John Dryden (in *The Conquest of Granada*) was the first to hail as the Noble Savage can and should be honored. The first nations in the Americas were not all noble, it is true; but they were not all savages, either. Most of all, in my opinion, we ought to honor them and keep what is left of their legacy to us, because, as the title of D'Arcy McNickle's study of the Amerindians in The Peoples of the America Series (1949) put it, *They Were Here First.*

Expect huge battles over whether, in fact, modern Amerindians were indeed "here first", or whether they possibly annihilated peoples who had come here by sea much earlier than those supposed to have crossed to the Americas on a land bridge from Asia. Disputes over the remains of very ancient people, found in what is now the United States and claimed by but very likely not related to modern Amerindians, are already making it difficult for science to determine facts which may or may not support the "here first" claims of Amerindians. Race has identified some questions that science raises as not politically correct. Few ordinary people want the Noble Savage to turn out to have been more savage and less noble than we have been saying. Political correctness threatens to go much farther than rewriting history by changing names on the land. Political correctness is more concerned with the political than the correct and inconsistent in whether it wants history revised or not. It wants 300,000 remains of Amerindians out of US museums and back in the ground. It wants no research to establish earlier presences. It demands change of ethnically offensive names, even of names in languages of oppressors of old. It will fight tooth and nail to resist any evidence that our Amerindians and the First Nations of Canada were not first after all. The ancient remains of earlier peoples the current Native Americans want totally ignored.

A NOTE ON PLACENAMES OF THE WELSH AND THEIR CONNECTION TO THE STUDY OF AMERINDIAN PLACENAMES IN CONNECTICUT AND ELSEWHERE IN THE UNITED STATES

**Lovely the woods, waters, combes, vales
All the air things wear that build this world of Wales.**

—Gerard Manley Hopkins, "In the Valley of the Elwy"

Diffusion studies are beginning to look seriously at last, not without controversy, of course, into the connections between the Welsh and other Europeans and aboriginal North America. This paper briefly treats of some connections between the placenames of the Welsh and the Amerindians. It may be stretching things, but it is interesting anyway.

The Welsh speak a Celtic language, related to Irish and Scots Gaelic, Cornish, Manx, and Breton. The Celts went to the islands of Britain in two waves from the Continent (where they were called Gauls and even earlier were noted by the ancient Greeks as coming from the East, perhaps Persia). Celts arrived in Britain about 1800 BC and again in 600 BC. They established trade connections between themselves and what are now France and Cornwall. They bartered with the Phoenicians and the Iberians, with Greek traders, with people from North Africa. The invading Romans conquered them (as late as the first century of our era, under Agricola) and pushed them westwards, making these Britons into Welsh.

Of those Welsh, Anthony Burgess writes in *Language Made Plain* (1964, revised 1975):

> When I say "British" I mean the original British, that is the Welsh. Those ancient Britons whom the Romans fought and subdued— Boadicea is a Welsh heroine, not an English one—were driven to Wales ('land of the foreigner') by the invading Anglo-Saxons. English is a foreign language as far as Britain is concerned. Welsh, or Cymric, was the tongue for many centuries of what is now called England. King Arthur held back the barbarous invader as long as he could, in the name of the Christian Roman Empire. He was a Romanized Welshman.

It has long been suggested that another Christian, St. Brendan the Navigator, brought the Irish to America. Very early the Vikings arrived in what is now Canada (Newfoundland) and maybe in what is now the United States. This was long before Columbus. It has been alleged that there were at least two Arthurs, leaders of the Welsh, and that one of them came to America and died, late in the sixth century of our era, in what is now Kentucky. (This Arthur is said to have been embalmed, the body taken back to Wales and buried at Mynydd-y-Gaer, which is near Bridgend.) Whatever you think of that theory, that a Welshman set up what Adrian Gilbert has described in a book called *The Holy Kingdom* (1998) in what is now the United States, it is certain that Europeans joined the people who had come to the North American continent over a land bridge from Siberia some 10,000 years ago. Some people are now known to have arrived by another route, in what is now Chile, long before the Siberians. Central and South America may have been partly settled by peoples of the Pacific, even China. Now recent archeological finds have established that Celts (wearing plaid) were in China thousands upon thousands of years ago. There are North African, Iberian, and Celtic inscriptions in our American archeology thousands of years older than the time of Columbus. Our continent has a long and complex history, not to be thought to commence with Columbus, but naturally the pre-history is spotty and in many aspects totally lost.

What I want to consider here are not diffusionist theories (5100 books on the topic are listed in the two giant volumes of *Pre-Columbian Contact With the Americas across the Oceans*) nor archeological facts but Welsh placenames in relation to placenames in the United States. One set of striking names may help us to think clearly about another such set. Members of the Connecticut Place Name Symposium, the first audience of this material, could connect the Welsh information with what they knew of Amerindian names in Connecticut. You can make connections, too. True, the Amerindian names of settlements have been almost entirely obliterated in Connecticut, but because no one can really own the mountains and rivers some geographical features continue to bear Amerindian names, one of which has been put on the state itself. All this you know. These Welsh names I shall mention resemble the descriptive names of the Amerindians: *Connecticut* means "great tidal river," and Pennsylvania's *Bryn Mawr* means "big hill." (In Welsh, *w* is a vowel.) *Bangor* (as in Maine) means "fence of wattles." Welsh and Cornish miners brought many Celtic names to the United States, while the Scots-Irish were important settlers of the South and the Irish were among the most numerous American immigrants of the nineteenth century and gave the United States a considerable percentage of its presidents (of that mostly Protestant Irish in origin), putting the presidential names as well as other Irish names on our land. Think of Mount McKinley (to which the Native Americans would like to restore the older name, Dinali). In Canada, the First

38

Nations have agitated to replace such names as that of the Mackenzie River with the old names.

Rivers in Wales, for instance, have names such as *Bargod* (border river), *Bran* (dark water), *Camddwr* (bent, winding water), *Carrog* (swift-flowing stream), *Cletwr* (rough water), *Clochnant* (with the sound of a bell, *cf.* French *cloche*), *Cowney* (reeds), *Hafesp* (it dries up), *Hydfer* (bold stream), *Llynfi* (smooth-flowing), *Magwr* (among rocks), *Melindwr* (water mill), *Pennal* (from high ground), *Rhiw* (slope), *Tanat* (shining water), and so on. I italicize to make them look even more unusual, to draw attention, I confess.

At first Welsh names of all kinds look forbidding. But *Aberystwyth* is just "mouth of the winding river." Look at these: *Pont Tyweli* (bridge over the bold stream) and *Pont Cynon* (Cynon's Bridge, that is the bridge over the river Cynon), *Blaen-gwrach* (source of the hag's river), *Caer Fadog* (Madoc's fortress), *Rhymney* (river that burrows its way along) and *Rhosilli* (*rhos* or moor of Sukien), *Dyffryn Dulas* (valley of the dark river) and *Dyffryn Tanad* (valley of the shining river). Do they not somewhat resemble Amerindian designations? Note that while in Wales each such name tends to be given to only one place, the Amerindian words for "big river" or "crooked river" or "shining water" could be and were applied to *any* such features, in any one of the hundreds of aboriginal languages. The Welsh names (those in Welsh) are all in one language.

None of the Amerindian languages was written down except in symbolic drawings until missionaries came with alphabets that they invented for the natives. These foreigners, missionaries and explorers and eventually settlers, transcribed the Amerindian tongues by filtering what they heard and putting it into their own writing system according to the orthography of Spanish, French, Dutch, English, and the like. That is always worth repeating: you hear what your own language predisposes you to hear. (Placenames are interesting evidence not only of what people hear but also what they perceive and decide to give a name to. This has a bearing on psychology.) So *Oregon* and *Wisconsin* come from different French renderings of a single Amerindian placename. What were *Sioux* or *Illinois* before the French took a crack at them?

An ancient literature preserves very ancient Welsh for us. The Welsh placenames even preserve pre-Christian cultural things. The names given in Britain by Eolithic, Paleolithic and Neolithic people are lost, but they must have had names. Neolithic Britons left us a village at Hayes Common (Kent), a large stone circle at Avebury (Wiltshire), and the well-known marvel we call Stonehenge (on Salisbury Plain), but no names for them. The Cromagnards, for instance, who took a name from France, had a cave in Wales, but its original name is lost and it bears a later name, *Paviland Cave,* the English helping to date it (and to underline it as a tourist site known to outsiders). It is possible that Cro-magnon people have living descendants in the Basques, but that is another

39

problem for another forum. But in Welsh placenames we have information about the Iron Age in placenames such as the following:

> *Aberaeron* (mouth of the river of the goddess Aeron)
> *Aberithon* (mouth of the river of the goddess Ithon)
> *Ciliau Aeron* (nooks [sources] of the river of Aeron)
> *Esgair Elan* (ridge of the goddess Elan's river)
> *Glan Ithon* (bank of Ithon's river)
> *Glyndyfrdwy* (glen of the goddess Dyfrdwy)
> *Pont ar Elan* (bridge of the river of the goddess Elan)
> *Pont ar Ithon* (bridge over Ithon's river)

The names of these deities must have had some meaning in themselves, but that is lost. It seems that rivers were often associated with female divinities (life-giving?), but *Ewenny* is for the goddess Aventi, and it is not a river. Contrast the Americas: aborigines in North America did not name places after persons, even divine persons. In Central and South America there are some old places named for aboriginal chieftains, if only those given by the Spanish, and in Wales there are personal names of that sort in the placenames.

The rules of Welsh that mutate the spelling of words in certain circumstances you do not need to have explained in detail here. Suffice it to say that if you see *gadair* (chair) you cannot look it up in the Welsh dictionary; it appears in the dictionary as *cadair*. One says *tref* for town—in Cornish a shift creates the prefix *tre* – but in Welsh "the town" is *y dref. Basged* (basket) is easy; but "the basket" is *y fasged.* An adjective varies with the gender of the noun it modifies. Some numbers have both masculine and feminine forms, and some do not. *Capel Ffraid* is partly simple for us—surely that's "chapel"—but why is *Ffraid* "of St. Bridget"? *Plumsaint* means "five saints," which five unspecified. *Gwyddelwern* means either "marsh of the alders" or "marsh of the Irishman," and no one knows which, or, if there is an Irishman involved, what his name was. The word for "blue" in Welsh is the same as the word for "green," and what we call "brown sugar" the Welsh would say is "gray." *Porthkerry* has no connection with the common Irish name; it is "the port of Ceri." Who he was, no one knows. When in Wales I reached what was indicated on my map as *Staylittle,* the locals said it was *Penfforddlas* or "the head of the road," and that seemed to be the local placename as well as a descriptor. A place whose name translates "warm meadow" actually is better rendered as "burnt meadow," and *Edwinsford* the locals call *Rhydodyn* (lime kiln ford). Who was Edwin? An Englishman or a Welshman? Or is it still another name distorted, as in Cornwall the English created *Penny-Come-Quick* (in which you can see the Brythonic prefix for "head of")? The English contributed some placenames in Wales that are not in Welsh and Anglicized some others, bending them quite out of shape.

The old Celtic names are everywhere on the Continent but bent out of shape, as you notice when *dwr* (water) yields names such as Don, Duoro, Danau (Danube), Dordogne, and in England there is a place called Doncaster, the Roman *castra* (camp) by the water. The Welsh were Celts, the Celts were Aryans, and the Aryans wandered widely. The non-Cymric Celts say *uisge* for "water," which is where we get *whisky. River Avon* is redundant: *avon* is Celtic "river." The Welsh say *afon*. Compare Welsh *wsyg* with the placenames Esk, Usk, Isis (at Cambridge, that name being half Celtic "crooked"), Exe, Ouse, Ischia, Ain, Aisne, Ausonne, Oise. Anthony Burgess added that Welsh *haul* (sun) has the ghost of Greek *helios* in it. Welsh is a complicated language, as many ancient languages are. This will be enough to convince you:

yr ydym ni (we are)
yr ydych chwi (you are)
yr maent hwy (they are)

Placename etymologists sometimes posit a personal name working backward from a placename, with what accuracy no one can tell. However, this occurs more often with Anglo-Saxon names than with Welsh or Cornish or Irish ones. Some people in placenames of Wales are to be noted in the following list. It is a lengthy list, agreed; but it will also bring up some of the problems of Welsh mutation in language as well as changes in the manners and lives of the Welsh people. In the early days they lived protected in hillside forts and castles, relying on rivers for water and transportation, fencing their churches to keep cattle out of graveyards and moving their flocks to summer pastures, and so on. Placenames always give valuable insights into the lives of people.

Abergwili (mouth of Gwili's river)
Alltwalis (Walis' hillside)
Alltwynog (Wnog's hillside, or perhaps wood)
Arwystli (Arwystli's land)
Beddugre (grave of Ugre)
Betws Bledrws (Bledrws' prayer house)
Betws Gwerful Goch (prayer house of Gwerful the Red)
Blaenau Ffestiniog (heads of the valley of Ffestin's land)
Bont Dolgadfan (bridge [*pont*] of Cadfan's meadow)
Brynberian (Berian's hill)
Bryn Cynfeln (Cynfelyn's hill)
Bryn Llici (Lucy's hill)
Brynllwarch (Llywarch's hill)
Caehopcin (Hopcin's field, never confuse with *caer* "fort")
Caer Fagu (actually *Gardd Fagu*, land of Fagu, not a fort)

Callwen (very rare example of a personal name used as a placename, *Cynwyd* is another example)

Cardigan (originally *Cerredigion,* Ceredig's land, now in the English lexicon)

Carmarthen (fort near the sea)

Cilcennin (source of Cennin's river)

Coed Owen (Owen's wood)

Cregrina (originally *Craig Furuna,* Furuna's rock)

Darowen (Owen's oaks)

Eglwyswrw (the church, *cf.* French *église,* of Wrw, clearly a person of the Christian era)

Eisteddfa Gurig (resting place of Curig, not a grave, which is *bedd*)

Ffridd Faldwyn (pasture of Maldwyn—in English we say Baldwin)

Garthbrengi (Brengi 's enclosure–in Welsh, as in Cornish, the word for "church" and the word for any "enclosure" is the same; this one is an enclosure, but with *Glansefin* or *Llansefin* one cannot be certain)

Glyndyfrdwy (here we glimpse Dyfrdwy, the goddess of water)

Gwely Melangell (land, possibly dwelling, of Melangell)

Hafoty Cedig (Cedic's summer home—in summer people moved flocks to better pasturage)

Llanfilo (Milo's church)

Llangollen (Church of St. Collen—but is there any such saint?)

Llan ShonDorthy (Shon Dorddu's church, parish, or enclosure)

Llaneyre (church, parish, or enclosure of Llyr—or maybe just *lir* "long")

Llowes (Llywes, Louis, a saint)

Llyn Tegid (Tegid's pool)

Machnynlleth (Cynllait's plain)

Maen Beuno (Beuno's rock—the Celtic noun often gets rendered in English as "maiden," as in the standing stones of Cornwall called The Seven Maidens)

Maes Machreth (meadow of Macreth, possibly "son of Hreth")

Nancol (*nant* stream or stream valley of Coel)

Pennally (actually *pen* headland of *Alun,* English Alan, Allan, Allen)

Pentrehyling (actually *pen Heilyn,* Heilyn's headland)

Plas Iolyn (Iolyn's mansion)

Tresilian (Silian's homestead or farm)

Wentloog (disguising the personal name Gwyllwg)

Ystradowen (Owen's vale)

The English-speakers have simplified for themselves and created familiar Welsh placenames such as Glamorgan, Raglan, and St. Lythan's (actually *Llwyneliddon,* Eliddon's Grove, and there is no St. Ellidon or St. Lythan). We even play with the dual names on road signs (said to cause accidents because they distract foreign travelers with odd spellings). I recall, the placename being familiar because Wales has a distinguished cheese of the name, seeing a joking sign that read:

YOU ARE ENTERING WALES.
DRIVE CAREPHILLY.

Carephilly is *caer* fort of Ffili—whoever he may have been.

You will note a placename that is familiar and even a personal name or two that is familiar, such as *Owen* (*Owain*, as with the Tudor or *Tewdwr* of whom you may have heard). The earliest names (ninth century) of the princes of Wales have English equivalents still but here are some Welsh names in the line from Rhodri Mawr (Roderick the Great, 844 – 878) down to Llywellen ap Gruffydd (1246 – 1282, Son of Griffith), the last native prince of Wales. His grandfather (Llywellen Fawr, "The Great," 1194 – 1240) had three children: Gryffydd (Griffith), Dafydd (David), and Gwladus Ddu (Gladys "The Dark"), and she married into the line of the princes of Deheubarth (South Wales) in the person of Reginald de Braose and, when he died, she married Ralph Mortimer, the line of the earls of March, ancestors of Elizabeth II. Elizabeth II is also related to the line of the Tudors—there are Owen and Edmund Tudor, Earl of Richmond, father of Henry VII of England. In the royal Welsh background are names such as Anarrawd, Hywel Dda (Howell "The Good"), Hywell the Bad, Idwel Foel ("The Bald"), Owain Gwynedd (of North Wales), Bleddyn, Tudor Hen ("The Old"), Maredudd ap Tudor (Meredith son of Tudor), and so on. These royal names do not often crop up in placenames, but these people also bear titles derived from placenames such as Mercia, Hereford, Richmond, Gloucester, Mortimer (from the French for "Dead Sea"), Cambridge, and March.

Usually the dates of important rulers are reliable, but we cannot give dates to the most ancient placenames containing personal names nor can we always easily distinguish between pre-Christian and more recent persons. There are, of course, a great many places in Wales bearing the names of Christian saints, and some of these places were formerly holy wells, etc., of an earlier religion, about which we know practically nothing. There is a lot of talk about druids, but nobody knows much about them except the sacred grove, holly and ivy, and misletoe (cut with a golden scythe). The modern bards of Wales, keeping the old traditions of song and poetry alive, have no more connection to druids, however they dress, than modern Freemasons have to The Temple of Solomon, maybe less. Modern druids do not sacrifice virgins as the old druids seem to have done.

Today Welsh has achieved official recognition in the Principality. I have written about the new language laws and their implications in Wales (*Geolinguistics* 25, 1998). Now business can be conducted officially in Welsh everywhere in Wales, although there are places in Wales where practically no one speaks Welsh, just as there are many more places in the United States where practically no one speaks one of the Native American languages. And some places where people do not speak English! In both Wales and the United States there are many old placenames simply translated and a great many old names wiped right off the map and replaced by placenames given by later settlers. In placenames, although they last longer than most personal names and certainly in most cases much longer than brandnames and such, one can see how language records history and changes over time. In Wales we see traces of the Romans in words derived from the Latin such as *coron* (crown), *gwin* (wine), and *ffenestr* (window). From the English there are words such as *breacwast* (breakfast), *cwnstabl* (constable), and *plismon* (policeman). The toponymy of Wales shows Latin and English and other influences and yet inevitably has a character all its own, connected to the Welsh language—from which also came the drive for independence which has now produced Welsh as official in Wales.

Welsh placenames (as most Celtic placenames do, and all North American Native American places names do) like to be clearly related to the features of the landscape. Many Welsh placenames are made with *allt* (hillside), *bryn* (hill, high places being more easily defended), *coed* (wood), *dol* (meadow), *esgair* (ridge), and so on down the alphabet. Common are *mynydd* (mountain), *nant* (stream), *craig* (rock), *pant* (hollow), *pen* (headland), and the odd-looking *cwm* (shallow valley or depression). Naturally there are many castles, huts, pastures, farms, bridges, and fords (but *Ffordd-fawr* is "main road"). Personal names occur, as in *Sancler* (St. Clare) and *Capel Isaac* (Isaac's Chapel), but sometimes there are problems: for instance, is *Bryn Camlo* a place with a personal name in it or just "crooked" (as in Gaelic surnames such as *Cameron* and *Campbell*)? Celtic personal names or even nicknames must have had some use in placenaming from pre-historic times onwards, but their whole history is a difficult one. Even places named for saints present us sometimes with holy persons not recognized in official Christian hagiography. In more recent times old personal names may have been put on the land of Wales as the names of Amerindians were adopted in the United States but not by the Amerindians themselves.

The most popularized Welsh names are both fakes, the extremely long placename some tailor in Wales thought up as a joke or an attention-getter—this section will be distinguished by the fact that I do not give you that name—and Llareggub (which Dylan Thomas invented for *Under Milk Wood* and which is "bugger all" backwards but looks Welsh because of the double-L beginning of the word).

So much here for literary Welsh placenames. There are some old personal names in the poetry of the sixth-century Welsh bard Taliesen (which seems to have been an epithet more than a name: His Brow is Radiant) but not enough there on placenames to discuss here his marvelous documents. We note that Frank Lloyd Wright (1869 – 1959) made Taliesen famous as an American placename. In fact, he established two places: Taliesen East in Spring Green, Wisconsin, and Taliesen West in Paradise Valley, Arizona. As for legend, legend if not history connects the Old World and the New World with one of the 19 sons of Owain Gwynedd (of Gwynedd, North Wales, 1137 - 1170). This notable person was Prince Madoc, and when his father died Madoc went off to visit one of his brothers in Ireland and either missed his destination (as did Eric the Red on another sea voyage) or just pressed on to land in America. That was 1170. Don't believe me? A plaque on a wall at Mobile Bay (Alabama) gives him credit for discovering America. Thomas Stephens demolished the claim in a talk at an Eisteddfod in 1858, but it will not die. People still speak of the "white Indians", early Europeans encountered in America, "speaking Welsh"! The legend lives on, more strongly than it ever did in Lloyd & Powell's *Cambria* (1584) or the verses of the nineteenth-century British poet laureate, Robert Southey.

This little look at some Welsh placenames can suggest things to keep in mind when we examine the placenames of the United States. In the United States you will find tens of thousands of descendants of the Welsh and, though you will not find many US places called *Wales* (New York has a South Wales), there are examples of certain Welsh names transposed here and many examples of both *Welch* and *Welsh* this or that, as well as lots of places called *Cardiff, Lloyd* and (closer to the pronunciation in our view) *Floyd.*

Unusual as Welsh sounds to American ears, the "funny names" of Connecticut are (as Prof. Kelsie B. Harder has shown in a paper delivered at The Connecticut Onomastic Symposium) not Welsh, or even the Amerindian, ones but the English ones. I can add names such as Folly Works Brook, Flying Point, Johnnycake Mountain, Vexation Hill, but very few of the likes of Waubeeka Lake, Wimisink Brook, and Wononskopomuc Lake.

We move on now to another branch of the Celtic people, the Cornish.

I have in the works, and probably will have published before you read this, a little book that undertakes to survey the whole subject of Cornish names, personal names and placenames, both major and minor (such as the names in Cornish that English people with summer cottages in the duchy of Cornwall love to put on their houses). I find a great deal of interest in the Cornish language because, though its last native speaker died before the end of the eighteenth century, in the nineteenth century Cornish patriots began efforts to revive the language and by the end of the twentieth century people were communicating in Cornish in on-line chat rooms.

Leonard R. N. Ashley

Here I am going to bring to your attention just a little of Cornish material. The next section deals with a lot of Cornish saints (some of whom are non-existent except in these placenames) and the placenames that are involved with them.

"THE SAINTS COME MARCHING IN": NAMES OF SAINTS IN THE PLACENAMES OF CORNWALL

This ancient Cornish language lies like a buried city under our feet—we pass to and fro above it but heed it not in the bustle of everyday life. Yet in its words there is as much reality as ever there was in the obelisks of Egypt....

—John Bellow, "On the Cornish Language" (1861)

There will be that whole book by me on *Cornish Names* and even now there is an article by me in *Names* on the names of Cornish saints in toponymy (in a *Festschrift* for a leading American toponymist, Donald J. Orth, edited by a leading Canadian toponymist Alan J. Rayburn). I have rewritten the latter for inclusion here, though I might have addressed saints' names in Roman Catholic areas such as Central and South America or even Quebec. I choose the names of saints on the Cornish landscape because they are neglected and because they bring in a folklore element here that I want to see stressed.

The Cornish are an ancient people, descended from the Celts who were the first Indo-Europeans to spread across Europe. The Celts were first noted in southern Europe around 500 BC. They went to the British Isles in two waves: to Ireland about 400 BC (whence Gaelic, later spread to Scotland and The Isle of Man); later to southern and western parts of Britain. Tribes coming from northern Europe pushed them westward and about 400 AD some were driven over to Brittany. The Cornish and the Bretons thus share Brythonic language. The last native speaker of Cornish, Dolly Pentreath, died at an advanced age in the last quarter of the eighteenth century, though Cornish lingered a bit longer in prayers and in common expressions. It remained in old literature and in the placenames.

Ancient Cornish placenames are found both in old forms (such as Carantoc) and in Middle Cornish (Merandoc became Meransek), the old stress on the final syllable shifting to the penultimate. Cornwall and Brittany share what is called P-Celtic, the *kw-* becoming *p-*, whereas in the Gaelic of Ireland, Scotland, and The Isle of Man the *kw-* was longer retained and later was *q-* or *c-*. There have been attempts since the nineteenth century to revive Cornish as a spoken and written language, based on the ancient forms. The placenames are firmly established; they still function for all the inhabitants of the duchy of Cornwall (of which the heir to the British throne, the prince of Wales, is always the duke). The Cornish placenames preserve a once-living language like a fly in amber.

Once the Cornish were converted to Christianity by monks from Ireland, Cornish baptisms created many saints' names eventually familiar to us in English forms such as John, Mary, Michael, and James (which, as Jago, produced such placenames as Trago and Treago). The Cornish for Constantine was Custentin. There were also some personal names recorded of the ancient kings and chieftains. The most famous of these is Tudor, from Teudar, king of Cornwall. Only three generations of Tudors reigned in England, but over a 120-year period: Henry VII (reigned 1485 – 1509, son of Edmund Tudor, Earl of Richmond, and grandchild of Owen Tudor and Catherine of France, widow of Henry V); Henry VIII (reigned 1509 – 1547); and three children of Henry VIII: Edward VI (reigned 1547 – 1553), Mary I (reigned 1553 – 1558), and Elizabeth I (reigned 1558 – 1601).

The Bodmin Gospels (a tenth-century manuscript once in Bodmin Abbey), also called the St. Petrock Gospels, give us the names of 33 persons who freed slaves at the altar of St. Petrock. Of those manumitting slaves, 24 had English names, 5 Cornish names, 4 Graeco-Roman names. Of the freed slaves, 12 had Latin names, 12 English names, and 98 Cornish names. That early, some Cornishmen had English names, some had Cornish names, some had one of each. At this time there were no surnames.

Eventually there were so many persons given the same Christian names at the font that the extra identification of a surname was necessary. I shall not deal with the given names and inherited surnames of the Cornish here, however; my subject will be the names of the locally revered saints who produced Cornish placenames.

These placenames are to be found not only in the names of churches and holy wells but also in the names of parishes (Budock recalls St. Budoc) and towns (Pinnock is for St. Pynoccus) and so on. Names sometimes undergo drastic alteration. Examples include Zennor (from St. Senara) and St. Veep (from St. Vepus). In placenames there was a Latinizing of Celtic names and a Celticizing of Latin names, and there are many names that look English (Penny-Come-Quick is well known and it signals distortion of a Cornish name, though most English names do not). Landrake goes back to an eleventh-century Landerhtun. That fact underlines the need to seek out the earliest forms of placenames in the archives. In this case, *lannergh* (clearing) and *tun* (town, or farm) are involved. This *tun* usually appears as *tre* in Cornish placenames (and in the surnames derived from them). The Anglicization of Cornish placenames occurs in Cornish surnames as well as in placenames: Tossell is from St. Austell. It is the same kind of thing that in English produced *tawdry* from St. Audrey.

There is a problem with placenames such as Virginstow, which was dedicated to St. Bridgit. Advent seems to come not from the season in the church calendar but from St. Adwena. Occasionally the *St.* designation is clear but the personal name is obscured: St. Winnock is for St. Winnocus, but some instances are less obvious. St. Tudy is one holy person honored on the maps of both Cornwall and Brittany. For a while I could find no person to go with the placename St. Issey but eventually I located a practically unknown saint called St. Idi. The lists of official saints of the Roman Catholic Church do not always contain the names of all the Cornish and Breton saints you may encounter. Some of those may be as fabulous as (say) St. Faith, St. Hope, St. Charity, or the well-known pious fraud of St. Christopher (whose name, too apt, should have made us doubt the story long before the church struck St. Christopher off the register). You will find in Jeffrey Spittle & John Field's *A Reader's Guide to the Place-Names of the United Kingdom* (1990) a considerable number of placenames deriving from saints not to be found in any official hagiographical lists.

Irish missionaries, "wandering for the love of God," were early sent by St. Patrick (who converted the Irish) to convert the Cornish. Famous was St. Peran, sometimes called Peiran or Piran, the patron saint of tin miners. Tin mining was begun very early in Cornwall (and could be a dangerous occupation requiring the protection of a saint). The Phoenicians traded for tin in Cornwall long before there were any saints there. When Cornish mines began to offer little work, tin miners left Cornwall for the United States, Canada, Australia, and elsewhere. In that way Cornish names of both persons and places spread all over the world. It was said at one time that wherever there was a deep hole you would find a Cornishman at the bottom of it.

Here are some saints remembered in the placenames still on the map of Cornwall. You will recognize Hilary because of Hillary Rodham Clinton (though the half dozen saints named Hilary are all male). There is also St. Michael of St. Michael's Mount in Cornwall, a sister establishment of the monks who built Mont St.-Michel in Brittany. The church of St. Peran at Perranporth is the oldest whose four walls are still standing in Britain: it dates from the sixth or seventh century. A Norman church was erected to house the relics of the saint but it sank into the sand in the nineteenth century and was not excavated until after World War II. You know the names of St. Mary, St. Martin, and St. Helen, and perhaps you also know that these names have been given to the smaller Isles of Scilly (whose inhabitants naturally do not like the term The Scilly Isles). St. Agnes, St. Austell, and some other saints are not in the following list but are to be found in Cornish placenames. The saints' names that follow will look strange to you, for the most part, and, even with names occasionally heard (Hyacinth as a forename, Hugo as both forename and surname) almost everyone would be hard pressed to say anything about any saint of that name. The name you will recognize is that of St. Ive, a very obscure person in hagiography but a famous one in a placename that has long been familiar in children's rhymes:

As I was going to St. Ives
I met a man with seven wives.

Leonard R. N. Ashley

St. Ives is therefore more famous than such Cornish tourist sites as Lord Robartes' seventeenth-century mansion at Lanhydrock, the Bronze-Age stones standing near St. Buryans (Boscawen-Un, The Merry Maidens—"maidens" and stones" confused again—and The Pipers), The Lizard, The Cheesewring (stones thought to resemble the device for pressing excess water out of cheese), Tintagel (alleged to be the site of King Arthur's castle and Merlin's cave), Lostwithiel Castle, Fowey (pronounced "Foy"), Mousehole (pronounced something like "Muzzle"), and the cathedral at the principal city, Truro (a Victorian cathedral tucked onto remnants of a sixteenth-century church).

Here is the list of strange saints I have been promising:

St. Anietus	St. Ervan	St. Hydrock	St. Mawes	St. Pierani di Udnoe
St. Blazey	St. Euny	St. Ida	St. Mawgan	St. Probus
St. Breage	St. Eval	St. Ildierna	St. Melanus	St. Rumonus
St. Breward	St. Ewe	St. Ive	St. Melor	St. Salwys
St. Clether	St. Felicitas	St. Julian	St. Mer[r]in	St. Sampson
St. Colanus	St. Feoca	St. Juliot	St. Merteriana	St. Sativola
St. Cornelly	St. Filius	St. Julitta	St. Mewen	St. Selevan
St. Credan	St. Gennys	St. Just	St. Moran	St. Sidinius
St. Crewenna	St. Germans	St. Kea	St. Morwena	St. Stedyana
St. Cubertus	St. Gerrans	St. Kerin	St. Mylor	St. Symphorian
St. Cuby	St. Gluvias	St. Kew	St. Nectan	St. Talian
St. Day	St. Gonandus	St. Keyn(e)	St. Neot	St. Teath
St. Dunstan	St. Gothian	St. Loe	St. Nivet	St. Tinney
St. Edelienta	St. Grada	St. Mabyn	St. Non	St. Uny
St. Enedoc	St. Gulval	St. Madsurnus	St. Nonna	St. Wendrona
St. Enoder	St. Guron	St. Manarca	St. Padernus	St. Wenn
St. Erme	St. wennarth	St. Marina	St. Pol de Leon	St. Wennapa
(St. Erney)	St. Hugo	St. Maudiz	St. Petherwin	
St. Erth	St. Hyacinth	St. Maunanas	St. Petroc(k)	

50

Spellings vary. In France you have heard of St. Lô. Some of these are known elsewhere (St. Dunstan appears in Canada, for instance) and some are imaginary or old divinities in Christian disguise. It was a habit of early Christianity to adopt and adapt pagan holidays (which early converts perhaps were going to celebrate out of habit anyway) and to turn pagan holy places into Christian shrines, just as a statue of Venus with Eros might be given halos and proclaimed to represent the Virgin and Child. It was part of a basic renaming, really. The statue did not change just because the figures it represented were renamed but the attitude toward it, its meaning, did change with the names.

Let us stray from the topic for just a moment to look at some English names of Cornish origin and you will see the placenaming at work:

Come-to-Good	Jesus Well	Rosewall Hill
Couch's Mill	Kingsand	The Rumps
Fire Beacon Point	Mother Ivey's Bay	Tideford
Hell's Mouth	Newland	Tucking Mill
Hole	Portholland	Widemouth Bay
Hore Stone Bridge	Rock	Yondertown

To these add what the English speakers have made of some Cornish names (with etymologies):

Arrow Park (*garrow* rough *parc* plowed field, or possibly *eru* one acre *parc*)
Bacchus Park (*bagus* bush *parc* plowed field)
Cold Harbour (*col* neck *ar* over *burg* the town)
Comfort (*cam* crooked *fordh* way)
Gold Arrows (*gweal* field *daras* by the door)
Well Man (*gweal* field *maen* stone)

So you can expect that some of the saints' names, as well as personal names in other placenames, will have suffered some in transition from Cornish to English times. Note also that the sort of corrupted names in the little list above leads inevitably to folk etymologies and legends. The English penchant for twisting foreign placenames out of shape matters less in Cornwall than in most places, because 90% of the placenames of Cornwall are Cornish and most, though not all, are pretty close to correct Cornish. A great many Cornish placenames still begin with *pen, pol,* and *tre,* about which there is a familiar rhyme in English:

> By *Tre*, *Pol*, and *Pen*,
> You shall know the Cornishmen.

Those of literary mind will think of the novel *Pendennis* and the 1898 Pinero play of *Trelawny of 'The Wells'* (Sadler's Wells is meant, a theater) and televsion viewers will know of *Poldark.* This also makes the point that many Cornish surnames are derived from the places from which the original bearers of the surnames came in Cornwall. The surnaming system in Cornwall relied heavily on placenames. The earliest extra names were the forenames of the fathers, however. Later placenames of origin were adopted as were occupation and –*son* names, along with the equivalents of English Black, White, Russell, and so on, from appearance. Cornwall produced John of Trevisa (1326 – 1412) and placenames such as Tremaine, Trenowth, Polglase, Polmear, Polwhele, Penprase, and Penrose produced inheritable surnames. The places named for saints did not often produce surnames, nor were surnames created in the Irish fashion that gave us the equivalent of (say) "follower of St. Finbar." Saints were remembered chiefly in baptismal names. Saints' names, therefore, served as surnames (we might say) only in the early period in which the forename of the father served as a kind of extra name. That attaching of the father's name to the child's is a Celtic custom which may be seen in John Millington Synge's well known play *The Playboy of the Western World*: in the play the heroine is Pegeen Mike (Little Margaret, daughter of Michael).

Informative and interesting as all Cornish placenames are, there is something special and worthy of notice, in my opinion, in the placenames of Cornwall that recall its saints, even the very obscure ones whose identities are shrouded in mysteries and whose shrines have long since disappeared so that the saints live on only in toponymy.

In Cornwall, the saint's name may be hidden inside a placename: Altarnun is for St. Non. This means that there are more saints' names than at first glance appears to be the case. There is even greater piety expressed than we may find in such Roman Catholic areas in Canada (such as Quebec) and Mexico today, although Cornwall has been for a very long time Protestant in general and Low Church (Chapel) in particular. It is true that in the reign of Protestant Edward VI the Cornish retained the Roman Catholicism that Edward VI's father (Henry VIII) tried to sweep away. In fact, Cornwall rose in protest against the new Church of England. It is also true that John Wesley's Methodism made a strong appeal to the Cornish (all those Methodist chapels). Cornwall became more Methodist than Wesley (who never himself left the Church of England). Now it is a long time since Roman Catholic placenames such as Altarnun and Bodmin

(Monk's House) or even Penzance (Holy Headland) were especially appropriate in Cornwall. Now Cornwall is basically dour Methodist. Methodism is a faith that seems to me to go well with the great Atlantic storms and the granite and shale of the severe landscape.

The Roman Catholic saints are an inheritance of the distant past—and a reminder that placenames preserve the old even through great social changes. Some few of them, as I said before, may be pre-Christian deities in disguise, particularly (in my view) those saints associated with holy wells, very early dedicated to pagan deities of water. As elsewhere in Britain, on occasion these wells are still decorated ceremonially by the folk, recalling old rites. In the nineteenth century Britain in a fit of antiquarianism revived many old customs, even Harvest Home, especially in the West Country, and wells that had not been decorated for centuries were suddenly decked again, not, of course, to please pagan deities. The names of pagan deities have to be guessed at, just as is the case with the names of old chieftains. Some chieftain's names are obvious in Bod Annam (Annam's Home, in St. Breoc parish) or Bod-Dell (Dell's Home—from which we derived surnames such as Biddle as well as the current placename). What some of the old saints' (and chieftains') names mean may be uncertain.

That at least a large number of places were actually named for persons is suggested by a manuscript in the library of Cambridge University, *Register of British Saints*, which was the work of an Elizabethan scholar, Nicholas Roscarrock. Roscarrock was put in prison because he continued to adhere to his Roman Catholic faith and this was a work of his Roman Catholic piety. Of course in some cases Roscarrock may have counted fictious saints as real. Those that the church recognizes as real can be checked in other hagiographies. All the saints' names recall the Christian missionaries from Ireland ("The Land of Saints and Scholars") who were responsible for bringing their fellow Celts in Cornwall into their communion. If, in the process, some of the old divinities and customs were quietly incorporated into the new Christians' faith, this would not be surprising. The same thing happened, as we can see from early Anglo-Saxon chronicles, in England. Everywhere the new religion built on the old (sometimes, in erecting churches over the ruins of pagan temples, literally), as when Christianity chose the Saturnalia's date for Christmas and set Easter to correspond with rites of Dionysus, and so on. In Mexico they actually used the stones of the Aztec temples to build churches. The early history of Cornwall is less well recorded, but the earliest laws of the English, for instance, show how hard a time Christians had in stamping old pre-Christian customs. (I write about this in my books on magic and witchcraft.) We still recall the Teutonic worship of gods in trees, at Christmas. This actually came back into fashion as an "old custom" in Victorian times. Such nature divinities (famously Teutonic) lurked long in Cornwall.

The worship of older divinities and the veneration of Christian saints were especially to be noted in the bleak parts of Cornwall where the people had special reason to pray for protection and solace. The holy names remind us now. In an area such as Cornwall where so many of the placenames are directly descriptive and pragmatic, there were also religious needs and religious names.

Indeed, there were some extraordinary religious figures who have places named for them still. Let us look briefly at the people behind placenames such as St. Budoc(k), St. Neot, St. Endellion, and St. Cleer. Region, folklore, and placenames all come together in this.

St. Budoc(k)'s mother, Azenor, had been declared unfaithful and had been cast out to sea in a barrel. She had been up to something, because St. Budoc(k) was born in that barrel. His name may seem to English speakers to be perilously close to *buttock* but it was much revered in Cornwall. Mother and child were washed ashore and the mother found employment as a washerwoman. The boy grew up to be a saint.

St. Neot was given two fish by an angel and told that if he ate only one each day he would always have fish for dinner. One day his servant made a mistake. (It was hard to get good help even at that early date.) The servant cooked not one but both of the fish. St. Neot promptly threw them both into a holy well, and everything was—well. St. Neot is said to have been only 15 inches tall, and he had an arm preserved as a relic in Cornwall. The rest of his relics were stolen— the practice was common in the Middle Ages—for a church in Cambridgeshire. Stealing of relics reminds us that one good reason for naming a place after a saint was to establish it as the place to come to ask for that saint's intercession. Pilgrims would visit the relics and leave offerings. In a sense, this is commercial placenaming: the influence of monetary considerations on the bestowing of placenames is something I have written about in connection with SoHo and NoHo, etc., but the subject deserves more attention from placename scholars of olden times. We must always consider not only what the namers called a place but why, something which geographers and even linguists often fail to do.

St. Edellion (or Endillion) had a cow. A nasty man killed it. Her father killed the man, in revenge. The saint kindly brought him back to life. (No news of the cow.) Her shrine and holy well are at Wadebridge, and *Wadebridge* is an odder name than it looks: *waed* is Old English for "ford" and *bryog* was the "bridge" that replaced the need for fording the water. The bridge was put up in the fourteenth century, by which time the Old English language was out of business.

St. Cleer, a sixth-century hermit in Cornwall, was outraged to see hurlers out playing games on a Sunday. Hurling is a rather violent game of Celtic origin in which the players often bash each other with sticks; it resembles the Amerindian game that the French christened *lacrosse*. To preserve the quiet of the Lord's Day, St. Cleer turned the players, magically, to stone. Don't believe it? At Liskeard (a placename that has traveled as far as Canada), the *lys* (court) of someone called Kerwyd, you can see the stone circle for yourself. It is, naturally, called The Hurlers. Note, in passing, that the names of Cornish tourist sites seem always to be in English. Tourists speak English.

I hope you will agree that the saints' names on the map of Cornwall are interesting. I hope you will further agree that there is much to be learned from even this tiny topic and the place that has, among other striking names, the *pen von lass* (end of the earth) at Land's End. These placenames bring to you something of a people with a long and colorful history and a fascinating folklore. They are people who are more than wild Britons, smugglers, wreckers, miners, and (like the Welsh, whose Celtic origins they share) "strangers" —that is what *Welsh* means—to the English. The Cornish race of people is also of interest to us in North America. In our history are such Cornish names as those of John Hancock and Dashiell Hammett, Ezra Cornell and John Berryman. Our Canadian cousins can note the famous twentieth-century physician Wilder Penfield and James Yeo, a prominent figure in Prince Edward Island in the nineteenth century.

A FEW FRENCH SURNAMES FOR THE ENGLISH

You have to know a man very well in Canada to know his surname.

—John Buchan, Lord Tweedsmuir,
"Sayings of the Week" *Observer,* 21 May 1950

William the Bastard did not have, because of his birth, the career prospects in the duchy of Normandy that he wanted. So he determined to take the kingdom of England. This he did, in 1066, from Harold the Saxon. After all, there were various claimants and William may have had as much right to the crown as Harold. In any case, might makes right, and Harold, exhausted from a victory over another contender, could not resist defeat by William. William probably did not kill Harold in personal combat, but the comic ballad tells us:

'E went right up to 'Arold and shot 'im.
'E were offside, but what could they do?

William the Bastard became William the Conqueror. He had himself crowned twice, just to make sure. He took a survey of his newfound kingdom (called *Domesday Book* because its decisions were as binding if not as significant as those to be made at the Last Judgment). He brought many of his Norman friends to positions of power in England, giving them land for loyalty. Their forenames (such as *Robert* and *Richard*) became popular, and their surnames were living proof that they were socially very much higher than the Saxon churls. That local bunch who went around speaking Old English and knew little either of French (the language of government) or Latin (the language of the Church).

If you have read the novels of William Makepeace Thackeray, you may remember Miss Crawley, who loved "French novels, French cooking, and French wine." The English admired French surnames. What some of those became in the mouths of the speakers of English is the subject of this short take on a very large subject. Surnames are of great importance in Britain, whatever a British governor-general said about Canada. That is true whatever the American habit may be regarding the use of given rather than inherited names and a certain freedom in changing the latter.

Now, this is a book about placenames. However, in any discussion of placenames there must be at least a nod in the direction of surnames. So many family names derive from places from which ancestors came or with which they were associated, either specifically or in names such as *Fleming.* Here you will

Leonard R. N. Ashley

learn something about Lewis Mumford and Frank Purdue and William F. Buckley, Jr., and Buffy the Vampire Slayer.

The French influence actually reached England before the Conqueror. The Anglo-Saxon king and saint Edward the Confessor had a Norman mother, and she brought to England with her a retinue of French courtiers. But it was William and his Normans who imposed French on England, where it was more important than English from the eleventh to the fourteenth centuries. Even when, in the late fourteenth century, Geoffrey Chaucer—note his French surname, derived from some French maker or seller of *chausses*, leggings or boots—undertook to write his masterpiece in English, in the first 18 lines of *The Canterbury Tales* he used at least 18 words of French origin.

The French influence declining in Chaucer's day had so long been pervasive that many of the names that we think of as particularly English are, in fact, derived from the Norman nobility, the occupations of their servants, or objects familiar to them. The nobles tended to have titles or surnames from placenames in France.

A typically Norman surname could have something to do with physical appearance (one of the main sources of surnames), such as Algernon (from French *aux gernons*, "bewhiskered"). The village that the first Algernon left behind, Percé, near St. Lô, gave us the surname Percy (later used as a forename as well). Algernon and Percy and similar Norman names started out as the identifiers of stalwart fighters. It was not until the nineteenth-century adoption of such Norman names (along with Norman, Marmaduke, Percival and such) for mommas' boys that these bellicose names took on a stuffy, weak, or effeminate character. Even Chester (from Latin *castra*, soldiers' camp) has moved from warlike to weak. Today Percy is such that one man is said to have named his son Percy not to commemorate any burly warrior but to make the lad himself a fighter. "Anyone named Percy," the father explained, aware of the cruel taunts of the playground, "has got to learn how to fight."

Percival is an even more sissified name now. It came from a different French source and was invented for an epic hero in a twelfth-century romance by Chrêtien de Troyes. Naturally, in addition to employing real placenames for their associations, significant placenames are created by writers of poetry and also by writers of prose fiction: think of the imaginary places in Cervantes' *Don Quixote*, one of which translates as Rogue's Island (the residence of a deep dyed villain). French romances in verse and prose contributed a good deal to the names in English.

Other names now weak but once soldierly are Bruce (from the ancestral estates, near Chérbourg, of Robert de Bruis, who was a forebear of Scotland's great hero, Robert the Bruce); Chauncey (from a village near Amiens); and Bayard (from *le chevalier sans peur et sans réproche*, "the knight without fear or reproach," Pierre de Terrail, Chevalier de Bayard). We have forgotten the

58

warriors whose lands were made memorable in names such as Chesney (Le Quesney), Lacey (Lassy), Lester (Lestre), Lucy (Luce), and Munsey or Muncie (Monceaux, Calvados). If you didn't have any land you were not much of a noble. King John was mocked as Lackland. If the French noted you were *sans terre* you might have got the nickname and then the surname that survives as Santer, Samter, or even (looking like an English stroller) Saunter.

The forenames of old French figures are also in use. "Saki" (H. H. Munro) has a character called Clovis. That Clovis is very unlike the fifth-century Chlodowig, or Clovis, first Frankish ruler of what we now call France. His name was Latinized—those who could write wrote Latin—as both Clovis and Ludowicus. So from Clovis we got not just Louis and Lewis but also Lüdwig.

You see that words change, though names change more slowly than most. In England, where Calais is pronounced like *callous* and garage is pronounced to rhyme with *carriage,* the French names were battered. Bacquepuis became Bagpuz, Giboin was demoted to Gubbins, Brett came from Bretagne, Boyce from some *bois* (woods), and Miners—which looks very English—is really French Minières (which as early as 1204 had become Mineres in England). Students of English placenames like to tell the story of Shotover Hill. For a long time it baffled researchers, for they found the name used in eras when there was nothing powerful enough to shoot over the hill. Eventually they discovered it had been the site of a *Château Vert,* Green House. There is still an argument going on as to whether London's Rotten Row comes from *ratton row* or *route du roi.* I tend to believe the latter; it would be just like the English.

Equally radical changes disguise many other origins undoubtedly French. Beecham is from some Beauchamp (a place with a pretty field), Bewley from some Beaulieu (Pretty Place), Mowbray from Montbrai, just as Buckley comes from some *beau clerc* (who could write well, or write at all), Bacon from Bacun le Molay, and Parlabean from *parle bien* (speak well). Crawcour or even Croker can be from some broken-hearted, or heart-breaking, French ancestor. Marbrow might look like Marlborough (also Marlboro) mangled, or suggest some ravaged forehead or hillside, but it is likely from French *marbrier*, someone who quarried marble. Occupation names are a common as names derived from places.

Not so clearly from the French are names such as Pierce. Pierce could be the French forename Piers (as with Piers Gaveston, the French boyfriend of Edward II), a forename more usually Pierre, or it could come from the English verb. It might even be from a French placename. Duffy can be an Irish surname or from the French (*homme*) *de fer*, which makes it rather like Smith. Brimson has more than one origin, but one of them is Briençun, Normandy. Boffey and Buff(e)y come either from *beau foy* (good faith) or from Beaufour, a Calvados placename. Keynes comes from Cahagnes, and some say Mumford comes from Montford-sur-Risle. Passmore sounds very English but is somewhat related to French geography: the Passmores originally arrived (French for came to the river bank) *passe mer* (across the sea). Bigot is either a placenane or "By God!" (The swearers in French, *"Par Dieu!,* received surnames such as Pardo and Purdue.) People can be named grandly from a place (de la Haye, de la Warre—whence Delaware) or they can fake it: Dan Foe becomes Daniel Defoe, Oscar Renta becomes Oscar de la Renta, or, not so grandly (Bunn[e]y can come from a rabbit or a swelling, *beugne*).

If you think that Pardo and Purdue are extraordinary, consider the surname Butter. English? Possibly. But also very possibly from *butor* (bittern); that bird booms so resoundingly during the mating season that the nickname and eventual surname was perfect for a loudmouth, just as Italian Parlaparla suited someone we might nickname Mighty Mouth. Because places can take their names from animals, objects, and so on, one can never be absolutely certain in certain cases whether a person's surname can be found on some old map or not.

On top of that, even if the name can be found on a map, surnames cannot always be traced back to one particular place. There are a number of English places named Ashley, for an ash tree in a field, or a sacred grove of ash trees of the druids. Nor can we always settle on one explanation: Warren may come from Varenne or from *warrenier* (sometimes *garennier*) the game warden. Marshall is a high title but also comes from *mareschault*, the fellow who looked after the horses. Even higher were the royal Stuarts or Stewarts, but they started out tending pigstys. At the same time, surnames can come down in the world: LeRoy or Leroy was related to the king, and Fitzroy was a royal bastard. (Better to be the illegitimate son of somebody important—FitzGerald, from a great Irish earl, for instance—than the legitimate son of a nobody!) All the English and Irish names with *Fitz* in them refer to French *fils* (son)—but now you know the son was born, as they used to say, on the wrong side of the blanket. Surnames from places can over time become more or less dignified.

Fitz and *fils* have come down practically unchanged. So have many of the estate names that aristocrats took for their surnames or their noble titles. When you get to be a peer, you sign your title, not your surname—say, Bath for that marquess, not Thynne, Bedford for that duke, not Russell—so the skinny and redhaired ancestors disappear. Those estate names, originally in France, produced such quintessentially British surnames as the following: Balliol (Bailleul-sur-Eaulne), Chandos (Candos, Eure), Curzon (from Hubert de Curçun), Giffard (Longueville-la-Gifart), Grenville (Grainville-la-Teinturière, a dyers' place), Marmion (Fontenay-le-Marmion), Vere (Ver, La Manche), Sackville (Saugeville), Talbot (Talebot), Buckerell (Bouquerel), Quincy (Cuinchy), Fancourt (Fallencourt, which by William the Conqueror's century was already Fanucurt), even Haig (La Hague, west of Chérbourg). From the French we also got Harcourt, Trac(e)y, Darry (d'Orrell), Redvers (Reviers), Montgomery (Mont Goumeril), Granville ("large city"), Pomeroy ("of the apple orchard"), and much more. The Ros family (of Kent and elsewhere) has no Celtic background (in

Celtic languages *ros* is "heath," though Cornwall's St. Just-in-Roseland makes it look as if roses were involved); these Ros people trace themselves back to Rots (Calvados). Some of the Briands, Brians, Briens, Bryants, etc., are of Irish origin, of course—there are many O'Briens, O'Bryans, and so on, but I've never heard of a McBrien—but some go all the way back to the Old Norse *Brjan*. That reached Britain from Brittany (or maybe the reverse).

Who would guess that some people named West (also Wast) come from La Vast in La Manche (The Sleeve)? Or that Sandlers and Santlers may be from St.-Lô (Somme, La Manche) or St.-Laud (Maine-et-Loire)? The saints are hidden by the English pronunciations of Seymour (St.-Maur), Sidney (St.-Denis), Simmery (Ste.-Marie), Sinclair (St.-Clair), and even Marleybone (Ste.-Marie-la-bonne, St. Mary the Good). In the same sort of way the English say Morris for Maur or Maurice and that disguises the word for "Moor," as in Morris dancing. Some of these are just personal names and some are both personal names and the names of places in Britain and wherever British culture spread. Morristown (New Jersey) does not register as "Blackamoor Town" to us.

Who thinks, in terms of personal names (which can also be made into placenames) of a small beak when he hears Becket(t) or of *la biguerie* when Bygore is heard? How many people named Fletcher realize that some ancestor put the feathers on arrows (made by Arrowsmith for bows strung by Stringer)? How many Faulkners (or Falkners) know an ancestor cared for falcons (*fau[l]connier* was "falconer") or operated a *fauçon* (windlass or crane)? The first Pauncefote had an "arched belly" (or, worse, was "belly faced") and the first Belcher had a pretty face, the first Vernon reminded people of Spring, the first René (and at least some of the Raineys) were thought of as "reborn." The Parsloes and Pashleys, and such Parsleys as were not named for plants, came from across the sea (Old French *passelewe*, "crossing the water," water as *l'eau* also proving the English with the loo, or toilet). Some people were named for places where there were certain trees: Perry (pear tree), Laverne (alder), Cheyney (*chênaie*, "oak grove"). Some persons were associated with—perhaps thought to resemble—birds: Merle (Blackbird), Russell can be "red-haired" or from *roselle* (redwing). Arundel (a placename as well as a personal name) is from *arondel* (little swallow). These names, once appropriate for an individual or a place, have been inherited by generations that do not even know what they mean, very often, and whom they no more suit that Mr. Long suits the short person or Mr. Short suits the tall one.

We already had a mention of *"Par Dieu!"* and some reference to surnames (Don Pardo has another, and you might add Pardew, Purday, Purdy, and perhaps Purefoy, even Pepperday) and some of my favorite British names from the French come from the hard-swearing Normans: Dabney and Debney are from the way they said "God bless!" and Dugard from "God save!" I particularly like Bonger, which comes from the way they said good day: *"Bon jour!"* Some of these surnames, thus derived, were put on places, institutions (Purdue University), and so on.

The Normans and the Anglo-Saxons intermarried, and their surnames and placenames include hybrids: Melville is half English "hill" and half French "city." But Neville is Neville and not "new city" and Dunstanville has nothing to do with St. Dunstan: it came from Denestanville in France. When is Grant from *grand(e)* and when not? Cummings may come in some cases from Bose-Benard-Commin (Eure) but usually it is of Irish origin.

Today the French are mourning the loss of overseas empire (though promoting *francophonie* in Africa and wherever else they can). The French are passing laws to keep *franglais* from proliferating. They are fighting a last-ditch battle to prevent English from becoming not only the second language of the whole world but even the replacement of French in diplomacy and trade, aviation and finance, and much more. (French terms remain in ballet and fencing and cooking and such.) French is on the defensive, except in Quebec, where English is taking a beating and so-called anglophones are leaving what used to be *la belle province* and now calls itself *le gouvernement du Québec*, as if it were a nation and not still just a part of Canada. In the battle, it is encouraging for lovers of French to consider how much the French language has contributed to English and—as this article illustrates—to placenames in English-speaking countries. We have stopped calling the Near East by the French name, Levant (the east, where *the rising* of the sun takes place), but the French influence remains strong, if not always noticed.

In as small a matter as the surprising number of surnames in English derived from the French and spread from Britain around the world, you can see how names and history are linked.

VERMONT

Freedom and Unity

—Motto of Vermont

I want to keep on the French tack for just a bit longer, so here are the placenames of a state with a French name, Vermont (for *les monts verts,* the Green Mountains, forever in our history because of Ethan Allen and his Green Mountain Boys of the eighteenth century). Vermont has 14 counties, with these county seats:

Addison	Middlebury
Bennington	Bennington
Caledonia	Saint Johnsbury
Chittenden	Burlington
Essex	Guildhall
Franklin	Saint Albans
Grand Isle	North Hero
Lamoille	Hyde Park
Orange	Chelsea
Orleans	Newport
Rutland	Rutland
Washington	Montpelier
Windham	Newfane
Windsor	Woodstock

Not much of a French connection there, though the capital of the state is Montpelier (which ought to have been Montpellier). There is also Barre and the French name of the nation's third oldest city (one that hoped at one time to become the capital of the state), Vergennes. The French names may be the most interesting in Vermont. The state has nothing to compare with the extraordinary placenames of (say) Texas, where a fellow named Joseph Howell in pioneer days refused to drink—the first building in town was a saloon—and so they named the town after him, St. Jo. There are elsewhere US towns named for a mule, a biscuit, and hot coffee, and staid Vermont cannot rival that.

The Vermont name *Vergennes* derives from a more dignified character. He was Charles Gravier, Comte de Vergénnes, the French diplomat who negotiated the Treaty of Paris (1783), which brought the American Revolution to an end. Vergennes bears one of three names adopted—others he suggested were not picked up—by Michel-Guillaume St.-Jean de Crévecoeur. He was a Frenchman who settled in Vermont, called a daughter America Frances, and became a citizen of the Vermont Republic. He wrote under the pseudonym J. Hector St.-John the famous *Letters from an American Farmer* (1782). To this St.-John we owe Saint Johnsbury and Danville (which he urged we adopt in honor of Jean-Baptiste Bourguignon d'Anville).

The intrepid explorers were early active in Vermont territory. During the French and Indian Wars, the Winooski River was so crowded with French ships that it was called French River. But many of the names given by Frenchmen did not stick, not even those bestowed by the great Samuel de Champlain. You know it has been a habit for each new wave of explorers to be ignorant of or simply replace placenames given by earlier explorers. What Champlain called *Rivière aux Loutres,* Vermonters christened Otter Creek. You can see that the name Grand Isle was once French; that was one of Champlain's names (Big Island) that stuck, and it is the name of a county (albeit the smallest one), often called The Islands. Champlain's *Rivière de la Mouette*—he saw some gulls, and he was a busy man, quick to give a name—was corrupted when an equally busy cartographer in 1744 failed to cross the *tt*'s. *La Mouette* became *La Mouille* and wound up as *Lamoille,* and that is another county name today. It is the most recent country, carpentered together from bits of other counties in 1835—way back when the United States for the last time didn't have any national debt. At one point, a lot of Vermont's latest county was part of the state of New York. Today, some parts of Vermont are filling up with New Yorkers, changing the nature of the state at least as much as has (say) the habit Canadians developed of crossing the border for better bargains in Burlington.

That trade brought Vermonters modern French speakers, but that did not stop Vermonters from continuing to manhandle French names. This only worsened when people began to forget some of their French and speak a kind of broken English, ever more English, ever less French. That twisting out of shape of French names was echoed in what they did with some other names of European origin. Recently, Vermonters have seen even Asian names. Germany's Mecklenburg (involved with the British royals) Vermonters made into

Meckelenbergh. From Wales came Penrhyn, but they made it Penryn. Dummersto(w)n once was Fullum, which Vermonters got from the pronunciation of the name of the Fulham area of London. Pronunciation also accounts for the fact that, as is to be expected from the early history and from the proximity of a part of Canada where the French language was, and is, important, there are a lot of French surnames among Vermont residents that are spelled as said, rather than "correctly." I shall not pause to debate whether personal names can have standard pronunciations or spellings or whether it is best to consider *Aline* a different name than *Eileen*, *Brytney* a different name than *Brittany*, *LaSeel* an unusual rather than "illiterate" male forename, and *Smythe* something other than a misspelled *Smith*. The implications for placenames, however, lurk around the edges of this sort of thing. If, for instance, Vermonters spell or pronounce a word that differs from your idea of how the spelling or pronunciation ought to be, are they "wrong"? Surely *the* name of Cairo (Illinois) is CAY-row, and surely the citizens of New Orleans know how to say its name, even if you say it differently. I don't like MON-peeler any more than BALL-mer MURR-land, but when in Rome....

Like it or not, there is a Vermont English (or Vermont American). It changes over time. I can hear the influx of back-to-nature New Vermonters beginning to affect the local speech more than it seems to affect them. (Or perhaps TV and movies are to be considered.) Interesting clues as to the older speech of the area are to be found in the facts that occur in Ralph Nading Hill's book on the "contrary county" of Vergennes: *Vergennes* over the years was rendered *Vergeens, Devergeens, Devergensburg, Vargeensburg*, and so on.

It must be admitted that this problem with the foreign was not unusual. The Amerindian word which we have now settled on calling *Connecticut* was even harder for the rural people to handle and appeared in a dazzlingly long list of variations, as Prof. Allen Walker Read and others have documented. Knowledge of French or Ameridian languages was not demanded of all Vermonters, and their scant Dutch (if any) permitted them occasionally to refer to the Batten Kill River (a *kill* is not a river but a stream). We cannot decide whether the Vermont toponym Okema is Abnaki for "louse" or Chippewa for "chief." Keep in mind that our state borders do not correspond to the residences or hunting grounds of the first peoples here, so when we speak of Amerindian names we are speaking of names in hundreds of languages (some of them dead) and when we say "the Indian language of —state" we may be mixing up a number of languages. Sometimes tribes and nations had languages much like their neighbors; sometimes they could communicate with each other only by gestures or picture writing. Vermont Amerindians were mostly, not completely, Abnaki, the last of whose keepers of the tribal traditions was Obum Sawin. His English name was William Simon. He died in 1959. His Abnaki name we actually do not know, for *obum sawin* is not a name but a title: *obum sawin* translates as "keeper of the fire."

In Vermont as everywhere in these United States and Canada, the non-English placenames were translated (*Lac Superior*/ Lake Superior), hybridized (*Rivière du Crédit*/ Credit River), agglutinated (*Rivière aux Sables*/Ausable River), assimilated (*Wequapauset*/ Wickaboxet), or simply discarded in favor of an English name (*Pointe de Mont-Réal*/ Sandwich). So much change took place in Vermont placenames that it could almost be compared to British Columbia, the Canadian province that has *British* in its name and a higher percentage of British names on the land than any other province of Canada. Despite the French origin of its name, Vermont seems at first glance to have little at all but British placenames.

The Amerindian names were (as in Connecticut) wiped off almost everything that could be taken as property of the white settlers. Now in Connecticut few people think of *Norwalk* as an Amerindian name, and in Vermont few think of *Jamaica* as an Amerindian name. Of what is left of aboriginal names, the most attractive may be those of Winona Lake (*Winona* is often used as a white forename, and here it is combined with an English generic) and Passumpsic (sandy bottom). But, like saying that Snowflake House is a pleasant name, all this is merely subjective. It was a subjective decision that Amerindian names sounded funny or were hard to say (along with the desire to rename in order to take) that changed so many aboriginal American names in the first place.

What we do find, to pass over negative remarks on defective names, is a very positive history of Yankee practicality. In the state's so-called Equivalent Lands there is a hint as to the battles between Massachusetts and Connecticut over territory. In Eastern Union and Western Union we have evidence of other political moves. In New France and New England there sound echoes of old imperialism. In the tales of Yorkers and the Green Mountain Boys we learn of the struggles between New York State and the Vermonters who held grants from New Hampshire and fought around Bennington and Arlington to defend them against a New York State (The Empire State) that wanted to extend its empire in all directions possible.

After the French and Amerindians ceased to be a threat in the area, royal governors of nearby areas created settlements in what is now Vermont. Homesteaders appeared from New Hampshire. Patroons and tenants were encouraged by New York. Britons already established in the Massachusetts Bay Colony, not wanting very much to go into Maine (which the Bay Colony actually owned), moved into certain Green Mountain areas. They took there with them imported names from Britain such as Charlestown, Durham, Dunbar, and Rockingham; they put those names on the land in place of any aboriginal or French names that might be there.

Much of what is now the state of Vermont was a grant from the British Crown to Bennington Wentworth, an ambitious man who had agitated for the creation of New Hampshire and had become its governor. The next step up was a peerage. He never did attain one; however, in the course of trying, he named many of 113 new towns (chartered in some three million acres) after influential lords and powerful families back in Britain whom he hoped to get behind his push for a lordship of his own. All but a dozen or so of the names he gave remain. His interest in British aristocracy, therefore, gives the small state of Vermont a very big dose of important British names of his period. Actually few or none of these important people had anything significant to do with settling and building up the state of Vermont.

Delaware and Lord de la Warre are more connected; Lord Baltimore and others are relevant there. In South Carolina, the case is different: the Ashley River (they say) meets the Cooper River "to form the Atlantic Ocean," but Anthony Ashley Cooper (Earl of Shaftesbury) never set foot in the colony, any more than did King Charles, for whom Charleston is named. Placenaming over here was a bid for money or for patronage. With no great connection to Vermont, I must say the Ashleys did pretty well: Ashley Cooper's county (Dorset, originally in Vermont called Dorsett), his mother's surname (Ashley Pond), and his earldom (misspelled, Shaftsbury) are all there in Vermont. And as for that spelling slip, the same day Shaftsbury was chartered (1761) there was also a grant for "Glossenbury" which was as close as they could come to Glastonbury and which now is officially Glastenbury, still "wrong," still very Vermont.

In the same way, Nieuw Amsterdam was renamed New York for a Duke of York who did nothing for that colony. William Penn deserved to have Pennsylvania named for him; he did so much to start and support it. In the end, Pennsylvania was not named for him. Earlier you learned that, as a Quaker, he said that the honor was too great for a humble man such as himself. Why not, he suggested, name it Pennsylvania after his *father*?

Vermont might well have been named for some American, but it was not, and few of its towns were, either. Vermont wanted to join the other colonies of the newly United States but for various reasons did not get unto the Union with the 13 original states. It had to be content with being late. By that time it did join the union there were only half a dozen town-sized places (30,000 acres each) left to be chartered and named.

Between independence (declared in 1777) and statehood (1791) naturally the republic of Vermont turned aggressively away from naming after British models, though they did pick up from other Americans some names that those Americans had brought from Britain. At long last, they actively sought some Amerindian names. Adopted then (or earlier or later) were some comparatively few Amerindian names (with the sometimes shaky spelling of Vermont, which has a Lake Abenaki and a populated place called Abnaki for a start). For the most part,

67

only the places that people couldn't own, such as the Missisquoi, Nulhegan, and Passumpsic rivers, have Amerindian names, and in the town of Missisquoi they like to call the place East Richford. For Missisquoi, Zadek Thompson in 1842 listed 24 Vermont spellings. You know that *Mohican, Mahegan, Mohegan*, etc., are all still on maps.

The one good thing Vermonters seem to have done in relation to aboriginal names is not to have made them seem childish by hyphenating them, as New Jersey did with the likes of Ho-Ho-Kus. When you read of Go-Wa-Ha-Su-A-Sing (Place of Hedges, I believe) elsewhere it is almost like running into Mew-Niss-Uh-Pul-Bill-Ding. Lake Memphramagog is pronunceable without hyphens, even Ottauquechee River (for which Vermont makes up with rivers named Black, White, West, etc.).

The white man named the likes of Indian Bay, Indian Brook, Indian Point, Indian River, and Indian Stones. He picked up a few Amerindian words (*musquash* is "muskrat," but he used neither the Abnaki nor the American in a placename) and whites even introduced the local Amerindians to the white man's way of naming places for people (which most Amerindians would never do). That seems to have started with white men naming Joe's Pond and Molly's Pond for two Abnaki.

It may be that some names that look like settler names to us are actually corrupted Amerindian words: I think that Tunket (which does not appear in the *Omni Gazetteer of the United States* I, under Vermont) may possibly be *k't-hunk* (Abnaki "very large stream"). The white man may possibly have translated some Amerindian names; and a few Amerindian names may be translated from names the white man gave. The French created the name *Iroquois* ("real adders," an insult that one tribe flung at another, *Irinakowi*), but the lake they gave *Iroquois* to is now Lake Champlain. What it was called before the French saw it, no one knows. Whole languages disappear. The Iroquois pretty much wiped out the Hurons and the Huron language has long been dead.

After the red man was no longer a danger, a romance began to surround Amerindian names. *Hiawatha* may have helped. There was scant opportunity by that time, however, for Vermont to start bestowing major Amerindian placenames. In The Bronx, in 1896 Katonah Avenue was named. It had originally been simply Second Street. By the way, *Second Street* is the commonest street name in the US. *First Street* would seem even more likely, but *First Street* was often High Street, Market Street, Front Street, Main Street, or named for some local hero or imported famous name. So Second ranks first.

Vermont has many Main Streets and numbered streets and lots of the expectable British names of New England. Vermont has a lot of famous or local personal names (Averys Gore and Buels Gore are names for odd-shaped pieces of land resulting from trying to map squares on a globe, one expert says). Vermont has a few foreign city names (Athens, Berlin, Calais). Vermont has the inevitable biblical names. The first town chartered was named Bethel and then came Canaan, Eden, Goshen, Mt. Pisgah, and so on, but I like Balm of Gilead Point and Brimstone Corner. Vermont, in addition, also has some unusual names. Here's a start on the alphabet: The Alps, Baby Stark Mountain, Biddie Knob, Big Dam, Bluff Mountain, Bow Arrow Point, Bread Loaf, Camel's Hump (also The Lion), Chiselville, Dog River, Domeys Dome, the Experiment School, Foolsville, the Goodnough School...even North Hero and South Hero. It was usual to name after people's surnames (the most important early families were Allen, Dwight, Wentworth—and there were Bakersfield, Starksboro, Pittsford, Whitingham, etc., while Gunners Brook is named for the Gunnison family) but a forename or two could creep in. There is Ira for Ira Allen—probably too many Allens around— but none of the truly unusual forenames of early Vermont, such as Remember, were used. A surveyor gave his name to Saxtons River (fortunately Vermont made no errors as with Maine's Savayed Pond, which was "surveyed"). There is Warners Grant, an Isle La Motte, and areas at different times in Manchester named Cook Hollow, Jameson Flats, etc. New streets and malls and so on are constantly being created, but not (say) for the whole state at the rate seen annually in the single city of Los Angeles.

The counties have English and French names and so do the county seats. There are no Amerindian ones. Special features have names such as Bread Loaf, Camels Hump, Haystack and Hunger mountains, Pico Peak, the Little River, Mad River, and White rivers—nothing very notable. Vermonters appear to be practical, literal-minded people, so that even that town named North Hero looks way out of place.

Heroes and at least one lady from elsewhere were noted in the placenames of Vermont: Prince Rupert of the Rhine, William of Orange, King Charles, Queen Charlotte, and so on. I think the state ought to have been named for Ethan Allen—he did get an air force base named for him—but I also am sad to see other US opportunities missed as with the fact that the southern state of Franklin disappeared. Franklin was another great American. In Vermont he gets a notice. Jefferson does not. There ought to be a state called Jefferson, who doesn't even have a Day, while the Rev. Martin Luther King, Jr., does. Jefferson ought to have one, *too*!

That, of course, like which names of the 400-year history of the Vermont area (which of course had a history before the white man came along, but we don't pay attention to that kind of thing these days) are fine or funny, etc., is a matter of personal opinion. What we surely can agree upon is that in the placenames of Vermont there is a lot of folklore and history. For example, Providence Island is said to have sheltered Benedict Arnold's fleet when the British threatened it during The Revolution. There is a lot of color and interest. There are folk etymologies, too, worthless linguistically, valuable culturally, always illustrative of the human desire to see meaning in the world. The French language may still be heard in Vermont. So are other immigrant languages, though they have to get their recognition in minor names, such as those of streets, because most big things were named before (say)

Koreans or Mexicans arrived. Nonetheless, the overall impression one gets from Vermont names is of a WASP, New England, Yankee place. LaPlatte and Ompompanoosic sound less Vermont-like than Brattelboro and Essex Junction. Until one goes there in person one cannot believe how many of the people one assiduously seeks to avoid in New York have moved to Vermont, and how much it has changed is constantly remarked.

You will find interesting names in the histories from that of Ira Allen (*The Natural and Political History of the State of Vermont*, 1798, reprinted) and that of Hosea Beckley (*History of Vermont,* 1849) down through the local and county histories and larger summaries such as the five volumes by Walter Hill Crockett (*Vermont: The Green Mountain State,* 1921), state papers, gazetteers, various yearbooks, etc. As is the case with other states, the Federal Writer's Project Administration (WPA) guide (*Vermont: A Guide to the Green Mountain State,* 1937) is useful. The second edition (by Ray Bearse, 1966) has become outdated but it remains as basic as W. R. Hard *et al.*'s *New Vermont Guide* (1964). For the Amerindian names I wish I had more time for here, see John C. Hutten's *Indian Place Names of New England* (1962), never completely surpassed. For placenames specifically, there is the admirable (but in need of updating) book by Esther Munroe Swift, *Vermont Place-Names: Footprints of History* (1977).

Next we are going farther afield, to the heart of the country (or flyover country), however you look at it, to examine some of the Amerindian names of Iowa. There are a huge number of different approaches we could take to American placenames. One could, for instance, concentrate on the names given by early explorers, or how the names of pioneers in the middle and far west showed where they came from and what their attitudes were toward the new homes and new lives they built, or how the railroads of the nineteenth century had an immense influence on the naming as well as the development of settlements. Or one could go far from the US to look at strange names in foreign countries, or (say) contrast the kinds of people who are commemorated in one country with the different kinds commemorated in the placenames of another country.

I choose to write a little about Amerindian names, largely because it is a too neglected topic and very important in our American cultural history, and to speak of Amerindian names in various parts of our country. To write about all aspects of all placenames all over the globe in all ages would be to write the complete history of the world. Medieval monks may have had the intestinal fortitude to launch on universal history, but I don't. I simply express my personal preferences and hope by indulging them to bring to your attention some of the lore and learning of placenames and to interest you a little in topics that I find fascinating.

Now Iowa, and some Amerindian names.

A NOTE ON AMERINDIAN COUNTY NAMES IN IOWA

**From red-skin tongues, and traders' lingo
Apache, Sac, Olgonquin, Mongo,
Sioux, Maha, Loup, and bright Musquakee,·
The way is long, the muse is balky....
The question ask: "Oh, warrior, say,
Did Indian tongue name Iowa?"**

—Iowa Historical Record 1: 2 (April 1885), 71

Iowa—which, as you see in the epigraph, was also pronounced Eye-oh-WAY—is the Hawkeye State. It has 99 counties, and the expert on Amerindian names, my late friend Virgil J. Vogel, identified 22 of them as related to aboriginal languages. When *Midwestern Folkore* in 1995 decided to publish a special double issue (Spring/Fall) on "Names in the Mid West," I contributed not only an article on the placenames of Kansas but attempted, in memory of Vogel, a native of Iowa, to present something such as he might have created for the issue. That note I revise and present to you here. I draw from Vogel's work on *Iowa Place Names of Indian Origin* (1983) and also am indebted to another inspiring friend in the American Name Society, Allen Walker Read, whose master's thesis on the placenames of Iowa counties beginning with the letters A through F was a very early attempt to give Iowan toponymy a scholarly basis. I offer remarks on the county names of Iowa that relate to the first peoples there. I must repeat at the outset that the Amerindians did not create or use placenames in the same ways that later European explorers and American settlers did. What we have here is a Euro-Americanized version of Iowa "Indian" names.

The 22 relevant county names of Iowa are these:

Allamakee	Muscatine
Appanoose	Oscelo
Black Hawk	Pocahontas
Cedar	Pottawattamie
Cherokee	Powesheik
Chickasaw	Sac
Iowa	Sioux
Des Moines	Tama
Keokuk	Wapello
Mahaska	Winnebago
Monoma	Winnesheik

Two of these names (Black Hawk and Cedar) are in English, translated from the language of the Sac (or Sauk). Black Hawk is an Anglicized version of an Amerindian occasion name, that is a name given to commemorate some special event. It was borne by a subordinate chief. It would really be better translated as Black Sparrow Hawk. As you know, no Amerindian would have named a place after an individual such as Black Hawk. Cedar is a partial translation of the Amerindian name of a river, Mosk-wah-wak-wah (Red Cedar). That need not be syllabified like that, but it is.

Some of the county names in Iowa derived from early French encounters with the natives. Sac comes from Osauaki in the Sac language and Sioux is the French version of a derogatory name used by the Chippewa (or Ojibway) to compare the Dakotas (Allies) to adders. Muscatine is as close as the French explorers could get to *mascoutin* or *mascouten*, which may not be a name in the ordinary sense at all. It means "prairie". Des Moines, is also, obviously, from the French and it suggests "monks" but it actually is a corruption of the name of the Amerindians who called themselves Moingwenas or Moingwena or Moinguoena. Interestingly, Des Moines as the name not just of a county but also of a river and a city, has itself had various spellings: Du Moine, De Moyen, even Demon. It has been on various occasions translated as having to do with "monks," "mines," "means," "the lesser," "the middle," "mounds," and "at the road."

The French were not the only ones to folk-etymologize or reinterpret the sounds of Amerindian words. Allamakee, which begins our list of Amerindian-named Iowan counties, is Sac and Fox *an-a-mee-kee* (thunder). Despite folklore, it has nothing whatever to do with Amerindians trying to pronounce the name of Alexander McKee, a British agent among the tribes (but in nearby areas, never in what is now the state of Iowa). Appenoose has nothing to do with apes or nooses; it is merely the surviving spelling of the Sac and Fox word for "little child" (often rendered as *pappoose* in English). Today that word for child and *squaw* for women are taboo, politically incorrect.

The Kituwagi or Tsalagi (The People or The Real People), whom others called the Cherokee, gave the name Cherokee to an Iowa county. Actually, the Cherokee never had any real connection with the territory. They began in the southeast and were later driven into what was then designated Indian Territory or what is today called Oklahoma (Red Men). Similarly, the Chickasaw, native to the region which today is the state of Mississippi, were forced to go west but do have a county named for them in Iowa. How did these names land there?

It has often been remarked that as the nineteenth century wore on the Amerindian population had been so reduced by disease and neglect and war that it no longer offered any threat to the expansion of the white population and at that point Euro-Americans felt that they could afford to regard the natives with a sentimental eye. They wrote poems about the braves who died in battle. They created legends about broken-hearted Indian maidens who flung themselves off cliffs. They enjoyed the Wild West shows and Longfellow's *Hiawatha*. They created "Indian" names for everything from raw towns to fancy camps and from country houses to Boy Scout jamboree sites. They began to collect "Indian" jewelry and pottery and rugs, much of it fake, and equally fake were many of the "Indian" names that were created, stringing one nonsense syllable after another, making Ed-an-pa-pa, let us say, the name of the cabin where Edwin, Anne, and their children Patrick and Patricia, roughed it in the summer time, bringing pots and pans and dishes and furniture and food from the city for an idyll by the lake. These "Indian" names, even real ones that were recovered, were usually put on places they did not fit at all. The effect of fake, "Indian," names on real Amerindian names is a subject in itself.

The name borne by Iowa Co., however, is another matter entirely. It is real and it has true significance. It goes back to the first group of Amerindians encountered by white explorers in the area. But if the white man got the name Iowa right he certainly made mistakes elsewhere, and not just in the pronunciation of placenames. Keokuk, for example, honors the Sac and Fox chieftain of that name who lived from 1780 to 1848. The red man would not have named a place after him and, in fact, it was the white man, in the person of Gen. Winfield Scott, who made Keokuk a chief, during the Black Hawk War. Mashaska Co. is named for another chief, that one of the early eighteenth century, whose name is translated as White Cloud. There is also a place named for him in Mills Co. White Cloud Township, however, is not named for that man. It is named for his son who, most unusually, bore the same name—or perhaps the white man just assumed he did—and who signed the Treaty of Nemaha (1838) with "Frank White Cloud."

The name of Monona Co. seems to have been selected for euphony. Fine sounding though it is, it is, in fact, the name of the villain of Lewis Deebach's melodrama, *Oolaitalor, The Indian Heroine* (1821). Such dramas had been welcomed since James Nelson Baker's *The Indian Princess; or, La Belle Sauvage* (staged in 1808), based on the story of "Pocahontas." You know her father was a "king" of Amerindians in Virginia and that she married an Englishman and for a time was a popular curiosity in London society. American dramatists had a vogue of writing "Indian" plays, colorful if inaccurate.

"Indian" maidens were exotic and could be presented to the public wearing fewer clothes than usual, though not naked, as they sometimes appeared in early drawings of the natives of North America; the extent to which that factor accounts for the popularity of certain types of plays has, unfortunately, never been the subject of exhaustive scholarly research. The native men (all characters played by whites, of course) could be presented wearing about as much as Tarzan, but we preferred the great feather hearddresses, the war bonnets, of the Plains Indians, the most dashing. It was "Injuns" like that who confronted the cowboys and the US cavalry in the western movies, the twentieth-century equivalents of the nineteenth-century melodramas. Beautifully sounding names such as Monoma seemed appropriate, part of the romance of the red man.

Osceola Co. commemorates another Amerindian leader who was not directly connected with the Iowa area. When the Seminoles, who lived in what is now the state of Florida, were ordered to move west (1832), some rallied around Osceola (1803 – 1838) and managed to resist displacement until 1842; indeed, some were not displaced even then and today there are more Seminoles in Florida than in Oklahoma, to which the white man wanted to exile them all. Osceola was a hero to his people, even a martyr, because he was captured by the devious Gen. T. S. Jesup while parleying under a flag of truce, and Osceola later perished while in detention at Ft. Moultrie (South Carolina). He became famous among whites when the Irish writer Mayne Reid, who lived in the US and found romance in the tales of Amerindians, wrote *Osceola, the Seminole* (1858), an inaccurate but colorful biography. In all, Osceola's name now survives in nearly 100 US placenames; his name is on counties, townships, lakes and mountains in more than a dozen states. His name is on the land in Iowa.

Pocahontas Co. commemorates the nickname of a more famous Amerindian; she was actually called Pokachantesu (d. 1617) and it means Playful Girl. Her real name was Matoaka, but the aborigines tended to keep their real names secret, believing that enemies could use such information for evil purposes in much the same way that a lock of hair or a personal possession might be used in magic. As I said, she was regarded as an Indian princess and her marriage to John Rolfe (1614) sealed the peace that had been achieved between the English and some 30 Algonkian (or Algonquian) tribes ruled by her father. He was Wahunsonacock (d. 1618) but the English called him Powhatan, which was the name of his confederacy in Tidewater Virginia. Pocahontas was baptised in the Christian faith and took the name Rebecca. Like Osceola, she had no connection whatever with Iowa. The appearance of her name in Iowa, as is true of most of the 50 other instances of it in other places across the US, is due simply to the fact that she was at the center of a romantic story of Capt. John Smith and the Amerindians of Virginia. Prof. Read, in that master's thesis I mentioned, mentions (pp. 21 – 22) that Pocahontas Co., Iowa, contains a township named Powhatan, a village of Rolfe, and another village named Varina (which was the home that Rolfe and Pocahontas briefly occupied after their marriage).

Between 1835 and 1848, part of the Iowa territory served as a reservation for a tribe called the Pottawattamie, and there is a Pottawattamie Co. today. The name has been translated as Keepers of the Fire, Makers of the Fire, People of the Place of the Fire. The only common element is *fire*, and most people know that among the Amerindians the keeper of the fire is the one who, like the griots of Africa, preserves and hands down the traditions of his people. Besides providing them with heating and cooking and keeping wild animals from invading their camps, fire was a symbol of life and independence and often of peace-making among the aborigines. The fire was passed from hand to hand with the peace pipe, which the French called the *calumet*.

Powesheik Co. recalls the Fox chief of that name (1749 – 1848?), also called Pawishika ([Bear] Shaking Off). He was an important member of the Bear Clan, the most important society among the Fox people, and apparently was a leader who cared much for his people. On numerous occasions, to avoid further conflict, he ceded to the white man various lands of those people until, at last, they were pushed right out of what is now Iowa into what is now Kansas.

Another Fox chieftan was Ty-ee-ma (Strawberry, *c.* 1780 – 1833); he led the Grand Medicine of the Fox. After him Iowa has named Tama Co. That was first named Iuka, a name transplanted from a town in Mississippi.

The principal chieftain of the Fox nation was Wapello (1787 – 1842). His name has been spelled in numerous ways; I give it as it appears in Wapello Co. Remember that the Amerindians had no alphabets. Their names, like all their speech, were written down by the white man phonetically—and filtered through whatever language those whites, educated or not, happened to have. The whites, particularly the missionaries, did, however, make great efforts to learn and record in a Roman alphabet the languages of the red men, so we know that Wapello's name meant Painted White, even though the Fox language tells us—it has no *l* sound—that we cannot be rendering it correctly. In Illinois and Saskatchewan, we find the name as Wapella. Wapana (Morning One) is a said to be a close alternative possibility, but it does not appear as a placename anywhere in the US.

Now we come to a name you surely know: Winnebago. Winnebago names not just an Iowa county but counties, townships, rivers, creeks, public schools and more in numerous states and is, of course, internationally known as the name of an RV (recreation vehicle), which I do not think now is manufactured in Iowa. In the language of the Cree, Winnebago may be a corruption of Wenipek (Great Water, Sea) and famous in the Canadian rendering: Winnipeg. In any case, the Winnebago people were driven out of what are now Illinois and Wisconsin and dwelt for a while in Iowa, then Minnesota, then farther west. The history of Iowa, as you realize, is closely connected with Amerindians being driven across it and right out of it as the Manifest Destiny of white Americans pushed more and more natives off their lands. In this way names such as Winnebago are shared by counties and townships, and so on, in Iowa and in other areas.

Finally, the story of Winnesheik Co. is that of a Winnebago chief (1812 – 1872) who was the second to bear that name (which suggests it may be a title rather than a personal appellation). In translation, however, this appears unlikely, because it carries derogatory connotations, "dirty" or "stinking" or (some scholars say) "muddy" or even "bearded." (Bearded would be unusual indeed for a red man.) It is odd than the white man would want to give the name to any place, but then he accepted the name Chicago, which also suggests "stinking" (being connected with wild onions or garlic). The Amerindian names on the map of the US, however, were often put there by people who mistook them or even did not have any idea what they meant in our languages. There were hundreds upon hundreds of Amerindian languages with which the white man came into contact, and most of such white men who did were not well educated even in their own languages: it was not, usually, the scholar who became an adventurer in the wilderness. Even today, when many of the aboriginal languages have disappeared, there are very few whites who know anything about the ones that remain, and nineteenth-century attempts to re-educate in the ways of white men such Amerindians as the white man did not otherwise exterminate have left even those Amerindians who want to cling to their cultures and their languages with great problems in achieving their goals. In the twenty-first century many Amerindian languages will be silenced forever as the last speakers pass away.

Vogel's *Iowa Place Names of Indian Origin* (1983, mentioned earlier) is unusual among the works specifically on Iowa placenames—such as Allen Walker Read's "Observations on Iowa Place Names" in *American Speech* 5 (1929) and Harold Dilts' *From Ackley to Zwingle* (1975)—or general studies such as George R. Stewart's *American Place Names* (1970) and Joseph N. Kane's *The American Counties* (revised, 1962), Kelsie B. Harder's *Illustrated Dictionary of Place Names* (1976), and the *Omni Gazetteer of the United States* (edited by Frank R. Abate, 1991).

With that I leave my comment in honor of Virgil J. Vogel on Amerindian names of the counties of Iowa. As I have tried to make clear, some of those names importantly reflect Iowa's colorful history and bring to mind otherwise too-neglected figures of our American past. The Amerindian names remain on the land of Iowa despite the fact that some of them are not part of Iowa's history and others are reminders only of how Amerindian peoples were pushed out of the way as the US expanded to create a nation stretching from coast to coast with Iowa part of the center of it all.

Iowa also has an Indiana and a Sioux township, an Indianapolis, an Indian Bluffs Wildlife Area, various Indian Creeks, Indian Hills, Indian Villages, an Okamanpeedam State Park, a North Wyaconda River and a South Wyaconda River, a Sac and Fox Indian Reservation, a couple of places called Camp Sacalawea, a Kennbec, and more. The names that people talk about include the North Skunk River, the Turkey River, and places you may like to think about are called Agency, Brooklyn, Correctionville, Dubuque, Exira, Forest City, Guttenberg, Harpers Ferry, Iconium, Joice, Kiron, Lost Nation, Mediapolis, Nodaway, Oto, Promise City, Quasqueton, Rake, Spillville, Tiffin, Ute, Volga, What Cheer, Yetter, and Zwingle.

THE PLACENAMES OF KANSAS

The literature of place-names in Kansas
seems to be confined to some local
pamphlets and newspaper articles and a
brief series of papers by W. H. Carruth
published in 1901 – 1902. There is a card
index in the headquarters of the State
Historical Society, but it is far from
complete.

—H. L. Mencken, *The American Language* (1962)

I. INTRODUCTION

Mencken's comment in his fourth edition (revised with two supplements) on
the work of Carruth in the nineteenth century (in *Kansas University Quarterly* 1,
1892 – 1893, and 6, 1897) was true enough in the sixties, but in the latter part of
the twentieth century Kansas was included in the *Omni Gazetteer of the United
States* (1991) and there have been two relevant books by John Rydjord (*Indian
Place Names* of 1968 and *Kansas Place Names* of 1972), enough scholarship on
the subject to warrant a survey of it by William E. Koch (in *Heritage of the Great
Plains* 19, 1986), plus various articles in scholarly journals since then (such as
that by Karl Rosen in *Names* 21, 1973, and by myself in *Midwestern Folklore* 21,
1995). Sondra Van Meter McCoy & Jan Hults published *1001 Kansas Place
Names* (1989). That many placenames cannot be said to suggest the nature of all
of the 12,000 or so placenames of the Sunflower State, but they did pick out the
entertaining ones. My article, "The Placenames of Kansas," is here rewritten for
inclusion in this book. It is meant to use Kansas placenames as proof of the
assertion of Robert Louis Stevenson:

> There is no part of the world where nomenclature is so rich, poetical,
> humourous and picturesque as the United States of America. All times,
> races and languages have brought their contribution.

I propose briefly to outline the overall picture of the placenames of Kansas,
territory and state. I take up the aboriginal names, insofar as they survive; the
French and Spanish names bestowed by early explorers and adventurers; the
names given by early settlers, including post office names from the early

nineteenth century on (Robert W. Baughman covered 29 May 1828 to 3 August 1961 in *Kansas Post Offices,* 1961); the names dating from the boom of 1869 – 1889, when railroad construction and other factors caused Kansas to bloom onomastically; and the names that have been discarded and the names that have been added in the development of Kansas throughout the twentieth century. I shall discuss placenames that range from commemoration and description to those resulting from clever wordplay and simple error, and I shall include incidental and associative placenames, possessive and commendatory names, made-up names, and names borrowed from other places and other cultures. I shall also touch on name change, folk etymology, and some other aspects of the placename history of Kansas. A similar survey could be made of the names of any other American state, but I choose Kansas because of its color, variety, and the convenient size of the corpus. I shall try to communicate the general flavor of Kansas names. This is a sort of sample of what could be done for any county or any country.

All the names of this particular state are part of the history of our heartland. Many of the names preserve something of the hard lives and light hearts of pioneer days in a very American place. In my general survey of all aspects of names elsewhere I undertook at one point to list the best publications on placenames for each of the states and possessions of the US—and in error Kansas was left out! So I welcome this opportunity to rectify the error, made in the first printing and not possible to correct until the revised edition of *What's in a Name?* (1995). Here, then, is my apology to the Jayhawkers and others who complained of the omission and to all who expressed interest in the Great American Desert, in the famous Kansan local names, the transferred names indicative of movements of population, the odd names redolent of American character, the names of simple farmers and famous men (and a few women) of Kansas and wider renown, the names that constitute a brief history of life in earlier days, and, in short, a lot of names that are historical, even "funny" or puzzling.

II. EVERYBODY IS FROM SOMEWHERE ELSE: "FOREIGN" PLACENAMES IN KANSAS

It is common for new settlers in any region to transfer placenames from the old homes to the new. Thus there used to be in Kansas a New Chicago, New Memphis, New Rochester, New Brighton, as well as a Paris, a Michigan and a London (later renamed Circleville, after a town in Ohio). There still exist a New Albany (the namesake of which is in Indiana, not New York), New Cambria, New Salem, as well as Rome and Arcadia, Augusta, Beloit, Columbus, Independence, Manhattan, Minneapolis, Pittsburgh, and Toledo, among many others. Sometimes such names provided reliable clues to the ethnicity of the settlers. Witness Pesth (now gone), Zurich, Lindsborg, Bern, Berlin (now gone), Weimar, Nueva Gallicia, Nuevo Leon, Nueva Italia, New Scandinavia (today called Scandia), Orleans (now vanished), Portage (also gone), Voltaire (also gone), Bourbon, Ozark (from the French *aux arcs*), and Little Balkans. Little Balkans was the nickname given to the southeastern corner of the state where more than 50 different ethnic groups originally settled peacefully. Often we find that what looks like a transfer has another explanation, however: Frankfort looks as if it might be a respelling of *Frankfurt* but it documents the fact that Frank Schmidt built the first house (fort) in the area. Ironically, Frank Schmidt was originally from Frankfurt.

This last example makes the point that there may be more to a placename that first meets the eye. Consider Moscow, located in the southwestern corner of Kansas. Did the original settler have connections to Europe? No. Did they transplant the placename from some US Moscow, such as Moscow in Pennsylvania? No. In fact the place seems to be named for one of the officers of Coronado's expedition of the 1540s. His name was Moscoso, and the modern townspeople shortened it by one syllable. When the placename reached the post office people in Washington, they improved the spelling (as they thought) from Mosco to Moscow. That's one story. Another is that there was a Colorado pioneer named Mosco, once again the post office being said to "correct" the spelling. In any case, the point remains: placenames cannot always be taken at face value.

Of course most of the places, though new to white settlers, already had Amerindian designations, but these were very often discarded in favor of labels which the Euro-Americans found more familiar and easier to pronounce. The Kiowan *Tsodalhented Pa* (which McCoy & Hults say means Armless Man Creek) became Walnut Creek. Thus was a colorful name replaced by a blander one, perhaps in the spirit of Shakespeare's "a poor thing, but mine own." Occasionally the descriptive Amerindian names, however, were replaced by more inspiring ones (Enterprise, Industry, Union) and important psychological groundwork was laid for future generations.

All the places called Pleasant are evidence of hope as much as reality and public relations as much as appreciation of a promising landscape. Plainville isn't plain; it looks out over the plains. Golden Belt and Mount Hope (which has no appreciable elevation) also mislead a little, and one trusts that Fairview, Protection, and Pleasant Valley deliver on their promises. Roseland seems to be the victim of public relations gone astray but, like St. Just-in-Roseland (Cornwall), mentioned earlier in this book, even if there were no roses there to start with—in Cornwall *ros* is heath, as you know now—the inhabitants may well have planted some. On occasion it was hoped that by calling a place (say) Junction City or Central City it would in fact come to deserve the name. Oddly,

Cimmaron in Kansas was named for a destination one reached by passing through this Kansas station on the Santa Fe Trail.

The first Europeans in the Kansas area were not homesteaders but Spanish explorers looking for fabled wealth in the "desert." They found little and soon left. Perhaps the natives knew enough to take the shrewd advice of Jack Handey, one of whose *Deep Thoughts* is: If you were a poor Indian with no weapons, and a bunch of conquistadors came up to you and asked where the gold was, I don't think it would be a good idea to say, "I swallowed it. So sue me."

It was not the Spanish but later white men, seeking land, not gold, who really proved to be the nemesis of the aborigines in the area which is now Kansas. Not much Spanish influence remains in the placenames of Kansas, but I would be remiss if I failed to mention Alamo Ditch, El Quartelejo, El Dorado, DeSoto, Potosi, Rio, Bonita, Fonda, Loco, and Valverde. There have been other names of Spanish origin in Kansas, too, but transferred from towns elsewhere in the US. For an area that was so early an interest of the Spanish in the New World, Kansas seems worlds away from New Mexico, Arizona, and California.

After the Spanish came the French and others seeking possession of the riches of North America. Therefore Kansas, like many other places, has a lot of names from forts and from the colonels and generals associated with those forts. Over the last century or two, Kansas had forts named Aubrey, Cavagnolle, Downer, Harker, Riley, Scott, and Wallace, as well as the famous Fort Leavenworth and Fort Dodge. There were also, once upon a time, Kansas forts named Hays, Jewell, Larned, Mann, Wallace, and Zarah, evidence of early insecurities.

The most notable French influence on Kansas placenames is to be seen in the use of Grand (as in Grand Junction); the British would have named it Great Junction. French influence is also to be seen in names such as Lake Fort Scott, Lake Chapparal Dam, and Lake of the Forest, where *Lake* precedes rather than follows the name, even if other words are Spanish or English. English would have called the places Fort Scott Lake, Chapparal Dam Lake, and Forest Lake. Kansans have also adopted a few French surnames as labels for the places they live (LeRoy, LaHarpe, Marquette) and some other placenames (such as Potwin for early settler Charles Potwin) may be derived from Anglicized versions of French surnames. Finally—perhaps most importantly—French gave us *prairie*. The word appears in Kansas placenames such as Prairie Dog Township, Prairie Grove, Pretty Prairie, Prairie Home, Prairie Lake, Prairie View, Prairie Vista, Prairie National Park, and several Prairie Creeks. A state cannot conveniently have two towns of the same name but often has various creeks with the same name.

Spanish and French settlers arrived in what is now Kansas long before the first American immigrant rushes in the middle and latter parts of the nineteenth century. However, there are fewer Spanish or French placenames than those which can be traced to speakers of English. Some of the names the English speakers brought were classical (such as Attica and Agenda), and others are linguistic blends (Norcatur, for example, comes from combining English Norton with originally-French Decatur). Others celebrate the local flora and fauna (Antelope Creek, Deer Run, Grasshopper). Much more often than one might expect, *city* occurs. Here are some Kansas examples: Agnes City, America City, Bird City, Bull City, Bush City, Cain City, Cawker City, Elk City, Empire City, Fowler City, Hill City, Home City, Johnson City, King City Township, Maple City, Mound City, Ness City, Ohio City, Pearl City, Pioneer City, Sherman City, Silver City Oil Field, Slab City, Strong City, and Sun City. There were probably more, but *city* often had a boomtown feel to it and was dropped—or there really was a boomtown, which faded away. Cain City is now just Cain, Home City now just Home. Bull City was improved to Afton. Solomon City became a ghost town and no longer exists. Slab City is an unattractive name, and retirement havens in sunnier climes deserve the name Sun City more than anywhere in Kansas.

The placenames of Kansas, like placenames everywhere, contain a lot of information about the people who settled the area and in Kansas, as in many other places, the names that were put on the land very frankly express the hopes and aspirations and the actual origins or experiences of the settlers. Pioneers there were usually very direct in their naming.

III. CHARACTERS AND CHARACTER IN THE PLACENAMES OF KANSAS

Placenames can derive from the aboriginal descriptives (such as Mississippi, Big River), from descriptions (such as Flint Hills) given by early explorers or settlers, from incidents which early people experienced (Horseheads), from the saints' days on which early explorers first saw or first established places (in Brazil a river was named for the month, January, in which it was discovered), from the names of foreign royalty (Charleston) or national heroes (Madison), or even from the names of ordinary people (Jack's Creek). In this section I deal with what, in Kansas, is arguably the most important group of placenames, placenames commemorating individuals.

David Rice Atchison was born in Kentucky and made raids into Kansas from Missouri in 1855 and 1856. Later he became involved in the Great Plains railroad. You know his name from "the Atchison, Topeka, and the Sana Fe" in the Judy Garland song. Amos Adams Lawrence was born in Boston and founded a college in northeastern Kansas; it became the nucleus of the University of Kansas. It is easy to see why locals as well as people like Atchison and Lawrence had places named for them. Beeler and Basor were so honored, as were Palmer and Downs (two railroad officials), and Cawker (who won the honor in a poker game). After people were named the airports called Harry Bivens, Bob Faler, Mark Hoard, Colonel James Jabara, Harold Krier, and F. M. Stout, with varying degrees of formality in the names, as you see. After Eugene Field (which would not have been good for an airport), Walter Johnson, George E. Nettles and others, schools were named. There is a wildlife area named for Thomas Granville Barcus, a state park for John Brown, a canyon for Governor Harvey, viaducts for Lewis and Clark, a street for Seth Child, and so on.

It is no accident that all the names cited in the previous paragraph are those of white males. Very infrequently have Kansas placenames involved white females or any African-Americans. The town of Nicodemus, named for a black slave, was an exception to the rule. Even the towns called Narka (for a railroader's daughter) and Florence (for a governor's daughter) may be said to have been intended primarily to please those women's fathers. Amelia Earhart, the first woman to fly solo across the Atlantic and the first woman to fly the entire width of the United States, though promoted by a powerful public relations machine, has little more than the house she was born in named after her. It is located in Atchison.

While full names often indicate that the geographic feature or town or building or street has been named by someone not very well remembered, shortened forenames reflect the informality of pioneer days and, in fact, an era when surnames might not easily be revealed. People who "lit out for the territory" often wanted to cut all ties, and starting a new life is very American indeed. Kansas has many creeks named for Joe, Jim, Jack, Little John, Little Gun, and so forth, and further investigation will have to answer the question of whether Jacobs Creek recalls a forename or a surname. Bens Branch, Bills Creek, and perhaps Eddy Creek (unless that's an eddy) bespeak the common forename uses in frontier society, but Franks Creek and Jacobs Creek (the way the US Board on Geographical Names likes things, without apostrophes) leave us uncertain as to whether we have there forenames or surnames. Is Guzzlers Creek in memory of one guzzler or more than one? And what was his name/their names? We shall never know.

Sometimes Kansans attached suffixes to personal names; often these suffixes were French or German. French *–ville* appears in such placenames as Forest Ville, Foxville, Harveyville, Mullinville, Smileyville (which once was Smileyburg), Sodville, Turnersville, Vanceville, Wilsonville, and Abbyville (named for Abby McLean, the first baby born there). German *–burg* was especially popular in rural areas (Pottersburg and Swedesburg). Over time, some of these clunky suffixes were dropped: Haysville became Hays. For French toponymy in Kansas, see Karl Rosen in *450 ans des nom de lieu français en Amérique du Nord* (1984).

These names, of course, reflect the ethnicities of the early pioneers of Kansas, but what of the classical names that appear? There are Argentine (from the Latin for "silver"), Carthage, Pliny (now gone), as well as Homer, Achilles, Bucyrus, Cadmus, Cato, Cyrus, Emporia, Flavius, Germania, Hermes, Horace, Opolis, Kanopolis, and Elyria. These names harken back to the classical revival in America when the United States was almost ready to name the capital Rome and the Potomac "Tyber". That was the period in which a postmaster in Upstate New York dotted the landscape with classical names and, across much of the country, classical ornaments and facades were plastered on wooden as well as stone buildings. All those columns, all that fakery! We have grown so used to the classical revival style that we can hardly see any more how truly silly it was, but we can appreciate the ideals expressed, whether in calling Gen. Washington our new Cincinnatus or putting a classical portico on some county seat. Richard A. & Pauline Sealock's bibliography of US and Canadian placename literature is good as far as it goes. It will give you a lot of information on classical revival, and other, names. Major writers on US placenames include George R. Stewart and Kelsie B. Harder and Wilbur Zelinsky.

It was less foolish to honor Amerindian individuals or, more frequently, tribes. Kansas did that, too. Cloud was named for Chief Cloud, and there were Cheyenne, Comanche, Kiowa, Pawnee, Nemaha, Waubansee, Ottawa, Chatauqua, Cherokee, Osage, Miami, and Potawatami (this name is variously spelled in the US) counties. Witchita and Topeka became the names of large cities. Chanute and Chikaskia and Kechi named smaller towns. Capioma (for the Kickapoo chieftain Kapioma) named a township; another used Chiaskia again. There is dispute as to whether Kansas itself is an Amerindian name. Spelled Kamnzas, Kansé, Kanseis, Kanzan, Kanzon, Konza, Konsas, Canceas, Cansa, Cansés, Cansez, Canzes, Canses, and Canzon, and maybe more, the name has been argued to derive from the Spanish verb *cansar* (molest, harass) or from the Spanish noun *cansado* (troublesome fellow). I do not believe there is much to be gained by sorting through illiterate spellings or impossible arguments at this point. I believe that most people believe Kansas to be one of the states bearing an Amerindian name. See John P. Harrington, *Our State Names* (1955). Students may wish to consult the standard histories of Kansas by John N. Holloway (1868), William G. Cutler (1883), and William E. Conneley (1918) and works on Amerindians by Henry R. Schoolcraft (1851 – 1856), Louise Seymour Houghton (1918), Thomas McKenny & James Hall (1934), William Brandon (1964), George Catlin (nineteenth-century, reprinted 1973), etc. H. B. Staples wrote on the "Origin of the Names of the States of the Union" in *Proceedings of the American Antiquarian Society* New Style 1 (1880 – 1881) and a "monograph on the name of the state" by Robert Hay (1906) appears in the *Transactions of the Kansas State Historical Society* 9 (1905 – 1906). Wayne Corley (1962) has a study of *County and Community Names in Kansas* and there is more *passim* in general books about US placenames, of which George R. Stewart's two books (*Names on the Land*, 1967, and *American Place Names*, 1970) are the most famous. There is also for the US Kelsie B. Harder's *Illustrated Dictionary of Place Names* (1976).

The great variety of origins of Kansans is reflected in the placenames. Here is an alphabet of examples I choose: Achning, Bismark, Coronado, Decatur, Epler, Finney, Gueda, Halstead, Ivanpah, Juse, Kolackny, Laclede, Munkers, Ness, Olson, Pfister, Quinadaro, Reno, Severance, Techgrabber, Ulrich, Van Slyke, Winhorst, Yokum, and Zimmerman.

You have already seen that Kansans have not restricted themselves to adopting only the surnames of the people whom they choose to honor in placenames. Here are some more forenames used: Gladys, Hugo, Ida, Ole, Irene, Maud, Mona, Myra, and Mary. There are also Anness (Ann S. Wilson), Beulah, Celia, Cora, Edna, Elsie (Chapel), Emma (Creek), Eudora, Elmer, Louisa (Creek), Elmo (Lake), Jeanette, Katy (Lake), Leona, Letitia, Lorena, Loretta, Lyona, Mildred (Mount), Lulu (Township), Melvin (Creek), and Milo. Though no one could ever trace them all, and today many people do not care at all, dozens of old forenames are there on the map, the names of dozens of persons once honored and now unidentifiable. They were the wives and girlfriends and relatives and buddies of the men—the naming was invariably done by the men—of old Kansas. There is some evidence there of the sorts of forenames women pioneers bore.

Times change and certain forenames go from fashionable to unfashionable, others from objectionable to picturesque, and so do the placenames that incorporate these personal names. Because of what we may call "the people in them," a lot of Kansas placenames have a distinctly nineteenth-century feel, but they are distinctive enough, and characteristic. Recalling the lives and adventures of characters from generations past, they have a character and a life of their own.

IV. THE JAYHAWKER STATE

The origins of Jayhawk(er), associated with Kansas since the Civil War, are shrouded in mystery. *Jayhawker* was flung around in the free-state debates in the Kansas Territory and the term came to be applied to James Montgomery (who now has a county named for him). Montgomery was a fiery preacher and abolitionist who settled in the town of Linn. Montgomery's bandlttl, who ferociously preyed on pro-slavery believers, were widely denounced as Jayhawks, a title they proudly accepted. By the time that Kansas gained statehood (29 January 1861) and entered the Civil War, the Seventh Kansas Cavalry under the command of Col. Charles R. Jennison was being called Jennison's Jayhawks.

Stephen Z. Starr wrote a book on *Jennison's Jayhawks* (1993). The application to Jennison and his troops appears to be the beginning of the use of the term *Jayhawks* in a non-derogatory way, the way it is to this day applied to all Kansans. But whence the term in the first place?

I can offer no better answer to that question than to quote some facts concisely presented by trivia buff George R. Stimpson in his *Why Do Some Shoes Squeak?* (1992, pp. 107 – 108):

> The Kansas Historical Society mentions...that the term is supposed to have been used by [Sam] Houston's troops during the war of Texas independence, but there is no confirmatory evidence. M. Schele de Vere in 1871 thought *jaywalker* had been coined by convicts in Australia and imported by way of California. Alexander Majors in *Seventy Years on the Frontier* says the name *Jayhawkers* was adopted playfully by a party which started for California in 1849 from Galesburg, Illinois....The New York *World* discussed the origin of the term as early as January 8, 1862. That paper, quoting the Leavenworth *Conservative*, stated that the term was first applied to Colonel [Charles R.] Jennison himself, who was from New York. He was called the *Gay New Yorker* because of his festive habits.

> His men were called *Gay Yorkers* and as the word traveled it underwent many changes, finally crystallizing as *Jayhawker*. This theory is disposed of by the fact that the term was previously applied to [the abolitionist James] Montgomery's men. A curious story...is often told by Kansas writers. In 1856...an Irishman named Pat Devlin rode into Osawatomie with his horse heavily laden with booty. When his neighbors asked him how he had obtained the goods, Pat replied: "I jayhawked them." Upon being asked to explain what he meant, the Irishman said that he obtained the booty in the same manner that the jayhawk made its living. The jayhawk, he explained, was a fierce bird of prey in Ireland. Pat became known to the community as the *Jayhawker,* and upon the outbreak of the Civil War enlisted in Jennison's regiment, which became known as the Jayhawkers. There are several obvious objections to this story, aside from the fact that it lacks authenticity and smacks of pure fiction. The word *Jayhawker*, it is quite well established, was in use before 1856. There is not now and never has been a bird known as the jayhawk, either in this country or in Ireland....There are jays and hawks in Ireland, but no jayhawks. Notwithstanding these facts, many people have a strong feeling that the word was suggested by the habits of some predatory bird. The assertion...that jayhawkers were so called from their quick movements, and their habit of "suddenly pouncing upon an enemy," implies a comparison between the anti-slavery band and a predatory creature capturing its victim.

Cartoonists generally assume that the name was suggested by a bird, either imaginary or real, and have invented a grotesque representation to supply the public demand. *Jayhawker*, it has been suggested, may have been derived from a combination of the names of the blue jay and the sparrow hawk, both of which are plunderers.

Malcolm Townsend's *U.S.: An Index to the United States of America* (1890) a century ago seconded the idea that Col. Jennison's men were nicknamed Gay Yorkers, but recent alteration in the meaning of *gay* seems to have scotched that supposed origin for the word *Jayhawkers*. Stimpson notes that Jayhawkers predates Gay Yorkers (if indeed that term was ever actually used) by many years. The safest conclusion for me to reach here, and the most telling, is to agree with William E. Conneley's standard *History of Kansas and Kansans* (1918, mentioned above). In the second of his five volumes, Conneley notes (II: 712) that "the origin of the term [Jayhawker] is unknown." Naturally that will be found unsatisfactory by anyone who likes any of the old stories. Allen Walker Read is but one of many serious scholars of language to have discovered that there is no end to competing and sometimes obviously foolish theories about the origin of even more common terms, such as *Yankee*.

The Kansans are Jayhawkers. Let us leave it at that.

V. THE BIBLE BELT: KANSAS RELIGIOUS PLACENAMES

Kansas is smack in the Bible Belt. Thomas Pyles, mocking Kansas' outrageous forenames, called his article in *Names* 7 (1959, reprinted in his *Selected Essays* edited by John Algeo, 1979) "Bible Belt Onomastics or Some Curiosities of Anti-Pedobaptist Nomenclature." To some, the Bible Belt names of Kansas are the essence of hick; and, while some of the forenames of Kansas today may still be laughable, now it is because some Kansans share the lowbrow taste of the rest of the country, not because they have unusually odd names. The awkward placenames, however, though some of them have been erased from the maps and memories of Kansas, generally remain, stressing the Bible Belt identity.

Consider Abilene (Grassy Plain, see *Luke* 3: 1, descriptive of an ancient tetrarchy located some 40 miles north of the Sea of Galilee), the more obviously religious St. Paul (formerly Osage Mission and Catholic Mission), St. Mary (another reminder of the Roman Catholics), Beulah (originally an all-Methodist settlement, the name literally meaning a land in which Jehovah reigns), Mount Jesus (which non-Kansans find a bit startling, because we find anything named for Jesus a trifle disconcerting, not only the disrespectful East Jesus and the Jesus bug but even Hispanics forenamed Jesús), Olivet (the Mount of Olives), Sabetha (named by a young man whose ox died at the location on the Sabbath—and serve him right if he was working, you might say), and St. Jacob's Well, St. Francis, and more.

Many of the religious names are from the Old Testament, preferred by the Protestants; the saints' names are usually from the Roman Catholics, who foregrounded—to use the modern jargon—the New Testament. The term *mission* occurs in Friends Mission and Mission Creek, and there are also Quaker Vale and Quaker Valley, Mormon Spring, Angelus, Bethel, Hebron, Goshen, Xavier (actually named for Sister Xavier Ross), and the Miracle Revival Center.

The names of Kansas churches give one an idea of the breadth of religious experience in the state. Some, though they must compete in the US with the likes of Church of Bob, Church of Elvis, Church of Satan, and some show-stopping storefront establishments, are startling. Here is a list: Adventist Church, Allegheny Wesleyan Methodist Church, All Saints Roman Catholic Church, Amish Church, Antioch Baptist Church, Apostolic Christian Church, Apostolic Church of Jesus Christ, Beecher Bible and Rifle Church, First Congregational Church, St. George's Church (Greek Orthodox), American Muslim Mission, Open Bible Mennonite Church, Temple Church of God in Christ, Bibleway Pentecostal Assembly, Bethel Life Center, West Congregation Jehovah's Witnesses, West Douglas Church of Christ, Arkansas Valley Christian Church, Zion Norwegian Church, Grace Lutheran Church, West Side Free Will Baptist Church, and Johnson Tabernacle Christian Methodist Episcopal Church. There are, of course, many hundreds more.

VI. GAS, TROUBLESOME, AND LAKE DE LAGO: HUMOR IN KANSAS PLACENAMES

In both *What's in a Name?* and in my essay on "Weird and Wonderful U. S. Place Names" in the first of the 11 volumes of the *Omni Gazetteer of the United States* (1991) I touched on the odd or mirth-provoking names on the map of this country. Here I have space only to mention a few of the stranger names of Kansas created by the rip-roarin' frontiersmen, the schoolmarms who attempted to put a little polish on them, the speculators and boosters who participated in the expansion of the Middle West, the land sharks titling their plats, and the good ol' boys around the cracker barrel or the hot stove in some backwater, chewing tobacco and chewing the fat in regard to what to name the place so that mail could reach them from the great world outside. Defiant or now defunct, some of the names these amateur onomasts came up with are captivating, and some tell us of the wit and wisdom, occasionally the witlessness and folly, of early Kansas residents.

We shall probably never know for sure why Moody Intersection was so named, though I suspect it was for some Mr. Moody. The surname was not unknown in the early US. You may know that the clergyman on whom Nathaniel Hawthorne based his character in "The Minister's Black Veil" was actually a Rev. Mr. Moody; Hawthorne changed the surname for the story lest the black view of humanity be attributed to moodiness and not to Calvinism's bleak outlook.

What explains Eff Creek? We can only guess at the motive of calling a place Fancy Oil Field. Here are some other remarkable placenames of Kansas: Air, Equity, Fact, Farmers Ditch, Feteria, Frisbie Landing Strip, Gas, Good Intent, Genola, Hard Cash Creek, Hasty, Hay Hollow, Headquarters Draw, Heir Airport, Hell Creek, Hoffnungsay Church, and Hungry Hollow. Some were originally not as funny as you may find them now: Frisbie and Grenola, for instance, have been affected by extraneous factors. Do you find amusing names such as Industry, The Island (there are two of these in Kansas), Jingo, Kippo, and Klendike [*sic*]? Over time weird names may be dropped or the locals may come to love them.

Some names are amusing only when you know the story behind them. Garland was named when those hot-stove boys I mentioned earlier sat around to choose a name and settled on the name of the manufacturer on the stove. Threshing Machine Canyon goes back to the day when a band of Amerindians ambushed some settlers and threw that machine of theirs into a deep ravine. Dexter was named for a racehorse. Durham was named for a breed of cattle. Ashland was named for a famous southern mansion. You may think the spelling odd for Arcansas River, but I happen to like it and I think that pronouncing *Arkansas* the way the French did is absolutely ridiculous if, at this point in history, not to be corrected. Rannamead for Runnymead is illiterate and indelible; it does, at least, tell us how people pronounced the name in Kansas.

Does Mount Lookout sound redundant to you? Not to me. Why is the Manure River also the Republican River? I want to know. What lies behind (or in the middle of) Shoo Fly Creek? What could be the origin of Penis Creek? And those are only the beginning. Kansas also has the following placenames. Again I apologize for lists, inevitable in name study, but I notice that, whenever I get to the level of "funny" names, people actively want long lists. Here we go: Knowledge High School, Niotaze, Plumb, Rest, Rural, Sawlog Township, Shook, Skunkie Arroyo, Smute Canyon, Snoopy's Airport, Speed, Starvation Creek, Sublette, Sugar, Suicide Bluffs, Toad Hollow, Two Duck Site, Walkinghood, Way, Wego-Wego, Yaggy, Zarah (named by Gen. Samuel Curtis for his son), and Zenda (originally Rochester, then renamed after Sir Anthony Hope Hawkins' novel *The Prisoner of Zenda* in the same spirit which elsewhere in the country produced Ramona, Tarzania, and such).

Most of those names I just listed still exist on the map, but Kansas has lost, for example, Example. Kansas used to have the following notable placenames:

Buffalo Park, Dogtrot (now Galatia), Fame, Four Houses (the namers may have been reacting to Horace Greeley's snide remark that it took only three houses to make a Kansas town), Free Will, Frisco, Grass, Green Top, Half Way, Hooker, Hole in the Prairie, Hot Hill, Hourglass, Igo, Lithium, Lone Cone, Loyal, Magic, Mirage, Motor, Rain Belt, Senith [*sic*] and Rotate Township. Farewell as well to Success, Surprise, Troublesome—you knew that one was coming!—Violenta, Wano, Wild Horse, Survey, and Zella.

Even the cemeteries of Kansas have lively names. There is one called Life Cemetery. Mount Olivet is more traditional, biblical, but what of Economy and Elevation, Radical and Wooden? What we have here is the cemetery taking an ill-fitting name from the town it serves, the same way that a Quaker meeting house in Pennsylvania got the inappropriate name Gunpowder. The name Fix may recall an important settler, maybe even the founder, maybe even a resident of the cemetery, but what about Silent Skiddy? One Kansas cemetery is named Welcome, but others are called Wait and Work. Why Old Black Jack? (I think the black jack oak is the reason.) Why IXL and why Home Holding?

In addition to the usual "funny" names of European origin there have been some from homemade religion (Lodi) and commerce (Oxide) and railroads (Hog Back Station), not to mention the likes of Westkan (abbreviating *West Kansas*) and Kanorado (*Kansas + Colorado*). We find both learning (Ivanhoe, Kenilworth, Hiawatha) and ignorance (Lake De Lago, Lapeer, Kill Creek—*kill* is Dutch for "creek," as you know but some Kansans didn't), Le Grand Riviere, La Monts Hill, and so on. The US gazetteer, with Belle Vista and El Mesa and more along the same dumb lines, can assimilate all the Kansan errors. I don't think early Kansans were very much behind their fellow countrymen in education at the time they were creating placenames.

These days there is not much to be named in Kansas besides streets and housing developments and shopping malls and they do not make much of a demand on a naming public. Such names are often created for the stupid, seldom by them. Naturally, street-naming always goes on. When developers get going on a "theme," some of these can be as dumb as Thisa Way and Thata Way.

As always, some of the new names as well as the old have odd explanations. Hamburgh was named for its first postmaster, W. B. Hamm. I noted that in the *Omni Gazetteer* article I mentioned and said there:

> Someone who hears the names of crossings or odd post-office names may be led into the byways of our history. Another who notes Princeton moving westward with the pioneers may go on to read George R. Stewart on transferred names and settlement patterns....Stumbling on an oddity, one may be tempted to dig deeper, moving on to a serious interest, amateur or professional, in what names hold and can reveal about history, anthropology, ethnology, sociology, psychology, and other pursuits; what

names tell us about linguistics, or how they function in literature and folk tradition. Nothing is more interesting than people, and naming is one of the most interesting things people do, whether you just want to be amused by it or study and analyze its total meaning and effect. One could do worse than get involved in the fascination of name study by beginning with Hugoton. They wanted to honor Victor Hugo but they needed to distinguish this burg in Stevens Co. Kansas from Hugo, Colorado, so they added the *–ton.* Midian was named because two of the founders were members of the Midian Shrine. Boot Hill was where those who "died with their boots on" were interred in "wicked" Dodge City. Oketo was named for the Amerindian chieftain Areketah. Colony was named by residents who could think of no other name for their colony in Anderson Co. I like the erudite effort to marry Greek and Latin in Kalvesta. I was amused to discover that Buffalo Bills Well (in Rice Co.) had no connection with "Buffalo Bill" Cody but was dug by "Buffalo Bill" Matthewson. Agra (Phillips Co.) is named for Agra Phillips, not Agra of the famous Red Fort in India. There was a health experiment that came to nought on Vegetarian Creek (Neosho Co.). Moreover, times change and names change, as Adrian Room records in his general survey of *Place Name Changes Since 1900* (1979). His is a world gazetteer, so Kansas finds little place in it. However, Kansas, too, has its changed names as well as lost ones.

Kansas has thousands of placenames, and every placename has some kind of a story, some people who made a decision to call it what they did. The study of placenames goes far beyond giving the longitude and latitude and identifying the feature and stabilizing the spelling of the name. The full and proper science of toponymy involves the study of history and sociology and a number of other disciplines because it is, after all, the study not only of what was named but of what was chosen to have a name and what was in the minds of the namers, not to mention what has been added to the name, as it were, by the events which have followed the gift of a name. What do you think of the following names and what do you think people were thinking of when they named Admire, Basehor, Cassiday, Dillon, Elyria, Flush, Gypsum, Hiawatha, Iuka, Jetmore, Kipp, Leoti, Mound City, Narka, Ozawki, Protection, Quinter, Rest, Shady Bend, Tyro, Utica, Voda, Wayside, Yoder, and Zook?

VII. CONCLUSION: "WOES AND GLORIES" OF KANSAS PLACENAMES

It has been my purpose to present a study of the placenames of Kansas but to be selective so as to keep it short. I hope this has been enough to suggest the inherent appeal of these names. Though I have on occasion had to resort to mere lists, I have tried where possible to comment on the names that residents and visitors have put on the land. Those names, like names everywhere, tell of the expectations and experiences of the people who left their mark on Kansas, territory and state. In the placenames of Kansas we can read the minds of people dead and gone. We can read the story of exploration, settlement, development, Bloody Kansas of war and modern Kansas of peace and prosperity, and we can better understand those who lived and died and left "sunny Kansas with her woes and glories," as Eugene Fitch Ware (who called himself Ironquill) put it.

*

And now, having used one state to show the connections between pioneering settlement and names on the land, I turn to the connection between commerce and onomastics. For this I could have selected the topic of retirement villages or some other kinds of housing developments, or malls (which tend to have boring names, such as Mall of America), or something along those lines but I have decided to look at the named neighborhoods of Manhattan, some of which may be familiar to visitors to The Big Apple as well as to all or most residents.

Leonard R. N. Ashley

SoHo, NoHo, LoHo, AND JUST SoSo: THE COMMERCIAL AND CULTURAL IMPLICATIONS OF SOME NEW YORK CITY NEIGHBORHOOD NAMES

> **All nationalisms are at heart deeply concerned with names: with the most immaterial and original human invention. Those who dismiss names as a detail have never been displaced; but the peoples on the peripheries are always being displaced. That is why they insist upon their continuity—their links with their dead and the unborn.**

> —John Berger, "The Soul and the Operator," *Expressen* (Stockholm, 19 March 1990)

Placenames do more than promote admirable love of country and rabid nationalism; they can also express love of a part of the country or a neighborhood and sentimental attachments. Placenames can even contribute to the value of real estate in a suburb or section of a city. I have published on New York City neighborhood names and their commercial considerations in *Onomastica Canadiana* 55 (June 1979) and here I turn again to SoHo, NoHo, LoHo (all related to Houston—pronounced HOW-ston—Street in the city). It has inventive names there such as Tribeca (Triangle Below Canal Street) and Dumbo (Down Under the Manhattan Bridge Overpass). Over the years, New York has seen the passing of many local designations (The Ladies' Mile, The Five Points, Castle Gardens) and the creation of many new ones.

I write from the perspective of a resident of Brooklyn, and you may know (if you read Norman Podhoretz's shameless confession of his nasty attempts at *Making It*) that "[o]ne of the longest journeys in the world is the journey from Brooklyn to Manhattan—or at least from certain neighborhoods in Brooklyn to certain parts of Manhattan." That may be true of *Machers* like Podhortetz, careerwise, but I want to argue that my position is different and that, in fact, I look upon Manhattan as a nearby plaything, not a shining goal. I agree, in fact, with what Oliver Wendell Holmes wrote to Lewis Einstein and what Joseph Epstein, calling himself Aristides, quoted in the *American Scholar*: "New York would be disagreeable unless one were rich or beginning a career." Manhattan is, in my view, an industrial town for people who have to work for a living and a great place to visit for those seeking culture and fun.

I am trying to suggest to you that each and every New Yorker (not just Manhattanites) staunchly defends the 'Hood and feels, or at least acts, incredibly

93

superior to people who happen to live elsewhere, only occasionally granting that, possibly, they cannot help it or do not know any better. This stance one must keep in mind when dealing with the neighborhoods of NYC, from the get-go.

Neighborhoods are personal. I get personal here. I live in Fiske Terrace, a small enclave in Midwood. That is near the nationally known (and far less elegant) Flatbush section of Brooklyn, all of which will come into this discussion in their turn. Each of these names designates, according to the residents and outsiders, a certain kind of neighborhood. The city is full of so-called good addresses (Fifth Avenue, Sutton Place, Riverdale in The Bronx) and others not so good. Every neighborhood is in flux. The Lower East Side is now Loisada. The LES was formerly the East [Greenwich] Village. Now it has besides the tenement museum quite a few arty boutiques and one-room apartments renting for well over a thousand dollars a month. The names as well as the reputations are always changing.

Residents and realtors both make much of the cultural and economic ramifications of neighborhood names. There is more than a spelling change in Haarlem becoming Harlem. The Bowery still retains as the twenty-first century begins a little bit of the reputation it had in the nineteenth century, and New Yorkers habitually divide themselves into those who live Uptown and Downtown (though the border has shifted frequently over the years). They often think of Eastsiders and Westsiders (particularly Upper Westsiders) as different tribes altogether. Here you will get some of their history as well as some of the names. An accident may bring a Queens neighborhood into the headlines and you may discover that a place you always thought of as (say) an Italian or Irish neighborhood is, in fact, largely Dominican. Then you realize that there are more Dominicans, legally and illegally, in that part of Queens than anywhere else but Santo Domingo. Suddenly you may find that your Staten Island or City Island or some other area has drastically changed its ethnicities, but very likely not its name.

Names are usually a good way into history of any kind, whether it be business history or psychohistory. Placenames carry, as Grady Clay says in his incomparable *Closeup: How to Read the American City*, "huge layers of symbols that have the capacity to pack up emotions, energy, or history into a small space."

Clay in *Real Places* will explain to you a lot of placenames not on the map, such as the Lulu (Locally Unwanted Land Use), Combat Zone (formerly Red Light District), Bioregion, Complex, The Burn, The Lighting District, and more.

Neighborhood names and nicknames (P-Town for Provincetown, Big D for Dallas, The Slot for Market Street in San Francisco) do not get on the map either, but they are constantly in use. There are also names outsiders use that the locals hate (such as Frisco) and commercially invented names for suburban developments such as Deer Run or The Highlands at Brandon Woods.

These development names vary from one section of the country to another, though people all across the US like *Brook, Creek, Forest* and such almost everywhere and *Lake, Pond,* and riverine or shoreline or other water features (*Run,* seldom or never *Falls*) are among things useful to mention. Those who move out of cities may also like *Village* or *Park* or something similar to dignify their tract housing. These names chosen by builders may be related to the styles of architecture and the overall "feeling" of the places. These names are clearly understood as attempts to make developments more saleable by appealing to the desire of Americans to have comfort, elegance, a sense of history, a sense of proprietorship (*Manor* and *Estates* often occur in such names, even *Acres,* though one's plot may be small). People appreciate distinctiveness in the places they live. There may not be a fox or a meadow or ridge or crest or even a tree nearby, but the name may include one. Who would not rather say they lived in an Oak Park than a Streetersville? As you cross a desert, doesn't far-off Thousand Palms gleam as a goal? Will the great world treat you as seriously as you would like if you live in or even originally come from Possum Trot or Lick Skillet or Yazoo or Dullsville?

Names can change more than personal destinations (to which both personal names and placenames contribute). Would you retire to a community called Overda Hill?

What is not so often noted is that by changing Hell's Kitchen to Clinton, or, by nicknaming a gay ghetto Boys' Town, the way that people regard those neighborhoods may well be reflected in real estate values. This creates a reputation, just as do the booster names such as the Garlic Capital of the World or the Rose City, Star City, Auto Theft City (Newark, New Jersey), and so on. Who can be dour in Celebration? Who can ignore the past of a place called Yellow Knife? Isn't there a big difference in San Francisco now that Eureka Valley has become The Castro? Imagine—a nationally-known area named for an old movie theater!

Coming back to New York City, we see many changes have taken place as Gotham became Fun City and then The Big Apple. Over time, of course, the reputation of (say) The Village (for Greenwich Village) may undergo drastic changes, while efforts can be more effective to maintain the prestige of an address such as Sniffen Court or Patchen Place, even as the world around them changes. In every detail, such as the preference for British names, there is information.

British names are seen in many cities and towns in street names. Near where I live in Brooklyn, there are very few persons of British ancestry on Argyle, Albermarle, Marlborough, and other streets with aggressively British names. Where such names do not appear on the streets lined with big houses, they may well be found on large apartment blocks built in the first half of the twentieth century. The Dutch and the Spanish and the French were a part of our colonial history along with the British, but it is the British that most of us tend to think about in connection with early America. When we wish to evoke that as some kind of Golden Age, or give a haughtier tone to things, we may "think Yiddish but name British." As the British accent used to be assumed here, even in Brooklyn, so the British placenames are assumed here in Brooklyn where WASPS are rare. I seldom see another WASP on my subway line.

Those British placenames are very noticeable in suburban developments (which sometimes have British urban street features such as Crescent, Terrace, and Close). They remind us again of history and of the fact that the names of places where we live are of crucial importance to us. They contribute to our sense of place and to our sense of comfort. There is something very comforting to us to live in a town where the old system that William Penn devised for Philadelphia–a place named when Greek was as you might say not Greek to us all – and to have Pine Avenue and Elm Street and other thoroughfares given the names of trees. This is true even though the particular trees may not be planted along them. There may be no Beeches or Oaks or Magnolias along the streets that bear those names today. Even if there were it is doubtful that the varieties would all be known to city dwellers these days. Can you tell a cedar from a hemlock? I once said to a friend, "That's a plane tree," and she replied, "I think it looks fancy."

At the same time, at any time even so well-established a street name as Elm Street can be suddenly put in a whole new light by the success of a horror movie. The use of *City* for boom towns in the nineteenth century, you have heard, was eventually tarnished when the boom passed and the places became ghost towns. The use of *City* for retirement communities such as Sun City colored names still another way. There are patterns in placenaming as in every other kind of naming.

Numbered streets and avenues, grid plans, streets named with a pattern (letters in alphabetical order, names of presidents in chronological order, and so on), and other practical systems appeal less to most people than pretty or powerful names. Most of all, the overall neighborhood name is even more important to most people than *Drive* in their street address (which may indicate there are no sidewalks and no strange strollers are wanted).

We all prefer to say we live in a named neighborhood that is "ours." We would rather not have it called Bengali Alley, Chinatown, Odessa-by-the-Sea or anything like that, for people still judge us not only by our physical appearance and our clothes and manners but also according to whether we have a fashionable address or not. In Boston if you say you are a Southie you get a whole lot of baggage with that. Ours is an allegedly classless society. It is, however, really one with more classes than most (because so much attention is paid to financial status, and this can change rapidly and radically). How to establish your class? Get the right address. Your address may well be taken as a measure of your status. Are you on Easy Street? Do you feel more comfortable with neighbors of "your sort"? When the grocer speaks Korean and the taxi driver is Pakistani and the cops are no longer Irish, do you begin to feel "out of place"?

Developers create *places.* In order to take a rundown area and turn it into a fashionable neighborhood, real estate people wanted a name for a section south of Houston Street. They called it SoHo. The interior capital letter looked modern and flashy. Now you see it in a lot of new company names. The idea was to make everything new. The drive was to renovate and restore, and in the long run the neighborhood is far richer and far more attractive than it ever was before. It is not really restored; it is essentially brand new and oldtimers are out of place. It stands as a monument to the great American outlook that produced the "actual hatchet that George Washington used to chop down the cherry tree" (admittedly with two new heads and five new handles over the centuries) and a Colonial Williamsburg that has no eighteenth-century nightsoil and no shacks, sluts, bad smells, or other off-putting aspects. Our new SoHo may have some of those, because some old buildings and some old residents could not be completely eliminated, but they are being worked on. Meanwhile, there is no plastic perfection, as there is none in the place which inspired our SoHo, the Soho in London.

London's Soho is not exactly fashionable, though it is famous. It is bordered by Wardour Street (formerly Prince's Street), by Shaftesbury Avenue, by Charing Cross Road, and by Oxford Street. Each one of them has its particular flavor. Wardour Street (in the dictionary under Wardour Street English, which is a peculiarly fancy variety) means theatricality, extravagant tinsel, and it used to have a major concentration of the offices of film companies as well as some rather dubious antique shops. Shaftesbury Avenue is named for the seventh earl of that title, whose monument called Christian Charity—he was a philanthropist—stands in Piccadilly Circus and is usually called Eros. Shaftesbury Avenue is the London equivalent of Broadway; its name telegraphs big-time professional theater, the West End hits. Charing Cross (said to come from the French *ma chère reine,* "my dear queen" of one of the Edwards in the time when the aristocracy of England spoke French and not mere English) was long associated with bookshops, such as Foyle's. In recent times it has come down a bit in the world and is full of emporia where the musical instruments of rock 'n roll bands are to be bought. Or that was the way it was last time I looked, when it even peddled some of the rockers' gear (clothes). Oxford is a shopping street, resembling New York City's Fifth Avenue; it reads as big department stores. Within these borders is an enclave that has long had a bohemian reputation. Kate Simon in *London: Places & Pleasures* wrote of Soho a few decades back as a place for "prowling in tinsel and cheap satin evanescence," but today Carnaby Street, where people bought the clothes that the Beatles made popular, is quiet. Now Soho in London is tamer and not at all as flash as it used to be. Prostitution has been mostly cleared away. Soho is dingy. It used to be the

Little Italy of London, but almost all of that except for a few Italian restaurants, among many ethnic others, is gone. There are still street markets, but not lit at night with "the naphtha flares that glow" that once were there, even in Sir Noël Coward's youth. The Dolly Boys of Piccadilly Circus and the Piccadilly Commandos (pavement princesses of the Blitz) are gone. There are some gambling clubs, some porno parlors, some grunge, some shriek chic clothes still, and of course the graves of William Hazlitt (d. 1830) and even of Theodore, King of Corscia (d. 1756). These notables were buried in a churchyard there in palmier times, but few Soho residents today know that. Soho is a little tawdry.

At the heart of it is small Soho Square, formerly called Monmouth Square after that illegitimate son of Charles II. His mother kept referring to the baby as "you little bastard" until the king made the child duke of Monmouth. The duke once lived where Soho Square stands. The first earl of Shaftesbury got the young duke involved in a plan to ensure a Protestant succession to Charles II. This was an adventure that ended badly for all concerned. John Dryden wrote a beautiful poem on it, in which Monmouth is compared to Absalom, the rebellious son of King David, and the first earl of Shaftesbury is excoriated as the "false Achitophel." The square is too tiny and too quiet to suggest all that history. It is a locale for a music publisher now, not a grand London residential square.

Some say that *Soho* was the watchword of Monmouth at the Battle of Sedgemoor (1685), but I doubt that explanation. The story rings as false with that which connects the surname Home (pronounced "Hume") with a warcry. Had that surname been pronounced as spelled, it would have urged Scottish troops in battle not to rally but to retreat! You may know of Home as "Hume" because of a twentieth-century Scottish nobleman of the name who was for a while the British prime minister.

It is just possible that *Soho* was not a warcry but a hunting cry. Clunn, a writer about London history, claims that "the cry used to call off the harriers in the fields where the Lord Mayor and membres [*sic*] of the City Corporation hunted the hare in the days when this district lay far beyond the outer limits of [the City of] London."

Whatever the origin of *Soho*, the wars and the postwar tourist trade of the mid-century brought Soho to American attention. Despite its somewhat unsavory connotations, it was thus available to lend something to the clever *SoHo* label. The interior capital letter made the American name distinctive. It is not always spelled with the interior capital name, despite the popularity of the company names I mentioned and the African-American trend in names such as LaMarr, LeVar, LuEase, and BeverLeigh (also look-at-me names). While in some connections LeRoy has become Leroy, and Leroy has been replaced by Tyrone, ghetto mothers have increasingly sought to give their offspring attention-getting names. Through eminence in sports, on television, in the recording industry, and elsewhere, some of these unusually named children grew up to be rich and famous, much admired celebrities, household names. Their odd forenames became so familiar as to lose any taint, and (say) Deuin, Denzel, Dy-Anna, and such become as ordinary as Barbra, Luci, Lynda, or Notorious B.I.G., Tupac Shakur, and Puff Daddy. In this onomastic climate, Soho or SoHo looks anything but weird. Names function in contexts, of course.

In 1963, Chester A. Rapkin—a New York name with its assimilated forename and its Jewish surname combination, typically American with a middle initial—was retained by the New York City Planning Commission to study that area stretching north from Canal Street (where there used to be a canal connected to the Collect Pond) to Houston Street. The problem was that the area contained a lot of old factory buildings which light manufacture, leaving New York City, had left vacant and sometimes derelict. But the buildings were originally very solidly constructed and many had the old-fashioned cast-iron facades.

By 1966 the area was being referred to as the Cast-Iron District. The name gave more of an identity, a certain dignity, to the warehouses, factories, and loft buildings. Art historians and shrewd developers got together to appreciate and capitalize on the architectural features. Soon the city's Landmark Preservation Commission created official boundaries, slapped on some regulations about preservation, and declared the area was the SoHo Cast Iron Historic District. That was an ugly name but pointed up a clearly identifiable unit (like the renovated South Street Seaport). It constituted a commercially important step forward.

Suddenly, with local artists, "fashion victims" and visiting Eurotrash (who were later to contribute significantly to the rise of South Beach in Miami and its neglected Art Deco neighborhood), New York's SoHo was more in the news than London's Soho. Lofts and "raw [unfinished] spaces" in which illegal artist-tenants had hidden their lights behind blackout curtains now blazed forth. They were talked up, fixed up, hiked up. They went for ever-higher prices (so high that many artists were driven out). The larger buildings were converted to co-ops and condominiums, art galleries and boutiques; these brought crowds and crowds spawned vendors. A flood of weekend sightseers came, and the trendy and expensive bars and restaurants buzzed with activity every night. The press liked to write about this. The public relations were largely free, even free with the truth. The nineteenth-century traditions of boomtown, even gold rush, were seen right here in (Hudson) river city! SoHo became a fashionable place to live, if you could afford it. It became a name everyone knew. It became a "destination," which is what we now call a tourist attraction. A lawyer or accountant could acquire some polish by living in an artistic district. He did not need an artist's loft but he liked space.

Naturally, SoHo was hyped and over-hyped. Helene Zucker Seeman & Alanna Siegfried were just two of the would-be writers who saw the opportunity to make a buck in describing how others were making a buck there. By 1979, when they published their *SoHo* (from Neal-Schuman, New York), they had the *chutzpah* (nerve) to claim it was "a great guide to the hub of the world's avant-garde art activities." Their 274 pages promised "a behind-the-scenes story of SoHo from its settlement in the 1600s, as well as essays on cast iron buildings and loft living in the area." What the pages contained looks like quickie research, little behind-the-scenes facts are reported (if known), no substantial "essays" appear. Despite maps, illustrations, and so on, this is little but a shopping guide. Here, however, is the essence of SoHo: facades, first of cast-iron and then of blatant brass.

The story of SoHo is a familiar one. It is an example of the development of an area which can be identified as having a bohemian character (artists, in this case) into a fashionable shopping area for others (non-artists, in this case). It reflects the American delusion that one can become interesting by coming into contact with what is interesting. It is, *au fond*, a way to make money out of the insubstantial. It is a way to recycle rather than to respect history, to turn eating out or shopping into supposedly entrancing, life-enhancing occupations. It is the triumph of what I call the municipal mall. It belongs to the era of the *New Yorker* cartoon in which two DINKs (Double Income, No Kids) boast of how their lives consist of going to plays and movies and eating in expensive restaurants. In the cartoon we hear how they achieved freedom to do this: "We sold the kids." SoHo residents either never had kids or they have someone to look after them while the parents play in their status sandbox. If you are not wealthy you can nurse one drink and hang out with the rich.

The same malling was done with waterfronts in New York City and even Baltimore. All you needed in Boston was one historic building and you could wrap a mall around it, or you could even try to work from scratch in some other locations. Colonial Williamsburg was "restored" from the ground up. This is Disneyfication, which by now has turned The Deuce (42nd Street), from sleaze into Mousewitz. Theaters built there several generations ago for comparatively modest prices are redone at the cost of many millions now and turned into cinemas at best and shopping arcades at worst. You can get movie memorabilia where you used to get legitimate theater. The *kitsch* is here. The sleaze has had to be moved blocks away.

The area that became SoHo was more seedy than sleazy when the great renovation began. Lower Manhattan had already started to be a partly residential area for the higher-bracket renters. This was partly the result of the spanking new accommodations erected on the landfill (Battery Park City) that was dug out of the holes into which the twin towers of the (late, lamented) World Trade Center were put. Manhattan, always in flux, with basically nothing left from the Dutch and very little indeed from the British of the eighteenth-century, was always tearing down to put up something bigger. Manhattan grew taller with the Twin Towers (the legs of some colossus lacking all the rest of a body) and larger with the addition of this landfill on the bank of the Hudson. Wall Street, where the

Dutch had a wall to protect themselves against the Amerindians, as financial center served as something of a wall against a residential area. But Battery Park City was nearby, and north of that light manufacturing, forever deserting the city, had opened up some living space. Named right, this space might sell. Piled high enough, apartments might make the great cost per square foot of land *no problema.*

Uptown from this, more or less, but in every New York's speech identified as Downtown, there were Chinatown, Little Italy, and other enclaves that were long established. Those drew tourists to an incredible number of restaurants (and low-paid workers to secret sweatshops). A sort of secretarial school promoted itself into Pace University. The first skyscraper was there on Broadway, along with Trinity Church and Trinity Chapel and City Hall, from the days when this was center city. You get a real cute feel in this neighborhood. If you put the buildings to new use—the Old Custom House becomes a museum to house the Amerindian artifacts that were supposed to remain forever up at 100-Something Street, but Up There was thought too dangerous a neighborhood for tourists—and you put up some new buildings, why you'll have a high-end, in-city residential area!

Around City Hall and the World Trade Center, discount and computer stores now flourish. There are not a great many apartments. Wall Street means money, the New York Stock Exchange, the headquarters of large corporations ensconced in skyscrapers (possible because Manhattan had a strong rock substratum). Every neighborhood (Chinatown, etc.) and every street (Anne Street is porno shops) has a name and a character. Hunters Key used to be called Rotten Row. That was another import from London, just as Pearl Street here used to be Queen and Hanover streets (before the Revolution) and then The Strand (though there has not been a beach there in London for centuries nor was there one in Manhattan). Here and there you see a sign like Old Slip or Peck Slip. This used to be a busy port area, with all that meant. From Rotten Row, William Livingston said in 1755, there was "a putrid Stench arising from the Sink of Corruption."

With the Revolution, in downtown Manhattan (which is all there was of it at the time) King Street became Pine Street, Little Queen Street was rechristened Cedar Street, Crown turned into Liberty. "Candor" writing to a New York newspaper in 1794 was one of the few who resisted the republican changes. "Candor" replied to "Democrat" (who had called for American name changes to match the political changes) in the columns of the same paper:

> The names of towns, cities, and streets in America are standing historical monuments; they tell us from what countries, whether England, Holland, Germany, or France, the first settlers came; and the names of King and Queen Street[s – if King had been called George, it could simply have been attributed to George Washington] tell us we were once

subject to a sovereign monarch. This, so far as from being a reason for abolishing the names, should be a reason for preserving them.

Modern Americans think little of history. For most, history is something over and done with. Modern thinking easily alters names such as Nigger Creek with only a few people claiming that an historical name is disappearing, although the change is, typically, uneven and unpredictable. Squaw Valley stands unchallenged as a name while other placenames with *squaw* in them cause sqwawks and politicians quickly move to change the names rather than lose votes. Whatever the laws, typically again, some placenames defy them. For instance, the residents of (say) Martha's Vineyard have kept the apostrophe and the USBGN does nothing to arouse the Yankee cantankerousness.

In Africa in the twentieth century, country names changed. (Where was Rhodesia?) In some riotous overthrows all the street names in a capital might be painted out and replaced overnight. In African-America, old NYC names were easily swept away to create Adam Clayton Powell, Jr., Boulevard and Dr. Martin Luther King, Jr., Boulevard, as you read above. Minorities vote (not a lot, but they must be taken into account). The Ukrainians may get a one-block "way" for one of their poets, and Malcolm's name (well, the X substitute for Little) goes up.

So SoHo gets a name. It becomes a little country in the little empire that New York City is in New York State (The Empire State). SoHo now is comparable to (say) the towns in Brooklyn (Flatbush is the best known) that kept their names for neighborhoods even after Brooklyn joined them together to make a city and even after Brooklyn joined Manhattan to make a greater New York. Manhattan, by the way, is often called The City, as if the "outer boroughs" (Brooklyn, Queens, Bronx, and Staten Island) were not part of that City. SoHo was in the City (Manhattan)! The inhabitants of SoHo would refer to the influx from the "boros" dismissively as "the bridge and tunnel crowd," even though they themselves may have moved to SoHo from (say) Bronx or Cambodia. When I moved to Brooklyn (for more space) in the sixties, I noted that the sign in the subway said TO THE CITY and meant Manhattan. Thereafter I took the position that I have a country house and commute to Manhattan. People in SoHo commute to Wall Street or even (omigawd) work Uptown.

A *SoHo Reporter*— later called *SoHo News* and a bit less provincial— appears, and the full-time and weekend freaks begin to gather to be ogled by the yuppies in *après work* outfits. The Gay Activists' Alliance in The Firehouse drops out of sight. Singles bars for heterosexuals spring up. SoHo becomes a lifestyle. You have to dress appropriately to walk its streets now. If faced with fashion indecision, all-black will do in almost all cases. At the moment square toes are in, pointy toes are out, on shoes.

In "SoHo Loft For Sale: Artists Need Not Apply" (*Village Voice* 21 March 1977, p. 22), Richard Goldstein explained the metamorphosis of the area from cheap manufacturing to free artists' lofts to artists-become-entrepreneurs to expensive living, the shift to what culture critic Lucy Lippard called "a geography of boutiques, bars, and fancy food." The 42 blocks between Houston and Canal, once called The Valley, changed as much in NYC as Eureka Valley (now The Castro) did in San Francisco. The derelict buildings were spiffed up. The sweatshops moved away, or hidden better. What the local firehouse had called Hell's Hundred Acres, what the local police had once thought of as the dumping ground for victims of the Mafia, became the Hetero Castro of the East.

Robert Moses was once NYC czar of development. He brought Jones Beach to those in city pent, and anger to those in penthouses in the city. He once had plans for a cross-Manhattan expressway (that never got built) and plans for The Valley in Manhattan. An expressway would bisect it at Broome Street, and everything south of that would be rebuilt to match a new World Trade Center. In the fifties the threat of this grand design contributed to decline of The Valley, but subsequently a law was passed that mandated a survey of existing real estate. And that is when Chester A. Rapkin found cast-iron gold in the South Houston Industrial District.

The longtime residents of The Valley believed that nothing could stop Robert Moses, so they slipped away, to Queens, even, and left 3000-square-foot lofts to be occupied by artists paying $90 a month, or maybe just squatting. Had the oldtimers held on, they might have become rich, and not as artists, and *then* got out. But, with development, what usually happens is that oldtimers don't make the big money. The newcomers do.

The fire department was disturbed by the most notorious newcomers, the people living in squalor in "vacant" buildings. The NYFD launched a search and destroy campaign against the artists. 200 artists marched on City Hall and obtained a concession: approved artists could live in approved lofts if the NYFD was shown a sign that the building was not unoccupied, however much it looked to be. AIR: Artist in Residence. During the next year, 3000 "artists" registered with the city. By 1967 they were firmly entrenched in what was SoHo. People drtiven out of The Battery and Chelsea, and so on, by new construction projects, and a few prescient enough to spot the new trend, moved to SoHo. They added to the opposition to Robert Moses' plan to create a Lower Manhattan Expressway. The pressure became too strong for politicos to ignore. A New York politician is a pragmatist: she or he says with Robespierre, "The people are in the streets and I must find out where they are going, for I am their leader". Push pays.

SoHo was now an artists' colony, more or less, and the City Fathers accepted reality. In 1970 it became a "special use" district, with some political horse trading, and "artists" could have lofts of not less than 1200 square feet and not more than 3600 square feet, at $1.50 a square foot. The Rapkin report estimated renovation costs at $3.10 a square foot. In short, an "artist" could own a finished legal loft in SoHo for around $5000. Today that sum would be a month's rent for a nice loft or cheap for a two-bedroom flat in a good building there.

In real estate they say the three most important factors are (1) location, (2) location, and (3) location, but a location can change without moving an inch; it's a matter (as we say in politics) of perception. The area in the nineteenth century was called The Venice of Industry. In the twentieth century it was saved from the expressway and from decline. No expressway was never built. Manhattan got more tourists instead of alleviation of traffic problems. SoHo business boomed, the real estate business most of all. The "artists" turned *rentiers*. There was a fellow named Peter Gee. His was probably a Jewish surname abandoned, like Sammy Kaye or Danny Kaye, or Cecil Gee of pop clothes in London. Peter Gee declared: "If an artist has a chance to turn his loft around at three times the profit"—did he mean "three times the cost" or "three times the value"?—"he will." And why not? In NYC, everything is for sale if not on sale. What Peter Gee said was (a) true and (b) not a typically Jewish approach (as prejudice immediately alleged) but a basic, typical New York approach. The Big Apple believes that Business is Business.

So artist Peter Gee dabbled in real estate and did better than he ever did with his silk-screened creations. He was shrewd enough to see that SoHo was essentially not artists. It was "wealthy peripherals," the kind of people you saw at parties where you dropped in but didn't stay, the women who wore fur coats in the summer time (until activists with cans of paint made that "unwise") and the men who looked like barbered swine with blown hairdos. With enough cash, now you can live in an Ottistik Airya and rub elbows with other nobodies who like celebrities. *Dollink, it's thrilling!* So Claes Oldenburg and Robert Rauschenberg have moved away, but here are Dr. Berg the dentist from Brooklyn and the second (or later) Mrs. Berg, the trophy wife with extraordinary cosmetic surgery.

So that's SoHo, from *Genesis* to *Exodus*. *Revelations* will come. I don't know when. The artists? Some went to The Hamptons and some to Brooklyn or Down South or Out West. Some went Big Business. Some got real and got a job or got better and became MOMA's boys (Museum of Modern Art, with a branch in SoHo). Some died, and some went to Malibu or Taos or God knows where.

With the *nouveaux* who replaced most (but never all) of the artists, the *schlock* merchants and the yuppies moved in. Today SoHo faces competition for gays' disposable income from Chelsea, even Key West. Some of the art gallery owners are leaving the sinking ship. But other bohemias are also on the skids. The Village is "not what it used to be, and never was." Loisada is suffering from Puerto Ricans who burn their apartments (so the city will provide them with new furniture) and landlords who burn their buildings to get out of the landlord trap (terrible in a rent-controlled or rent-stabilized world left over from World War II and defended to the knife by tenants). Landlords want to collect insurance and go, or finance only market-rent building. Better life through arson. The LES is returning slowly, but it is still called The Jungle. It's just a higher-priced slum than it used to be, exciting, colorful, not as nearly as dangerous as New Yorkers like to think it is. Crime is down all over New York, lower than in a number of other US cities, but New Yorkers like to think they live on the edge. They just live on the edge of the continent, a bit out of touch with the rest of the country.

You never can tell what is coming in Mughattan, crime or no crime, plans or no plans. Manhattan itself is not so much a city—the center of which has moved progressively uptown to 14th Street by the Civil War, then to 23rd Street, 34th Street, 42nd Street, Central Park—as a collection of neighborhoods. Each neighborhood has a name. Every name has a story.

Take, for instance, the Lower East Side, the area which first provided the tenements into which the huge immigrant population, largely Jewish in this case, were packed in the nineteenth century and the early years of the twentieth century. Some of the space between the Third Avenue El (elevated railroad) and the East River became for a while the most densely populated region on earth, one and a half times more crowded than the most crowded city in India, almost 1000 persons to the tenemented acre. That was the LES (below 14th Street). That was the first American home of the ancestors of millions of Americans of today.

The Lower East Side or LES lost the original immigrant look when the Yiddish theaters of Second Avenue and environs and even a lot of the synagogues were abandoned. It got a new immigrant look with Puerto Ricans, from the fifties onwards. The look changed again when flower children flocked to St. Mark's Place (near the old churchyard where the grave of Peter Stuyvesant has been paved over and near where his pear tree stood for two centuries before it was chopped down). *EVO* (East Village Other, the alternate lifestyle paper) came and went, along with the Tenth Street Coffee House (on Seventh Street) and food co-ops (Cornucopia) and free used clothes and summers of love, winters of promiscuity. Addicts replaced freaks. Health-foodies gave way to the drug culture, sandals to motorcycle boots, Free Love to AIDS. The area became the swinging sixties East Village. Then the hippies OD'd or cut out and we had Loisada. But there are still some white faces, even a boutique called White Trash.

Loisada (Hispanic coinage for "Lower East Side," of course) points up the fact that people of color with some Spanish blood (Hispanics is a term that extends to African-Americans who speak no Spanish at all) lived there, chiefly in Alphabet City (Avenues A, B, C, etc.). Scarce apartments and rent control citywide raised rents wherever possible, so the area changed still once more, mixing in new populations with the Puerto Ricans who had come, replacing the Jews, Poles, Ukrainians, and the rest who moved out. *Dom Polski* (the Polish National Home) became the Dome disco and then the psychedelic Electric Circus. That gave way in turn to something else (I believe a city-sponsored project to teach lesbians to be carpenters and plumbers, but I may be wrong) and now St. Mark's is for T-shirts with outrageous remarks about NYC and sex on them, and *kitsch, kif,* etc.

The East Village (Greenwich Village was the west one) disappeared with Fillmore East (a rock venue). The area became a druggy playground and later home to real or pretend dropouts and trust-fund hippies, disco bunnies, gay bars (Dick's, The Fat Cock, etc.) and chic alternate culture. It became the new playground of yuppies and guppies and buppies and huppies (young and upwardly mobile professionals: white, gay, black, or hip), anyone who would pay over $600 for one room —politely called a "studio"—a cramped space in a semi-gentrified slum. Why would they? Christopher Mele (2000) in *Selling the Lower East Side: Culture, Real Estate and Resistance in New York City* says that

> [media] content workers pay high rents to tolerate the area's above normal levels of crime, noise, and drug-related social problems that are viewed as integral to the ambiance of Downtown urban living. Thus they derive social capital from occupying an area that the stereotypical middle class are reputed to avoid.

Studio suggests artists, but these *Rent* romancers and comfortable subversives (safe now that "Die, Yuppie Scum" writing on the wall has disappeared from the LES and there are concerts and Wigstock transvestites rather than riots in Tompkins Square Park), are office-workers. They are not artists. They just want to be rebels in some sense—or they cannot find apartments elsewhere, in a city with a vacancy rate of less than 5%. The artists who couldn't keep up with rents rising are gone. The new elite is netheads and Wall Streeters, geeks, not freaks. I call them freakoids: *like*, you know, like, freaks. The cyberworld will pay $40,000 a year and more to start to a twentysomething with piercings and a ponytail—if they know computers. These people are a new yuppie elite, and their way of dressing has already begun so to affect Wall Streeters (who envy their freedom and with-it status) that the word *suit* for an executive will soon not fit at all the casual clothes of the would-be nethead. The LES is in a similar sense fashionable. It is really not for artists but for cybernauts. They, too, will have their day and go.

Most artists, as I say, were pushed out of the East Village just as they previously had been pushed out of The Village by rising rents (ironically in new apartment buildings such as those named Van Gogh and Cezanne). They spilled onto The Bowery and then farther east still, then west into the factory lofts of what was to become SoHo. After SoHo they went to Williamsburg across the water in Brooklyn. A formerly almost exclusively Jewish community, Williamsburg was where the locals would have put chains across the streets to block Sabbath traffic if they had been able to get away with it. Williamsburg did not exactly welcome bohemian artists with open arms, but cheap rents made the move there irresistible. Today Williamsburgh is a very strange mix of bohemian and orthodox.

Where the artists can go next is anybody's guess, but in these days of what I call The Loft Generation, there are paintings so large they become *environments,* clutter is assembled into large *installations,* and sculptures are so huge they are called *constructions,* so artists demand not only big prices but also big spaces. Space is at a premium in big cities, so large spaces go beyond the price range of any but the most successful artists. The successful always flee the city for country estates, anyway, even if they go only as far as Long Island.

The artists' spaces were taken over by the likes of business people from the suburbs and singles—most New Yorkers live alone or in as-long-as-it-lasts relationships—who could fit into the big spaces broken up into small units. Then the new population, who moved to Greenwich Village for the "color," started to demand the close of the homosexual haunts (never accomplished), that authorities clear out the bohemians of all sorts (somewhat effected), spruce up the tenements (few could afford small houses whose prices soared into the millions), "clean up."

Residents in New York believe that because they rent rooms they own the streets and can control the whole environment. They organize. They get things done—or no longer done. They *kvetched* (a Noo Yawk word for whined and complained incessantly) about the tacky businesses that drew (horrors!) even New Jerseyites to crowd the narrow streets on weekends. There is still a bohemia of a sort in Greenwich Village, but it is a wealthier one and hardly an artistic one. There is more real bohemia in the French Quarter in New Orleans, in the gay areas of Chicago and San Francisco, even in Seattle (most famous for overpriced coffee and rainy days, but actually a thriving Microsoftia), than in Greenwich Village. We don't have a Microsoftia or Silicon Valley but we have a Silicon Alley in New York. It's Midtown, though not actually in the geographical middle.

Well, what is the use of all this history of just a patch like the LES of NYC, where some few artists and some Off- and Off-Off Broadway theater people and pop musicians still lurk, and where pushers of baby-buggies are beginning to appear in numbers though the pushers of drugs still are everywhere? Tuli Kupferberg's Fugs have fugged off long ago. Ed Saunders closed the Peace Eye Bookshop and went off to write about Charles Manson. There's no Auden there any more, not even Allen Ginsberg. Quentin Crisp is dead, too.

However, writers have been replaced by the new culture heroes, filmmakers and pop musicians. In the area of which I speak there are coffeeshops and bars where film *auteurs* are debated by very thin people. There is new jazz, and all-night discos, and CBGB, right along with nitespots with velvet ropes on The Bowery! Lofts with AIR signs seem to have disappeared. The Department of

Buildings always hated them anyway. Where do artists come off, bureaucrats asked, even as they kowtowed to political realities, demanding special privileges?

On The Bowery, not very far from the fleabag hotels and the discount-rate shops selling lighting fixtures or the places where you can buy the equipment of failed restaurants, some movie stars have bought lofts for staggering prices. They have lifted the local market, in which most people don't think for a moment about what something might be worth but want to know the price at which a comparable thing last sold. The people who ought to be able to live in elegant houses have drastically altered the original living loft décor. That I once described as Early Homosexual (expanses of bare floors, one wall of exposed brick and one of windows if you can manage it, big plants because there is little furniture, the coffee table on a rug forming an island with a few seating arrangements around).

Manhattan has the UWS (Upper West Side), with a grand apartment building once so far off the beaten track it was called Dakota. Manhattan also has the generally far more fashionable East Side (if largely owned by Europeans). Brooklyn has Park Slope and Howard Beach and the Italians of Bensonhurst and the refugees of Coney Island. The Bronx has posh Riverdale and utterly devastated slums. Staten Island has Todt Hill and historic Richmond and countless spreads of ticky-tacky box houses. To be brief, there are hundreds of neighborhoods. Each neighborhood has a character. Each has a name, traditional, forgotten then revived, or newly invented.

My point is that New York City is and always will be *becoming*—I shall not argue that it is progressing—and that every single area changes over time. Therefore, what a placename means at one point may differ incredibly from what it means at another time. Placenames look permanent, but in a sense they are not. This is a fact that gazetteers and government maps, concerned with precise geographical location, totally miss.

Most of all, I want to stress that placenames are charged with personality. I want to say that these neighborhood names are the names of the places people consider home. They are Park Slopers, not Brooklynites, and Brooklynites rather than NYC residents. Neighborhood names can keep (say) Sutton Place snooty for generations or rapidly transform some depressed areas (a polite way of putting it) near Brooklyn Heights into prettier and socially upgraded Boerum Hill, Cobble Hill, Carroll Gardens, more livable, more rewardingly rentable. On the other hand, a single crime can change what (say) Howard Beach means to all city people, even the majority who have no idea where Howard Beach is or what it looks like or who lives there. Who knew who lived in Belle Harbor until the plane crashed? Do you know where the Greeks or the Irish live?

The names put places on the map. Some are known to history (The Times Square Area, The Bowery), some to all New Yorkers (The Village, Flatbush, Coney Island), some to most New Yorkers (Bedford-Stuyvesant in Brooklyn, St.

George on Staten Island, Astoria in Queens, The South Bronx), some to a comparative few (Inwood, Midwood, Woodside). Some are promoted by realtors (Kipps Bay, Yorkville, Tribeca), and some are familiar only to local residents (my Fiske Terrace Association). Of course, with millions of fairly recent arrivals and with some 150 languages here, New Yorkers may hardly know or care that Chelsea has been created as a gay ghetto to replace Greenwich Village, that Hell's Kitchen (now officially Clinton) is jokingly Lewinsky, and that all over the place neighborhood names rise and fall.

Their borders change: what is in and what is not in Park Slope? The slope down from one edge of Brooklyn's Prospect Park? Not really. Where do (say) Crown Heights or Morningside Heights or Washington Heights begin and end? A New Yorker's idea of terms as basic as Uptown and Downtown may differ from the idea of the next New Yorker you ask (if he or she speaks English). A New Yorker knows that 125th Street is the Main Street of Harlem, but what New Yorker can give you the exact borders of Harlem? Or the Columbia University Area? Precisely where does the Upper East Side become upper (and lower in estimation than the East Side pure and simple)?

You probably cannot find Uptown and Downtown and the neighborhood names on maps in any case, but they are the New Yorkers' New York. There was a time in which Uptown meant going "to Harlem in ermines and pearls" for slumming. Today Downtown is, in the view of many, "where it's happening." Midtown has shifted over the years, ever farther north. Its location is vague. You know from the famous *New Yorker* cartoon what a vague idea any New Yorker has of the rest of the country: it's basically New York and The Coast with Flyover Country in between.

Today SoHo bids fair to become *the* "Soho." When English settlers arrived in Connecticut, they ditched an Amerindian name for the name London. The old London was going to be surpassed (as you read early in this book) as the settlers built the New Jerusalem in the New World (as if the geography was not as old as that of Europe), for the driving spirit of America was to be constant change, forever transforming, forever an improvement on the old, and on a bigger, better, more beautiful, more important continent! "Thine alabaster cities rise, undimmed by human tears." It was our Manifest Destiny.

In the name of that destiny we might forcibly move the Amerindian nations or the Fulton Street Fish Market. Every development means putting in new amenities and also pushing out businesses and relocating people who "do not belong" in the more expensive new real estate. That is one reason why New Yorkers resist gentrification, a word with a generally pejorative feel to it. Most New Yorkers resist gentrification with unexpected ferocity—if seldom with success, because "money talks." Their rents are already more than they want to pay!

Now let's go north of Houston Street. To NoHo. William Zimmer in "Noho Art" (*SoHo Weekly News*, 4 May 1978, p. 24), gave the earliest significant report on that fallout from SoHo:

> What Gertrude Stein said about Oakland, "There's no there, there," might have, until recently, applied to the area north of Houston St. covered by the umbrella term, Noho. An article last year in the [New York] Times calling the public's attention to the area began, "Noho is nowhere". Now the area is acquiring some "there" and is getting to be "somewhere"—as far as art is concerned. Noho has long been famous for music and theater—CBGB's and the Public Theater are landmarks—but now the blocks of gone-to-seed warehouses and men's shelters are being colonized by artists and are becoming revitalized. Artists always have this good effect: pioneering by artists in Soho and lower Manhattan made those areas, for good or ill, attractive to developers."

Mary Costanza chastised Zimmer in a letter to the same newspaper (11 May 1978, p. 20):

> "Noho IS the original artist center of New York—has been for over a century. Tenth St... has Zimmer ever heard of it? Or 12th St....or Edgar Allan Poe on Bond St., a building now occupied by 47 Bond Street Gallery and whose director, Marie Pellicone [is] quoted as saying, "Noho is the Bellybutton of New York" is nearer to the truth than Soho's columns allow. Jackson Pollock lived on Bond St. as did or does Stankiewicz, Jean Follet, Dubuffet, DeNiro, Kadish, Sugarman, Jan Muller—nearby, Rauchenberg, Resnick, Warhol, DeKooning, Kline—must I add more?

There are some problems here, quite apart from the fact that the most of the names you *recognize* in her list got the hell out of New York as soon as they could. The Public Theater is on Lafayette Street. I used to live across the street from it, near Astor Place, and I called the area The Village Verge: it is not The Village and it is not the East Village. It is a block east of Broadway, which is a kind of eastern limit to The Village, though never spoken of as belonging to The Village area. Once the East Village emerged, The Village broke up into The Village and The West Village, their borders unclear. The defining building in the vicinity of Astor Place is The Cooper Union, on Cooper Square, a block still farther east than Lafayette, basically The Bowery (where CBGB is). The East Village essentially began as you walked from Third to Second Avenue, and, if you went along East Fourth Street, before you went a block or two over there, *there* was the Off-Off Broadway theater row in the sixties. Not Noho.

Edgar Allan Poe gets mixed in with the painters somehow, but Poe's most noted residence is not in NYC and a house he did live in here is so gutted and redone so often and so badly that the Landmark Commission refused to save it. As I write, New York University (which some people say is spreading like a purple Karposi's sarcoma all over the area, even above 14th Street) is tearing it down in order to build another big building which, area residents predictably complain, will cast a shadow on Washington Square Park (once a graveyard and execution place, now a local gathering place). I would say nothing north of that square, and nothing east of it, is NoHo.

Noho is really a sort of South Village rather than a North SoHo, and SoHo has more cachet. Greenwich Village's Christopher Street was once called The Gay White Way. The Village, however, is really is nowhere as gay as Chelsea. You hear of Chelsoids but not Village-oids. Still, The Village's reputation remains such that sensitive straights and very closeted gays risk discomfort having it as an address. Brooklyn Heights has the same reputation from gays gone by, though the important gay bars of Brooklyn are elsewhere. Nor would The Bowery or Harlem (and both offer some nice accomodations, having housed the wealthy in earlier days) do for all of the career-minded.

One can always live in Chinatown or some other exotic locale and defy classification (unless one is Chinese). I once considered renting the loft over William Burroughs' in Chinatown but the skylights leaked. I bring myself into this still again but I have to drop a real name, that of Burroughs the Beat guru, for having a "name" in your building is another NYC feather in one's cap. Auden gave up a much nicer apartment in Brooklyn to move to one on St. Mark's Place because Trotsky had once lived in it. People say they live in the condo building of this or that celebrated Big Name, although they may try to keep out the likes of ex-Pres. Nixon because of all the fuss that Secret Serrvice guards bring, or the fans of (say) Barbra Streisand. Not all "names" are liked by condo boards.

Names are often fiddled in NYC, the way street numbers very reluctantly increase as one goes east of Fifth Avenue, the elegant and efficient east-west dividing line. Efforts to name numbered thoroughfares won't usually work. Fourth Avenue has, however, been upgraded to Park Avenue South. The Upper East Side used to stop at about 72nd Street; now it goes at least to 86th. A former slum is now Lincoln Center, and the United Nations Buildings stand on the site of another former slum, across town, about where the Dead End Kids once were.

As an area sinks into decline, most often a distressed place is left in search of a better one. Let it decline on its own; get out while the getting is good. As white New Yorkers lose more northern territory in The Big Apple (Harlem, Spanish Harlem, huge areas of Queens, Brooklyn, and Bronx), Manhattan's Deep South takes on more interest for them. The lower Houston area becomes LoHo for those who cannot afford the rents of The Real Thing (SoHo), and some pioneers ventured to Ft. Greene and other Brooklyn enclaves, even (convenient by PATH train under the Hudson) nearby Jersey. Many thousands of Jerseyites work in NYC.

The immigrants to Brooklyn from Manhattan reminded us that Booklyn was always a city of immigrants. One out of every six or seven Americans traces relatives back to Brooklyn, which early drew Jews and Germans and Irish and more and today has sections that are thoroughly Pakistani, West Indian, Haitian, and even Russian: Brighton Beach is that Odessa by the Sea. Williamsburg is a sort of new Greenwich Village, a more affordable SoHo, from which poorer artists were evicted in the last decades of the twentieth century. In the mid-eighties, for instance, NYNEX (the New York telephone company) published in *New Connections: The Magazine for New Movers* (to Brooklyn especially) David B. Konigsberg & Nancy Garfinkel's "Moving Out of Manhattan's Shadow." One paragraph ran:

> Today…many of the artists who made SoHo *the* place to be have been displaced by lawyers, brokers, doctors, and other wealthy citizens. Where have they gone? To Brooklyn's waterfront, where old factory buildings and warehouses have been remodeled as artists' lofts.

This phenomenon (of 1984) followed upon the gentrification of Brooklyn Heights and Park Slope and some other areas of Brooklyn by brownstoners from the fifties onward. These were still another class of immigrants to Brooklyn in the latter part of the twentieth century. That was a time when Asians and other persons of color were also moving into the borough and some public housing efforts (such as the Nehemiah Project and others) were creating houses for poorer locals, many of them people of color in Bedford Stuyvesant (sometimes spelled with a hyphen, sometimes not, often Bed-Stuy). Brooklyn, which would be, had it not been joined to Manhattan a century ago, one of the largest cities in the US, has seen immense demographic changes lately. Its neighborhoods have become more distinctive with every decade. It has old placenames and new neighborhood names.

So has, to a lesser extent, Staten Island, especially since (as a New Yorker might say) "the Verrazano Bridge has been constructed to connect it to the rest of the world." Staten Island is not just an "outer boro" but o-u-t. It is not only unfashionable but totally content to be so. It has even discussed breaking away from The City altogether. Mayor Guiliani says eventually he will retire there.

In The City, LoHo is "nowhere" and (cruelly) south of SoHo is just SoSo. Marjorie Pearson, however, years ago on the Landmark Commission, said that SoSo residents do not mind the joke and use the name themselves. (Better some designator than none!) More fashionable and at the turn of the century very expensive is Tribeca, now going to be much changed by the demise of WTC.

Tribeca is clearly defined—Triangle Below Canal, not a Three-Bridge Area as some dumb Men of Gotham believed—and it arose from still another City Planning Commission report. Tribeca is bounded by Broadway on the east, West Street on the west, and goes south to Barclay Street. Barclay is one of many British-inspired names (from the pronunciation of Berkeley) in the area, but old WASP associations do not keep ethnics who can afford it from moving in. (For some reason, a WASP is not an ethnic.) Many firetrap buildings, but don't worry; everything is heavily insured. Tribeca is nice and you are within walking distance of SoHo at somewhat lower prices. Tribeca may not be SoHo but in a couple of senses it's the next thing to it. In the age in which (to use one of my favorite expressions) every Billy Goat Hill wants to be Angora Heights, every little helps. If in New York you cannot have a dining room, you may have a dining area, or an EIK: eat-in kitchen. If you cannot have a garden, you may rent an apartment with a view of a garden out your back window. Views of Central Park, even if you have to stretch your neck, send the rents soaring even higher.

You will have noticed that concern with status is important to New Yorkers. Nobody says any more, for instance, that he lives in the East Thirties of Manhattan; he lives in Murray Hill. Once his telephone exchange boasted this, though it was not as uppity as PL(aza) 5 or BU(tterfield) 8. Today the 212s lord it over those with borough (718, etc.) exchanges and even those with Manhattan exchanges created when the 212s were used up (646). One Manhattan bank boasted East Side grandeur by saying it served "Dry Dock Country." That hinted: East Siders, not junk people. New York is a place where a person who anywhere else would have a large apartment is content to live in a hall bedroom hardly larger than a double bed so that he can have a Gramercy Park address. Gramercy Park is one of the best East Side addresses, and you get a key to the fenced square.

On the East Side there are newspapers such as the *Resident* promoting community causes. There may even be West Side papers—but lots of East Siders wouldn't know if that's true or not. Many East Siders would not go the West Side to see. One boy who went to the exclusive Dalton School (on the East Side, of course), on a scholarship, reported that East Side classmates were not allowed by their parents to visit his home because he lived on the West Side.

Murray Hill is comfortably East Side. Murray Hill isn't much of a hill but it survived a leveling off in the nineteenth century. There used to be a Bayard's Mount, Bestevaer's Cripplebush, Pot-Baker's Hill, Crazy Smith's Hill, and Crowfoot Hill. These and more of the vanished names are to be found in Leonard S. Marcus' "What's in a Street Name?" (*Seaport* 12: 2, Fall 1978, 14 – 19) and old histories. It is possible that some realtors will revive some of these names in Manhattan as they have revived others for "upwardly-mobile neighborhoods." If they can sell brick-front houses as "brownstones," they can sell anything. If they can call subsisting in an 18-foot wide floorthough "gracious living," rationality flies out the non-picture window. Moreover, new names can bring new vitality to the neighborhood economy, a new outlook, new pride and further projects and profits. But first, very often, comes a name. "In the Beginning, was The Word." It doesn't always work—Brooklyn Union Gas' Cinderella Project did not get a Flatbush Avenue and environs revamp really going—but it can. Hope springs eternal, except perhaps for Flatbush Avenue.

Where or what was that Flat Bush? Most studies of placenames deal with etymologies, and there are some interesting ones in NYC neighborhood names. I like DUMBO. Some scholars deal with placenames as clues to settlement patterns. Some critics deal with the evocative placenames in poetry. This article has taken you on a little trip around NYC real estate. I mean to suggest that a neighborhood, given the right name, can revitalize. With the right name cash may be forthcoming from venture capitalists to make investments in rehabilitation or replacement, enthusiasm infecting preservationists or fashionable newcomers, and the area may experience a real turn-around and a new commercial prosperity.

With this emphasis on names, I urge urban sociologists to pay attention to the phenomena I have mentioned here. It would be a good idea if economists and psychologists also had a look at the power of commercial names. Names in magic are said to be able to transform matter. Names in commerce perform magic, too: they are able to change the thinking of people and, as we see here, a whole cityscape changes. There's nothing either commercial or non-commercial but thinking makes it so, as the fellow said who should have sat tight until the job opened, should have waited to become king, and turned Elsinore into a Danishland attraction. A ghost might even draw more tourists. It seems to work for some bed & breakfast joints in the US and for musty castles in Britain.

Names put the *there* there for people, for a name is a name is a name and is much more than a name. A name naturally expresses the mind of the namer, but names once given, as Sir Winston Churchill said of buildings, have a life of their own. We create them but "thereafter, they shape us."

A name can move the product or spark the service (Takeout Taxi). A name can also put a piece of real estate in a certain light and make or break a business deal.

PLACENAMES IN CATCH PHRASES

A phrase that "catches" one's attention,
especially if often repeated and used as a
slogan, as with "read my lips, no new taxes"
(George Bush in his campaign for the US
presidency, 1988). Some catchphrases are
fashionable and ephemeral, others persist for
years and may become idioms...*For my next
trick* (followed by a pause, especially said by
someone who has just botched something;
dating from the 1930s patter of stage
magicians).

—Tom McArthur, "Catchphrase,"
The Oxford Companion to the English Language

I'm not casting nasturtiums, but nobody, so far as I can find out, has ever
written an article on the place of placenames in catch phrases. Because I was of
some help to Paul Beale in his edition of Eric Partridge's *A Dictionary of Catch
Phrases* (1985), and have always found catch phrases to be a curious sidelight on
popular speech, I offer a brief examination of the subject here. I draw my
examples mostly from Beale's revision and updating of Partridge. That will give
the whole thing a rather British slant. I wish someone would do a similar and
updated dictionary concentrating on the US, where advertising, other aspects of
the media (especially comedians), and further factors have contributed to a rich
store of US catch phrases that yield an insight into the public mind. While we
wait for that, let us look at the following. We cannot say (with the slogan of the
News of the World, joking called *The Screws of the World* because of the sex
scandals reported) "All Life is There," but there is some. Are you sitting
comfortably? Then I'm off to the races.

Abyssinia. "I'll be seein' ya." Goodbye.
Admiralty could not be more arch, the. Admiralty Arch is a London
landmark. Beale dates this playful "you're being arch" to approximately
1925 – 1960.
Alamo, remember The. A battlecry of the Mexican War. At The Alamo
in Texas, most American defenders died (the rest were captured and
shot).

Alice Springs to breakfast (time), from. Australian for "all over the country" or perhaps the Aussie equivalent of US "from hell to breakfast," the complete story.

Appleby, who has any land in? Why are you holding up the passing of the drink? Capt. Francis Grose noted this obsolete catch phrase in the eighteenth century.

Arizona, happy as ducks in. Unhappy. Arizona is supposed to have no water.

Barking Creek, like the ladies of. Refusing intercourse. Verses said these ladies "have their periods three times a week."

Bath (and get your head shaved), go to. Victorian "to Hell with you".

Belgium, if it's Tuesday this must be. Mocking fast-paced Continental tours.

Belgium, remember. A World War I slogan, to which the reply was from those who served there, "As if I could forget the bloody place!"

Berlin by Christmas. Hope of British soldiers in World War I. Like **Home by Christmas,"** in time it elicited **Which Christmas?**

Berlin or bust. US soldiers' equivalent of the above, influenced by **Pike's Peak or bust.**

Blackfriars! Victorian Londoner's equivalent of Public School *Cave*! (Latin for "Look out!") . Blackfriars was once a low section of London.

Blackpool, do you come from? US equivalent is "Were you born in a barn?" In the UK the suggestion may be that Blackpool has only swinging doors, like the saloons of the old West. The idea is: shut the door behind you, "put the wood in the hole," you clod.

Blackpool's a fool to it. Said of any lighting display that surpasses the "illuminations" at this British seaside resort.

Black Rock, bad day at. Any unpleasant time, from a western movie.

Blockhouse, better than dog-running from. Fair to middling, Royal Navy. This was the submarine base at Portsmouth. Add: **not as good as a run ashore in Istanbul** (the far end of the dog or morning run).

Borough Hill after Jackson's pig, it's gone to. It has disappeared [in Northamptonshire]. Mid-nineteenth-century origin.

Boulevard of Broken Queens, things are picking up on. "I see you have scored while cruising San Francisco's Polk Street." (Polk Street was also known as Pig Alley, Pigalle, Turkey Run, etc., according to "Bruce Rodgers"(1972).

Bourke, back o(f). In the boondocks. Bourke is in a remote part of Australia.

Bourke Street from Tuesday, he doesn't know. He's ignorant. Australian. The vulgar US equivalent is **he doesn't know his ass from a**

hole in the ground and less vulgar is **he doesn't know which way is up.**

Brazenose College, bred in. Impudent, has a lot of "brass" (nerve). Brasenose is a college at Oxford University. Seventeenth- or eighteenth-century.

Brazil, there's an awful lot of coffee in. From a popular song. Greets stale news, as "Queen Anne's dead" used to do.

Brazil—where the nuts come from. A laugh line from *Charley's Aunt* (1893).

Brighton, we're all going to. "I don't believe it!" (A girl caught *in flagrante* on a train makes this remark in a dirty joke.) Comparable to, "You come home with your knickers torn and tell me you found five pounds in the street."

Buffalo is redundant, suicide in. A line from one of the gypsies in *A Chorus Line*, but known before that pastiche was put together and repeated now by people who "lived in cave in Tibet for 10 years" and never heard of the musical.

Burbank, beautiful downtown. Rowan & Martin on TV mocked this California location. Catch phrases come from television now as they used to come from vaudeville and the music hall.

Calais, the wogs begin at. All people but the British are people of color.

California, if you tipped the United States everything loose would roll into. This can serve as a sample of the indefinite boundaries between more or less accurate quotation (in this case, from H. L. Mencken) and catch phrase or sociological observation, unwarranted insult, etc. With this one, **Los Angeles** is often substituted for **California** and sometimes people add: **and it has.**

California or bust. A slogan of the Gold Rush.

Casbah, come with me to the. A sexual invitation. One of those "quotations" from movies that were never said by the actors that impressionists imitated.

China, is there a flood in? Your trousers are too short.

China, not for all the tea in. Not for any price or under any circumstances. Tea = marijuana produces **not for all the tea in Mexico.**

China, oil for the lamps of. Any windfall. From a book title.

China, she thinks Fucking is a town in. She is very naïve.

China; what's that, the population of? Of any high number.

China with a cargo of tea, sailing to. Joke about training ship newcomers.

Christchurch. New Zealand equivalent of "Cripes" or "Crimminy."

City Hall, you can't fight. Bureaucracy baffles brains.

City Morgue—duty corpse speaking. Jocular way of answering the telephone. Variations include **Whore house—the customer comes first!** and **City Jail,** etc.

Cloud Nine, be on. Be ecstatic. Islam has only seven heavens.

Coliseum, like a beer bottle on the. Incongruous. Australian.

Colney Hatch for you. You belong in the "loony bin."

Connaught, go to Hell or. "I don't care where you go."

Cunnyborough, ask cheeks near. "Ask my arse!" Obsolete.

Denmark, something is rotten in the state of. I suspect foul play (from *Hamlet*). Distinguishing between a quotation and a catch phrase is hard.

Devil, gone to The. I include this as a sample of an explanation I do not believe. In Eliezer Edwards' *Word Facts and Phrases* (1881) it is claimed that this phrase refers to The Devil pub in London. "Businessmen and lawyers who closed up shop to have a few drinks would hang up a sign, 'gone to the Devil.'" By the way, I could not find in my researches a London pub called The Devil in this period but I presume that in most or all cases such a pub would have been named for a printer's devil (perhaps another story about an origin?) and not Satan.

Dodge, it's time to get the shit out of. It's time to move on.

Dover waggoner, put this reckoning up to the. Charge my bill to "Owen."

Drury Lane whore, always in trouble like a . Self-pitying, allegedly like the prostitutes in the street where The Theatre-Royal stands (and therefore over-dramatic).

Dumas, I'm a ding-dong daddy from. I'm a Texas he-man.

Dunkirk, biggest fuck-up/SNAFU since. The retreat from Dunkirk was a debacle for the British in World War II. In World War I, they said **since Mons.**

Dunkirk spirit, there's the (old). Ironic to a slacker.(UK)

Durban, off to. South African for going to "paint the town red" anywhere lively.

Egyptian medal. Fly button (UK, after the campaign in The Sudan).

England, close your eyes and think of. Instructions for the female during British intercourse. ("Did I hurt you? You moved.") Originally, more seriously, instruction on how to cope with nostalgia during overseas posting, etc.

England expects everyone to do his buddy. The English are all gay. A canard.

England, the things I do for. Self-congratulation for otherwise unappreciated efforts. From the film *The Private Life of Henry VIII*.

Erie, on the. Eavesdropping. Some scholars suggest the Erie Canal or the Erie Railroad, but it seems clear to me that "ear-y" is meant.

Fagshaft, having to spend a Queen's Christmas in. Stuck with visiting the family in Flagstaff (Arizona) over the holidays (or a similar awful place).

France, as we say in. Used to excuse a French phrase. Nineteenth century.

But **Pardon my French** excuses some expression too vulgar or obscene.

France, somewhere in. Heading of soldiers' letters home. World War I. Now equivalent to "I don't know/won't say where I'm writing from".

France the last drop always goes down your pants, when you dance in. Used by Australians to make fun of what they consider to be "fawncy" English speech.

Ft. Apache. From an oat opera (western movie) where Injuns attacked US troops. We took this name for any place where authorities (such as police in Bronx slums) were under attack by savages.

Gath, tell it not in. Victorians familiar with The Bible used this for, "Fancy you doing that!" It's a quotation from II *Samuel* 1: 20 but in that Victorian use a catch phrase.

Georgia, everything is peaches/peachy down in. Everything is "hunky-dory." UK: "Everything in the garden is lovely."

Gibraltar, the anniversary of the siege of. Any day at all. Gibralta was under siege continually 1779 – 1783.

Gomorrah. Raffish "Good morrow!" c. 1900 – 1914.

Halifax, Good Lord deliver us; from Hell, Hull, and. Seventeenth - or eighteenth-century.

Harwell (and no return ticket), he's/she's going to. That person is headed for the insane asylum (for a permanent stay).

Harwich, they're all up at. They're in a fine mess. Late nineteenth-early twentieth century.

Hell in a handcart, going to. Getting worse quickly.

Hell, he hasn't got the chance of a snowball in. He's "for it" (UK), "hasn't got a Chinaman's chance" (US).

Hell, it will be a cold day in. "That will be the day."

Holland is a low-lying country. The unkind English add, "full of low, lying people."

Holland, the Dutch are in/have taken. Greeting for stale news.

Hollywood on me, don't go. Don't start acting crazy or putting on airs like a movie star.

Hutton's is best. Don't argue. Australian. From an advertising slogan.

India, what's the rarest thing in? Answer from imperial days: "Guardmen's shit." The fancier (Guards) regiments did not draw this kind of peaceime oversea duty.

Jerusalem, all jam and. A criticism of The Women's Institutes, known for jam contests and the singing of the hymn *Jerusalem* (lyrics by William Blake).

Jerusalem, since Jesus played half-back for. A long time, especially in relation to army service or the RAF ("since Pontius was a pilot").

Key West; Key West, young gay. Modern "take" on "Go West, young man...."

Ladysmith has been relieved. From the Boer War. The response is: "Well, I'm glad for her." Still used jocularly in various circumstances, as are many of the old catch phrases. I have omitted the ones that require a special manner of delivery (difficult to detail in print), but these imitations are the soul of certain humor picked up from popular comedians. Perhaps you know how to say (for example): "Hey, Abbott!" with the correct Costello inflection.

Leicester landlady, you have a heart like a. You are ungenerous.

Liverpool landing-stage, the only stage you'll ever get on is the. You'll never succeed in the theater. (UK)

Lombard Street to a China orange/a Brummagem sixpence/ ninepence, etc., all. Everything from the wealth of bankers to a small amount. Lombard Street was famous for wealth in London in the eighteenth and nineteenth centuries.

London, carry on. Catch phrase from The Blitz of World War II.

London, don't turn that side to. The metropolis demands the best quality.

London, is that the way to? Said when someone raises an arm to wipe their nose on their sleeve.

London, it's raining in. Mocking cuffs (turn-ups) on trousers as affected. Obsolete. From the days when trouser ends were turned up (outdoors only) so as not to get muddy. J. Alfred Prufrock: "I shall wear the bottoms of my trousers rolled."

London on it bare-arsed, you could ride to. That's a very dull knife.

London to a brick, all. Odds on a horserace or any "sure thing."

London, Walker. Obsolete derisive cry of street urchins, from a business sign.

Madras for health, Bengal for wealth. Condition in India under the *Raj.*

Mafeking has been relieved. *Tant pis, tant mieux.* "My aunt has been to the toilet and is feeling much better."

Maine, remember The. A slogan of the Spanish-American War, precipitated by the battleship *Maine* blowing up in the harbor of Havana.

Manchester you've never seen anything, if you've never seen. Booster slogan.

Melbourne, all behind in. Aussie equivalent of US "fat-assed" or "broad in the beam."

Missouri, I'm from. You'll have to show me before I believe it.

Mons, gassed at/hanging on the wire at. Soldier's reply to where's —? World War I. There was no use of poison gas at Mons. *Wire* is barbed wire.

Naples and die, see. Not that it's that crime-ridden, rather that it was beauty never after to be experienced.

Nenagh, there's a barracks in. Ironic Irish for "Cheer up!"

Newark, if the world ever needs an enema it will be administered at. Calling a place—insert your own choice—the "asshole of the world."

Newgate may soon be afloat at Tyburn, he that is at a low ebb in. The prisoner in jail may soon be hanged. Things can get worse.

New Haven, we bombed in. The out of town tryout of the play was a failure. We never got a real opening for the play, the project, etc.

Newmarket Heath, a fine day to catch herring on. It's raining, "a fine day for ducks."

New York minute, I'd do it in a. I'd do it instantly.

North Carolina said to the governor of South Carolina, as the governor of. "It's a long time between drinks." Said to antedate the Civil War.

OK Corral, the. From a western movie we got various catch phrases related to this locale as the site of actual or impending trouble.

Oklahoma credit card, he uses an. He siphons gas out of other people's vehicles.

Paris, he fought the Battle of. He had a "cushy billet" in Paris in World War I.

Paris, it's snowing in. "Your slip is showing."

Pearl Harbor, remember. A slogan of World War II designed to stimulate revenge for 7 December 1941, "a day that will live in infamy" (in case you have forgotten). Australian has joking **remember pearl barley.**

Peoria, will it play in? Is this not too sophisticated for the rubes?

Persian Gulf's the arsehole of the world and Shaiba's half way up it, the. Often introduced with "you know the old saying." From British troops abroad. Many catch phrases are preceded by "As the man says" or "as the saying goes" or "You know the old saying," etc., but the fact you know does not stop the speaker any more than "Have you heard the one about...?" can stop the joker telling his story.

Philadelphia, on the whole I'd rather be in. Anything's better than being dead.

Philadelphia, the woods begin at. A snobbish Easterner's view of the country.

Piccadilly Circus shining out of his arsehole, he thinks he has the lights of. He has a too high opinion of himself, he's "stuck up," "thinks his shit don't stink," etc.

Pike's Peak or bust. A nineteenth-century travel destination. Now, any goal.

Pisa, as Big Ben said to the Leaning Tower of. "I've got the time (if you've got the inclination)."

Pitt Street from Christmas, he doesn't know. He's ignorant. Australian.

Poona…, Gad, Sir, when I was in. Take-off on that "monumental man, the officer and gentleman" of the British *Raj.* Delivered in the tones of a retired, red-faced, blustering colonel.

Poona, two other fellows from. US version: "It wasn't me; it was two other guys."

Portsmouth, consider all propositions like the nice girl of. Portsmouth, a sailors' town, had some nice girls as well as many whores.

Potomac, all quiet along the. From the Civil War song, *All Quiet along The Potomac Tonight* (1864), made popular again by Burl Ives in the twentieth century. See: **Western front, all quiet on the.**

Putney (on a pig); well, I'll go to! "Well, I'll be damned!" You can use any of the placename variants for "Hell," such as Hanover, Halifax, etc., also.

Pyramids, hence the. Pointing out a *non sequitur* or interjecting one.

Ruffians' Hall, he's only fit for. He's a ruffian.

San Anton'! The name of San Antonio (Texas) was used in the Wild West as an exclamation like "Wow!" or "Hoo-EEE!"

San Francisco, city of fruits and nuts. "If they aren't fruits, they're nuts."

Shit Creek without a paddle, up. In dire straits. A single example of a non- existent place, the rest of which I have omitted from this necessarily limited list. The most interesting are the wordplays. Example: "the walls of Jerry & Co. falling," the modern construction company (of jerrybuilt houses) being created to play on the biblical Jericho ("and the walls came a-tumblin' down").

Short's in The Strand, cheap and nasty like. Short's served inexpensive meals in Victorian London.

South America, God is alive and well and living in. God is not dead, He just does not care anymore.

St. Paul's (not forgetting the trunkmaker's daughter), all around. St. Paul's Churchyard was long famous for the outdoor sale of books.

Unsold books were broken up to provide paper for lining trunks. It means just "all over."

Starve 'em, Rot 'em, and Cheat 'em. This doesn't look as if it belongs here but it stands for three places (Stroud, Rochester, Chatham) used as military and naval bases mid-eighteenth to late-nineteenth century in England.

Stinking Yarra. Sydneyite derision at Melbourne's "only river that flows upside down, with the mud on top." The retort to Syndney is "Our 'Arbour!"

Stockholm tar, every drop of his blood is. He's a real sailor.

Sydney or the bush. An Australian betting all.

Swanee, down the. "On the skids." People were **sold down the river** sent to jail **up the river**, etc.

Texas, if I owned Hell and Texas I'd live in Hell and rent out. Lack of appreciation (of the heat, etc.) of The Lone Star State.

Thames in a wheelbarrow, you didn't travel up the. "You're no fool."

Tippecanoe and Tyler too. One of the electioneering slogans ("It's morning in America" was my favorite laugh) that has long survived. It is said to mean now "this is even more wonderful than I expected" or "that's very old-fashioned."

Tookarook and there's no bloody work at Bourke, things are crook in. Australian outback version of "things are tough all over." Any placenames that rhyme will do.

Toronto one Sunday, I spent a week in. "I felt as if it were Resurrection Day and I was the first one up." "Toronto the Good" has now lost its Scottish-Presbyterian dour reputation and is a very cosmopolitan city.

Tower Bridge, up and down like. Tower Bridge is a drawbridge. It's the one some Americans (I think) thought they were buying when they purchased the plainer London Bridge, which they installed in some desert. Better are the variants such as "up and down like a shit-house seat," "up and down like a whore's drawers (on Boat Race night)" and "up and down like a bride's nightie"….

23-Skidoo. In the early twentieth century, a skyscraper erected on the triangle where Broadway crosses Fifth Avenue in Manhattan (nicknamed "The Flatiron Building") created winds that caused skirts to fly up. To move along the gawkers, the police told them to skeedaddle—or skiddoo.

Victoria Station without the clock, like. Extremely crowded.

Vienna, goodnight. From an operetta of (German equivalent of) the same title.

Beale quotes Cyril Whelan: "a pen-knife phrase in that it can be put to a variety of uses…." We had a few drinks, back to her place, and Good Night Vienna."

West, young man, go West; go. Horace Greeley's advice to the mid-nineteenth century ambitious man. In slang, "gone West" = died.

Western Front, all quiet on the. Quiet, from World War I despatches. Used as the title of a famous film. That made it very popular in the early twentieth century.

Whitehall, he's been to. That (army officer) person has been granted an extension of leave. Victorian.

Wigan, he comes from. He's provincial.

Wigan, give it a. Give it a try. ("'Ave a go, Joe, the wife won't know.")

Wigan, that went better in. A comedian's comment when a joke gets few laughs. Other expressions for such an occasion include: "Thank you both," "Thank you, Mother," and "That must be the landlady." One member of a US comedy team is said to have announced, "My partner will now pass among you with a baseball bat and beat the bejeezus out of you." That became a catch phrase, too.

Wigan, twice removed from. Of people of Lancashire or Yorkshire origin but now living the in south of England.

Windmill girl said to the stock broker, as the. A variation on the more familiar "as the actress said to the bishop" (or *vice versa*), a way of making an innocent remark sound like sexual innuendo. The Windmill was a cheap theater in Piccadilly, more respected for staying open during The Blitz than for its shows.

Winnick for you. You belong in the [Lancashire] insane asylum.

Woolwich arsenal, make way for. Said of a heavily-laden infantryman. (UK)

Woolwich, I'm with the. UK reply to "Are you with me?" "I'm with the Woolwich" was the slogan of an insurance company.

Yorkshire compliment, that's a. "You give me this worthless thing because you have no use for it, and I have no desire for it." Yorkshire people (even in connection with delicious Yorkshire pudding, basically designed to flavor something cheaper than meat and fill you up on that, so you will "go easy" on the meat) are traditionally said to be tightfisted. We can learn from placenames in catch phrases is what stereotypes existed, maybe persist.

York Street is concerned. "Watch out, someone's watching us!" From the cant *York* = stare. The "is concerned" is typically Victorian. The expression is dead now. But in slang, catch phrases, and such, one never knows, do one? At any moment, to be facetious, someone can start the likes of "23-skidoo" up again. We also have Bedlam, Billingsgate, and recent Bollockshire in the UK.

PLACENAMES IN POETRY

Survey Mankind from China to Peru....

–Alexander Pope, *An Essay on Man*

You know that a placename is more than a matter of latitude and longitude. Some American placenames have been settled by the turn of a card at the gaming table and elsewhere some battles have been fought over what a place should be named. What happened at a place can instantly be brought to mind by the mention of the placename. A placename is a word charged with a freight of history, but it also can be charged with emotion: Auschwitz. Placenames work almost like characters in some fictions—think of Egdon Heath in the fiction of Thomas Hardy—going beyond functioning as setting to taking some part in shaping the plot. A placename can call up a memory or a feeling. One poet says our hometown or homeland is "beloved over all" and another refers to "England, my own," while Kipling wrote:

> If England were what England seems
> And not the England of our dreams...
> How quick we'd chuck 'er, but she ain't.

We must be aware that a placename can be "of our dreams," a symbol. It can have almost incredible power, like the name of a lover. Richard Curle in *Wanderings* (1920) gushed about "something in the very name of England that sounds like a sweet trumpet across the seas." But *England* has often been a call to action, like a trumpet call. Auden says that "poetry makes nothing happen," but *La Marseillaise* helped to start the blaze of the French Revolution. You would be hard pressed to find three non-placename words that accomplished as much in world revolution as the Russian we translate as "Peace, Land, Bread." Even highly-charged prose can stimulate. The cadences and haunting sounds of poetry can drive the point deeper. Advertising copywriters know this; they use it every day. Mnemosyne was the mother of all arts—Memory. Poetry is memorable.

As *Peace* and *Ritzy* are more than ordinary words, so a placename can be much more than a geographical location. With the mention of a familiar placename associations of all sorts come flooding in. With an appropriately sounding placename that we have never heard before, one that the poet may simply have made up, the creator can evoke a world for us. Literature is full of imaginary places, each with a name that works to make it seem real and resonant. Altruria and Utopia, Narnia and Ruritania are among those.

Then there are the real placenames. The white race, English says, comes from the Caucasus. How many overtones there are in *Caucasian*! Or *African*! "What is Africa to me?," asks one African-American poet; the answer is that the word conjures up all the history of suffering and loss, all the Golden Age, real or imagined, before Africans were sold by their enemies to be made slaves, mostly outside of what we called The Dark Continent. *Africa* triggers thoughts and reactions in people who have never been there, profound responses in people whose ancestors have been in America for several hundred years. *Africa* can be steeped in sorrow and anger in people whose roots were cut and who still mourn that and seek their heritage. And *America*, to Chinese immigrants The Golden Mountain, was to so many a beacon of hope and a new life on a new continent. The very word suffices, like the sight of the flag, to rouse us. Put *America* into your poem and it is something like George M. Cohan waving the Stars and Stripes to give his vaudeville act a big finish.

Put in *The Riviera* and we'll paint the scenery for you. Expressions like *banned in Boston* preserve prefabricated reputations that can be counted upon, once again working on people who were never in those places. Places have faces, like people. There are traditions: Anna Russell can make fun of operetta with the very title of *The Prince of Philadelphia*, and yet, if we had never heard of a Philadelphia, that word has an imposing rumble to it, a grandeur that might have worked (as in *Ruritania*) and passed as a suitable operetta title, comparable to *The Grand Duchess of Geroldstein.*

Literature, however, need not be limited to struggling with the already established reputations of places (the Barbary Coast of San Francisco, the French Quarter of New Orleans, the "little old lady from Dubuque" to whom one editor refused to tailor the *New Yorker* magazine); literature can bathe an existing placename in a light that will forever characterize it thereafter. The vampires of myth come from "across the woods," Transylvania. In our minds we hear the name ominously pronounced by Béla Lugosi.

Finally here, though the discussion of non-geographical aspects of placenames could be a long book, consider placenames and their various uses in ordinary language which approaches the heavy significances of poetry. Any long run (not on Broadway) recalls the delivering of the news of the result of the battle at Marathon. A crushing defeat is someone's Waterloo. An enchanted (or antipodean) country is Oz. A gleaming if insubstantial world of riches far away is an El Dorado, named from the "golden man" of the Amerindians, the naked chieftain covered with honey and gold dust to be presented in glory to his subjects. This man the *conquistadores* heard about; the tale fueled their lust for treasure. With nothing but the name of a fabled city of great wealth to drive him on, Coronado set off on an vast expedition which brought him into what is now the US. He never found the gold he sought but he opened up a huge territory.

From a goddess who had a river (the Volga) named for her, and from barbarians (people the Greeks contemptuously said could not speak Greek but merely babbled the equivalent of "blah-blah"), comes our word *rhubarb*. Not because of the meaning of the word now, but just from its sound, some poet of the people, hearing a crowd murmuring or shouting confusedly, put *rhubarb* into slang to mean a loud crowd or a riot. Then somebody called a mischievous cat Rhubarb in a sports story. A more formal poet wrote of "a peak in Darien" as the spot where the first white man saw the vast Pacific Ocean. John Keats actually got the name of that explorer wrong. The discoverer was Balboa, not Cortés, and the line stumbles over the correct place to put the accent in *Cortez*, which should be Cortés, and draws unwanted attention to the Keats mistake.

But, in poetry, placenames, like personal names (even if you get the wrong one), can do a lot of the work of the poet. This goes well beyond apostrophe. I mean apostrophe in the non-punctuation sense, the likes of "Oh, my America, my New found land!" or "America…stand beside us and guide us in the night with a light from above" or "O Canada, my home, my native land". Placenames are among the shiniest pebbles that poets like to play with. They can be precious or semi-precious gems.

Scholars of literary onomastics (how names function in fiction) have paid a certain amount of attention to placenames in poetry, but not much; and critics of poetry have said something in passing about the sonority of names or footnoted them, but there has not been a great deal of appreciation that is of use regarding how placenames can be incantatory or evocative in poetry. Even what we might today call Tom Wolfe's laundry lists of placenames, or other people's polysyllabic pilings-up, can be intoxicating. And fun, like wordplay with *funny money* and *loose tooth sleuth*.

Naturally, placenames also function in prose: think of "To Moscow, to Moscow, to Moscow" in *Three Sisters*, where Moscow is an El Dorado. Think of the songs in which *Paris* plays a part, or "Hell is a city very much like London," or Washington (or inside The Beltway) standing for government, or Roaring Camp of the Gold Rush, or the amusing names in juvenile fiction of Lemony Snicket, and much more. Real placename power, particularly the rattle of the polysyllabic one or the perfume of the mythological name, is to be found in poetry.

I resist the temptation to lecture you on alliteration and assonance, consonance and elision, the great variety of meters, the use of masculine and feminine rhymes, and all the other tricks of the poetic trade. But I will say here that placenames can not only anchor poetry in fact but can give it wings. If each placename is itself a little poem, then each placename in poetry should do something to add to the magic of the whole.

How does that work? Suppose, this once, you figure it out for yourself. I shall provide you with some seemingly random poetic fragments. Some are from

Leonard R. N. Ashley

world-famous poets in English; some were tremendously influential in their day because they were part of the lyrics of popular songs which people got by heart—and kept (as the poet would say) in their hearts their whole lives through. I ask you to read these poetic snatches. Read them aloud, as all poetry was first presented and deserves still to be presented. I ask you sing the lyrics, as poetry first was sung, if you know the melodies, for music adds immeasurably to the power of words. Doing that, try to discover for yourself how the sound adds to the sense of the line, how the placename contributes to what (even in snippets) you can guess is the overall tone and purpose of the poem.

This is a place where a very great number of placename tricks in literature could be demonstrated, but *Names in Literature* is another book. I shall be for once severely limited in my examples. Ordinarily, I fear—to put it poetically—reading essays on names, with all the examples that are usually heaped up, is like drinking from a firehose! Pause after each of these following examples and think about the *effect* the placename has.

"Now I see what there is in a name," wrote Whitman, "a word, liquid, sane, unruly, musical, self sufficient...."

Mention my name in Sheboygan,
It's the greatest little town in the world....

The isles of Greece, the isles of Greece!
Where burning Sappho loved and sung....

America, America, God shed His grace on thee....

Quinquereme of Nineveh from distant Ophir
Rowing home to haven in sunny Palestine....

The boy arrived from Mississippi
And got a room on Seventh Avenue the same day.

Well, we had a lot of luck on Venus.
We always had a ball on Mars....

In among the silver birches winding ways of tarmac wander
And the signs to Bussock Bottoms, Tussock Wood and Windy
      Brake....

128

Columbia, the gem of the ocean,
The land of the brave and the free....

You'll never see in Gay Paree,
In London or in Cork,
The queens you'll meet on any street
In old New York.

Asked me in demotic French
To luncheon at the Cannon Street Hotel
Followed by a weekend at the Metropole.

You're the Nile,
You're the Tower of Pisa....

who retired to Mexico to cultivate a habit, or Rocky Mount to tender
Buddha or Tangiers to boys or Southern Pacific to the black
locomotive or Harvard to Narcissus to Woodlawn to the daisy-chain
or grave....

Stilled for the passage of her dreaming feet
Over the seas, to silent Palestine....

Once Paumanok,
When the lilac-scent was in the air and the Fifth-month grass was
        growing,
Up this seashore, in some briers,
Two feathered guests from Alabama, two together....

Is it is not passing brave to be a king
And ride in triumph through Persepolis?

In Bengal to move at all
Is seldom if ever done,
But mad dogs and Englishmen
Go out in the noonday sun.

Swanee, how I love ya, how I love ya,
My dear old Swanee,

I'd give the world to be among the folks in D-I-X-I
E-Ven see my mammy....

The last bear, shot drinking in the Dakotas....

When I was but thirteen or so
I went into a golden land,
Chimborazo, Cotopaxi
Took me by the hand.

This blessed plot, this earth, this realm, this England....

A credible informant says
This conduct on the part of Chile
Was much discussed for several days
Both in Pall Mall and Piccadilly.

We'll have Manhattan, The Bronx and Staten
Island too....

It was down by the dark tarn of Auber,
In the ghoul-haunted woodland of Weir.

Piping Pebworth, Dancing Marston,
Haunted Hillborough, Hungry Grafton,
Dodging Exhall, Papist Wixford,
Beggarly Broom, and Drunken Bidford.

When awful darkness and silence reign
Over the great Gromboolian plain....

Like apples on the Dead Sea's shores,
All ashes to the taste.

And, as my way is, I begin to dream, resting my elbows on the desk
and leaning
out of the window a little
Of dim Guadalajara! City of rose-colored flowers!
City I wanted most to see, and most did not see, in Mexico!

The *Ballyshannon* foundered off the coast of Cariboo....

The harp that once through Tara's halls
The soul of music shed,
Now hangs as mute on Tara's walls
As if that soul were dead.

If you ask for the cause of our national flaws, and the reason we're
    blamed for our vices
We are too much controlled by Academies old on the banks of the
    Cam and the Isis....
Come my friends,
let us govern Canada,
let us find our serious heads,
let us dump asbestos on the White House....

[on the death of Sir Jacob Epstein:]
'A loss to Art,' say friends both proud and loyal.
'A loss,' say others, 'to the Café Royal.'

New York, New York, it's a wonderful town,
The Bronx is up and The Battery's down....

Here at the Vespasian-Carlton, it's just one
Religious activity after another....

...before we go to Paradise
By way of Kensal Green.

If you are coming down through the narrows of the river Kiang,
Please let me know beforehand,
And I will come out to meet you
As far as Cho-fu-sa.

"I had a son, who many a day
Sailed on the sea; but he is dead;
In Denmark he was cast away;
And I have travelled far as Hull to see

Leonard R. N. Ashley

What clothes he might have left, or other property."

Harry the king, Bedford and Exeter,
Salisbury and Gloucester....

O Shenandoah, I long to hear you,
Ha-ha, we're bound away
'Cross the wide Missouri.

Y-born he was in fer contree,
In Flaundres, al biyonde the see,
At Popering, in the place....

In Xanadu did Kubla Khan
A stately pleasure dome decree,
Where Alph, the sacred river, ran....

Old men with beautiful manners
Sitting in the Row of a morning;
Walking on the Chelsea Embankment.

'This was Mr Bleaney's room, He stayed
The whole time he was at the Bodies, till
They moved him....'

Ring-a-ring-o-geranium,
A pocketful of uranium,
Hir-o-shima,
All fall down.

THE FOLK AT WORK

A fair field full of folk found I there.

— William Langland, *The Vision of Piers Plowman*

Here is a brief essay on folklore in relation to placenames. The folk are always very active in the creation of and very inventive in the use of names. Placenames are no exception. The subject is important. Peggy A. Bulger ("Folklore Knowledge…," *Civilization* April/May 2000, p. 56) writes:

> The term *folklore* calls to mind a host of pejorative connotations: old-fashioned, unscientific, false. Modern Americans often don't see that we possess folklore, still less that we are possessed by it— but we are.

What is folklore? If you turn to volumes such as Kenneth S. Goldstein's *A Guide for Field Workers in Folklore* (1964) or Alan Dundes' *The Study of Folklore* (1965) you will see that much progress was made in folklore studies in the twentieth century. Folklore as a science is not old: the term *folkore* replaced *antiquarianism* in the nineteenth century. All through the twentieth century folklorists were still having a lot of trouble defining just what folklore is. They resembled to some extent the great lexicographer confronted with the word *wit* who said that he could better say what it was not than what it was. Even the leading American expert on how the folk concoct and transmit stories, Prof. Jan Harold Brunvand, in his book *The Study of American Folklore: An Introduction* (1968), begins by defining folklore as "the unrecorded traditions of a people" and therein (and for the rest of the twentieth century) proceeded to record it. Tristram P. Coffin and Henning Cohen in their anthology *Folklore in America* (1970) wrote that "literature flourishing in oral tradition is folklore". They admit that that definition is inadequate: "some people may quibble." Yes.

For my purpose here, it is enough to say that folklore is the product of the folk (rather than a single author, though you will quibble that everything that has ever been said must have first been said by some one individual). What I mean is that I want to think of folklore not as the folksy literature or fakelore of authors but as the narratives and songs, proverbs and jokes and riddles, behavior and beliefs, traditions (including celebrations and ceremonies and customs) and more or less primitive art (quilts and toys and even log cabins and sod houses), folk dances, festivals, popular culture in general, all the vulgar (in the best sense) work of the common people.

One could discuss names in folktales or popular sayings or children's rhymes for games, or the names of folk heroes and what they express of the ideals of the people who loved them, or any one of a number of other topics. I considered that one of the commonest applications of placenames was as nicknames of persons. Tex springs to mind. There are, however, the likes of Minnesota Fats, Sonny "The Bull" Gravano (which comes, I believe, not from the obvious but from the arcane: Bull's Head on Staten Island), and the numerous Caseys (some from the initials of Kansas City). I decided that because here my subject is placenames I had best concentrate on folk input in connection with the naming not of persons but of places. I insist on sidestepping that which is best discussed in a talk rather than in print, such as the strange pronunciations in the US of Bogota, Cairo, Madrid, Rio Grande, and so on. You know that *bed* is something like BAY-ed in the South, BAD in California, and BUD around the Great Lakes. People do "talk funny," don't they, when they do not live where you live! Let us forget about that for the moment. I suggest we look at the cleverness and occasional confusion preserved in American placenames.

One could go back to the Greeks. They delighted in producing perfectly groundless explanations of why this or that place bore this or that name. Our tradition of folk etymology goes back at least as far as the people who gave us that odd-sounding word *etymology*. The Greeks were very apt to create incredible but cherished myths to connect places with gods and goddesses. Moreover, the Greeks (who took so much from the Egyptians and the Phoenicians and other early people but always managed to steal rather than to borrow) had the reputation of being great innovators. To a notable extent, of course, they were, but they borrowed a lot, too. This dazzled the Romans. The Romans were immensely impressed with Greek culture. Some Roman historians report with straight faces the most ignorant etymologies that the Greeks taught them and even today physicians (who love their Greek and Latin terminologies) call a cupped or concave hand *poculum Diogenis* because "the ascetic Diogenes broke his only wooden bowl and drank from his cupped hands." Like some things in folklore, that is not impossible, just unlikely, perhaps. Equally unlikely is the story that when Alexander the Great, the world conqueror, asked the philosopher if there was anything at all he could do for him, Diogenes is said to have replied, "Yes, step out of my sunlight."

That ought to be true. We want it to be true, just as we wanted to believe Parson Weems' pious fiction about George Washington and the cherry tree ("I cannot tell a lie"). This is the reason that lies behind our thinking up stories to explain certain placenames, like that of the historic Pissing Tree. That tree was callously destroyed when they widened the old state highway from Petersburg to Surrey Court House in Virginia, but the stories remain. We need a story or two for Sunday Rock and No Law Rock in The Adirondacks. We cry out for one for Jackass Lane (now Landis Road) or Bull Pasture Brook or Cow Pasture Brook (which flow into Indian Lake up in Canada), or Grumble or Mousehole (corrupted Cornish names in Cornwall), or Dry Prong (Louisiana) or Joe Batt's Arm (Newfoundland), or Dog Walk (which, in our US style, we unfortunately have improved into Cedar Grove, Illinois). What could explain Accident (Maryland), Attaway (South Carolina), Eek (Arkansas), Booger Hole (West Virginia), Box Springs or Squabbletown or Winos Corner or Wimps (all in California), Henpeck or Needfull or Pee Pee (all Ohio), the ghost town of Shakespeare (New Mexico), Jot 'Em Down (Texas), Lickskillet (there is one in Kentucky, and it is not unique), Dead Irishman Gulch (South Dakota), Niggerhead Mountain (renamed, along with Niggerhead Brook and Niggerhead Pond in Vermont), Scarce Grease (Alabama), Gin City (Arkansas), Nowthen (Minnesota) Sweathouse River (renamed Swan River), Growlersburg (renamed Longview in California), or Bowlegs (Oklahoma).

I'll tell you about Bowlegs. *Bowlegs* was the closest the white man could get to pronouncing the name of an Amerindian chief named Bolek. (In the stories, every man is a chief.) Whisky Run Township commemorates an Amerindian named Ouiska. Whisky Chitto Creek is Choctaw *oski* (cane) plus *chitto* (large). Hog Shooter (Oklahoma) is named for Joe Hog Shooter, but what his name in Cherokee was I cannot for the life of me discover.

Kamulea (Hawaii) was named for Samuel Palmer. There are only about a thousand natural speakers of Hawaiian left but there a great many Hawaiian placenames; they seem to be mostly vowels and glottal stops. That's what we tend to notice, not wondering about their meaning. Anacortes Island (Washington) came from An[n]a Curtis. Noodle Doosey (Pennsylvania) came from Pennsylvania Dutch *nudel du sie* (your turn) and the story adds: "spoken according to legend by one lad to another while sharing the sexual favors of the same girl." Pocotaglio, "originally a town of the Yamasee Indians," according to Prof. George R. Stewart, is alleged to have received its name from a Negro's advice "for getting rid of a certain pest: 'Poke 'e tale, 'e go.'"

This evidences the same kind of handling of foreign languages that produced placenames such as Low Freight (from *l'eau fraiche*). *Cayo Hueso* has the bones picked out of it now: It's Key West. Faced with *cohuilla,* a Spanish term for an unbaptised Amerindian (which seems to come from a now dead language of Baja California) turned into a place name (in Riverside Co., California), the Average Joe may well reach for some "cow wheeler" or similarly outlandish explanation.

In "Weird and Wonderful U.S. Place Names" in the *Omni Gazetteer of the United States,* I mentioned among other placenames: Too Nigh (Georgia) and Bug Tussle (Texas), Top of the World and Hellhole Palms and Zzyzx (California), Bengay and Nutt and Possum Grape and One Horse Store (Arkansas), Errata and Gnatville and Who'd A Thought It (Alabama), Highjinks and Skull Valley (Arizona), Dry Tavern and Just a Farm (Pennsylvania), Wahoo (Nebraska), Tightwad (Missouri), and Why (Arizona) and Whynot (Mississippi), among others. I could have gone on and on, and I am not shy about repeating here what I did get in there.

We look back at early days when placenaming was more casual. Those were the days when the locals got together in the general store or local tavern, you know, and thought up some name to send off to Washington so that they could have a post office. The reply to one application said that the name chosen was already used in the state and that a "peculiar" name was necessary, so the citizens applied for and got Peculiar. Among names that also must have a story are Deadhorse (Alaska) and Fleatown (Ohio) and Bugtown (Indiana), and of course many a Last Chance and the likes of Angel's Roost, Poker Flat, and Bollibokka.

There is a story that once when they wanted a "good safe name" they took the brandname off the safe in the corner. That's how Marvin (South Dakota) got its name. Maybe looking around the store they also named Cocoa Beach or Hot Coffee (both in Florida) or Coffee (Indiana). In earlier days they gave places in Wyoming names such as Dull Center, Difficulty, Goose Egg, and Maggie's Nipples. In Illinois they named Bone Gap and Moonshine. In Texas there are lots of striking old names: Cut and Shoot is one. Once in a while invention gave out even in Texas. They named a street in Austin, Una Mas—just one more street.

Wouldn't you like to be able to give your return address as something lively like Humansville (Missouri), Hard Cash (Georgia), Intercourse (Pennsylvania), or Okay (Arkansas)? Wouldn't you like to be there in winter when Hell (Michigan) freezes over? Can't you see yourself as the king of the hill on Goon Dip Mountain (Arkansas) or Bastard Peak (Wyoming) or Two Teats (California)? Wouldn't Lower Bottom Road (instead of River Valley Road) or Zap (North Dakota) or Humptulips River (Washington) or Hen Scratch (Florida) be nice? Wouldn't French Broad (Tennessee) be a fine address? So much better than the very common Madison, Washington, Clinton, Franklin, Pleasantville, Springfield....Or you could go for something with music in it, like Onandaga (New York) or Aswaguscawadic (Maine). Some people care a lot about the name of their place. "How Bristol Pond Became Winona Lake" in *Vermont History* in 1968 recorded how much bickering even a pond name came create. By the way, what some people call a pond some others don't. That's a regional thing.

Humor can be regional or personal. It is true that some of the humor that people see in placenames derives solely from the fact that they are not familiar with geographical terms such as *hole* and *broad* and connect them with slang. Ignorance made people accept that Azusa (California) was "A to Z in the USA." The story went that the namer had said: "Well, we've suggested every name in the alphabet from A to Z in the United States of America, so why not just take the first letter of each word and call it Azusa?" Actually *azusa* is Gabrielino, an Amerindian word for "skunk." But there are some undeniably funny names—in both senses of the words—on the map. Some people always smile at anything with *Jackass* in it and at the duplications, such as our Walla Walla or the foreign Bio Bio.

Amerindian names open the door wide to folk interpretation. Take Tidioute (Pennsylvania). The name comes from what we call the Munsee Wolf language and means "he who looks far." But the story goes that an Indian maiden was bathing topless in the Allegheny. An easier to understand explanation involves a hard-of-hearing gandy dancer who asks about an engine driver, "Did he hoot?" Consider Tenino (Washington). Railroadmen say that was 10-9-0—I'm not sure how they explain what *that* was—but really the town is named from Chinook "fork" or "junction." During The Depression the town was called Wooden Money; thereby hangs another tale. I do not believe the story that Ogonquit (Maine) was named when some settler's gun failed to fire. (It is Abnaki "place of the waves".) I do not believe, but like, the story that Savannah (Georgia) was named for a drowning girl ("Save Anna!"). The folk hold that Enola (a town in Alabama, with a lady's name that became forever notorious with the *Enola May* and the dropping of the atom bomb) has a name that resulted from a lonely widower carving ALONE on a tree. "Not being exactly a college graduate," the tale goes, "he started carving from the wrong end." An ingenious story, but just an amusing fabrication.

Prof. Allen Walker Read investigated all the Podunks (New York, Massachusetts, etc.) in connection with the story that the name came from a waterwheel that went po-DUNK, po-DUNK, po-DUNK. In the sixties you could have bought all of Podunk Center for a mere $7000, so no wonder that Podunk meant a godforsaken community (like East Jesus, Nowheresville, Dogpatch of Al Capp's comicstrips, etc.) Once again we have folk invention, as when Sheboygan was said to come from some Injun's lament on still no success producing a daughter ("She boy agin'"). Funny, but Bayou Funny Creek (Louisiana) involves Choctaw *fani* (squirrel).

They say in Australia that Katamatite (Victoria) can be traced to some digger's question, "Kate, am I tight?" I don't think that's the explanation. Do you?

Here's a story that may well be true: Alexander McCune, an Indiana pioneer, remarked on people streaming into his store after an especially hard winter. "Here come the Arabians," he said. Parts of Ohio and Illinois were nicknamed Mesapotamia and Egypt and the poor area around McCune's place was often compared to the deserts. "Here come the Arabians on their annual pilgrimage to Mecca." So McCune's place is called Mecca today.

A man bought some swampland just outside Tampa (Florida) in the real-estate boondoggles of the nineteen-twenties. He discovered his only real crop was rattlesnakes. So he opened a factory to can rattlesnake meat and petitioned the post office for the name Rattlesnake. There might have been a Rattlesnake

(Florida) had not poor George been bitten by a rattlesnake and died before his application could be considered.

Similar colorful tales surround Starveout, Isolate, Nofog, Gladtidings, Mule, and other post offices now vanished (although Amity, Sublimity, and such remain). They must go far to explain Philadelphia (Tennessee), Laughing Pig (Wyoming), and Helpmejack Creek (Arkansas). The classic post office story is connected to Wewanta (West Virginia): "We want a post office" was the application.

The good people of Virginia applied for a post office under the name Noon, but they got Moon in error, and it stuck. Chance (Maryland) wanted to be called Rock Creek, but there already was a Rock Creek, and Capt. James Whitlock held as how there was little consarned *chance* they would ever get what they wanted from those blankety-blank bureaucrats up in Foggy Bottom. But Washington did come through, by chance—with Chance.

You will find that plenty of engaging stories have been preserved by local historians and in books such as Horace P. Beck's *The Folklore of Maine* (1957). You could amuse yourself with Ronald L. Baker's *From Needmore to Prosperity* (1993). It's about Hoosier placenames in folk history. Mary Abbott's review (*Journal of Arizona History* 20) of William Croft Barnes' *Arizona Place Names* (1936) refers to "a million dollars worth of fun." Think of what a million dollars meant then! There is very likely something available about the names in your city, county, or state that you will find informative and charming. You may come up with some explanation to equal that offered for Toad Suck (Arkansas): "They would suck up booze [while waiting to be ferried between Faulkner and Perry counties] until they swole up like toads." Or maybe the toads "swole up" after sucking water in dry seasons out of crawdad holes. Who can say? The historian of Smithtown (New York) wrote that Bread and Cheese Hollow Road near town is related to the fact that Richard "Bull" Smith used to lunch on such fare while inspecting fields there. People say that Deathball Creek (Oregon) was named to commemorate a bad cook's hard biscuits. I suspect it may have something to do with poisonous mushrooms or a fatal gunshot, but I do not want to ask the great expert on Oregon placenames, Lewis L. McArthur; the facts he has may ruin a good story! On the other hand, he has some odd stories of his own. He told me how one place was named for a horse, for instance.

Similarly, there are the stories about The Crawls in England (a dying woman was promised by her nasty husband she could have for the poor as much land as she could get around in a limited period of time—this tale seems to be true), the castles and old towns and holy wells, etc., in Wales and Cornwall, and some of the ancient place names of Scotland. Right here in the US of A we may have the Garden of Eden, say certain clergymen: Rev. D.O. van Slyke in 1886 argued the Garden of Eden must have been somewhere between what we now call LaCrosse (Wisconsin) and Winona (Minnesota), on the banks of the Mississippi, and Rev.

Elvey E. Calloway said it was on the banks of the Apachicola River at Bristol (Florida), the only place Noah could have found the gopher wood used to build the ark. Gen. "Chinese" Gordon was convinced the Garden of Eden was in the Vallé de Mai (Valley of May) on Praslin island in The Seychelles, where grows the coco-de-mer, the rare tree Gen. Gordon said must have been the tree of Good and Evil. Other sites suggested for Eden are in modern Iraq, Turkey, Egypt, Israel, China, and elsewhere, even the supposedly lost continent of Lemuria.

There is a lot of blarney in the folk etymologies of Ireland, too. The Irish language often gives English speakers the oddest ideas about places.

The folk stories can get out of hand, with Tywhoppety, Alpine, even Albany in the US being given implausible explanations (as implausible as the story that John Philip Sousa was a Chinaman called So who patriotically added USA to his surname). The folk say *bum* comes from a shelter (in Steyr, Austraia) decorated with the figure of a little dog (*bummerl*) and that Dixie "was the way plantation slaves pronounced the second surname in *Mason-Dixon Line*."

I feel certain that Yelltown (formerly Shawnee Town, near Hemmed-In Hollow, Arkansas) was named because Archibald Yell paid $50 for the honor. There was no yelling. I would gladly pay twice that sum for a place to be named for me (even the site of an annual Turkey Trot) but I am not ready to die to qualify for the honor, which is what (usually) one has to do these days. Maybe Hell's Half Acre (Wyoming) would change to Ashley. Another name that would be better off gone is Monguago, a site of a battle in the badly-named War of 1812, somewhere near Detroit, I believe. Henry Schoolcraft's *Personal Memoirs* say on page 576 that it is "No-guan-go-nong...a man's name signifying dirty backsides."

Do you want to hear a really way-out folk etymology? Actually it's joking, never intended to be believed. A New Jersey settlement was visited by the Earl of Perth. He wore a kilt. An Amerindian, seeing the kilt, asked: "Perth am girl?" "No," replied the earl. "Perth am boy!" The *Philadelphia Enquirer* soberly commented:

> Trouble with this lovely legend is that Perth never visited America. The town's "last" name came from an Indian word, "Emboyle," meaning a point or elbow of land. This later became "Amboyle" and finally "Amboy."

How about the very macho Am-Boy Dukes?
Here is the *New Haven Register* in 1975 on Galilee (Rhode Island):

> In 1902 Tom Mann, a fisherman from Nova Scotia who settled here, felt the village that had sprung up with its fishing shacks should be called Galilee after the Sea where disciples of the Galilean [Jesus]

fished in biblical times. One day an old timer happened to be repairing his nets when a stranger called out to him, "Where am I?" The answer was "Galilee." "And where is that?" he said, pointing to the other side. The old timer thought for a moment and said, "Jerusalem." And so henceforth the two names Galilee and Jerusalem were used to denote a most picturesque part of Rhode Island.

Here is the *Vicksburg* [Mississippi] *Sunday Post* for 1977 on Graball, in Tallacatchie Co. Graball's name is said to come from the fact that "some old guy ran a trade boat on the river and would allow customers to reach into a bag and pull out as many gifts as they could grab with one hand." The story adds that Shucktown (Lauderdale Co.) received its name from a farmer who had borrowed a wagonload of corn and was badgered about repayment. He irately dumped a wagonload of cornhusks in the lender's field. Ah, Shucks!

Helechwa in Wolfe Co. (Kentucky) has been explained as an Amerindian name but also was said to be on a road that was "hell each way." The chief executive of the Ohio & Kentucky Railroad, however, made up the name from the name of his daughter, Helen Chase Waldridge. In Canada, the so-called "Indian" name Hemaruka (Saskatchewan) came from the names of the daughters of a vice-president of the Canadian Pacific Railway: Helen, Margaret, Ruth, and Kathleen. In similar fashion the names of Boy Scout and other summer camps may be made up to look Amerindian, but they are not. In time the made-up names may be provided with false but interesting legends of origin.

Prof. W. F. H. Nicolaisen is correct in stating that "folk lore does create placenames through the application of facets of popular belief and the localization of migratory legends." Folk etymology often explains placenames by creating legends. Those in turn become part of the folk culture. The odder the name, the more likely it is that an attempt will be made to explain where it comes from. In places such as Cornwall, I discovered, where strange names abound because the Cornish language, though there have been attempts over the past century and more to revive it, is essentially a dead language, the folk are busy at explaining Lower Drift, Catchall, Gloweth, Twelve Heads, Goonhaven, Black Head, Gummow's Shop, Probus, Highway Fowey (pronounced "FOY"), Crafthole, Boot, Rhude Cross, Widemouth (pronounced "WID-ee-muth"), Zeah, and Broadwoodwidger. The stranger has to be careful not to be taken in by extraordinary explanations. These may simply be calculated to fool the tourist. There are as well folk etymologies intended to be acceptable to everyone.

Katherine Hart in the *Austin* [Texas] *American Statesman* for 29 August 1969 tells us in "How West Lynn St. Got Its Name" that even micronyms (you realize that the term refers to names of smaller things, in this case streets) can involve elaborate tales and obscure allusions. As summarized by Karl Ames in the *American Names Society Bulletin* 51 (December 1977), her story goes like this:

> The study has it that a Judge Robertson took his family to Fort Davis for the summer. Returning to Austin, he found that his elegant Victorian home was not finished. The family had to live for two months next to the Millet Opera House. The children of the family found a window in the Millet mansion through which they could peer down at the stage performance each night. This was the beginning of one of the children's interest in the theatre; her favorite came to be "East Lynne" [1861, a play version of Mrs. Henry Wood's sentimental melodramatic novel of the same name]. When Judge Robertson told his family he had been given permission to name their street, the "stage-struck" daughter spoke up: "West Lynn."

With such arbitrariness, and individuals "given permission" to name the streets on which their houses stood, it is not surprising that some nineteenth-century street names in the US are odd or that strange stories should be told about them.

Like most pioneers, those in the US recalled names from the places they had left behind or they made up simple new ones. The US is dotted with Greenvilles and Smithtowns. We are rich in names from The Bible (Salem, meaning "peace," was extremely popular, Sodom was not unheard of, but unofficial), names of heroes (Washington or some local), names from landscape features (Springfield, Walnut Grove) or local business (including Business Corners, Mechanicsville, Zincville, etc.), and the incidents of frontier life (Dead Valley, Dead Man's Gulch, and some more pleasant ones). The more informal the society, the more unusual the names might be. For instance, consider these Canadian placenames from Newfoundland: Famish Gut, Bumble Bee Bight, Fogo, Foxtrap, Whale Gulch, Horse Chops, Goobies, and Little Paradise. Compare those with the following, also chosen more or less at random, in this case from Louisiana: Advance, Retreat, Brimstone, Jigger, Plain Dealing, Welcome, Wham, Bob Acres, Chopique, Topsy, Ikes, Log Cabin, Long Straw, Hydropolis, and Zylks. Any one of these could give birth to to story. You could make up a story or two yourself, I'll bet.

Here are two true stories. The first concerns Charles W. Conner, an old guide for surveyors in the Great Smoky Mountains. Conner often complained of sore feet, so Horace Kephart named a hill Charlie's Bunnion. The second story explains Horseheads, a placename of New York State. In 1779, Gen. John Sullivan disposed of packhorses worn out in a campaign against the Iroquois. In 1789 white settlers in Upstate New York came upon the horses' bleached bones and called the place Horseheads.

Gasoline (Texas) was so called because the cotton gin there boasted a gasoline engine. Short Creek sounded better as Colorado City. Burford was more picturesque as Stinking Lake and Cape Despair more striking than *cap d'espoir* ("cape of hope"). A placename that might well mislead you is (say) Bantam. It doesn't mean anything small. It actually comes from the Narragansett for "he is praying" and referred to an Amerindian converted to Christianity (as if before Christianity the Amerindians did not pray!).

I think you will agree that we all like to be able to tell people what our names mean, why the place we live was called Aurora or Zion (one Zion is for a western pioneer surnamed Zion). It gives people pride in their communities to know (or make up out of whole cloth, as they say) a story about why it is called Clever (Missouri) or Chinchuba (Louisiana) or Fireworks (Illinois) or Joker (West Virginia). People like their placename pronounced their way (Noo York, Noo Yawk, *bois aux arcs* became Ozarks) and on occasion spelled their way. There is a place named Porto Rico (West Virginia).

It is my view that we ought to hold onto the old names. I think we are losing something when we turn Whisky Hill into bland Buena Vista or even change Trash to Treasure. I like the pioneering names of my state of New York (Potluck and Climax, even Index and Cuba and Swastika). We can no longer see the red stick for which Baton Rouge was named nor the *tête du mort* (either a skull and crossbones pirate flag or, more likely, a trader's head put on a pole by the savages) at Teddymore, but we can keep the history.

Sometimes a name is racist and sometimes the words conceal vulgarity (as *poppycock* comes from the Dutch for "soft shit") but that is part of our history, too. The stories may be entirely fabricated. But still there are folks who are certain that a king knighted a roast beef to make *sirloin* or that the inexplicable *kittycorner* relates to "the way a cat crosses the street." Who believes most of the placenames stories that the folk come up with? The same people who swear by urban legends, I suppose.

Nonetheless, these stories are part of our culture, as are the placenames, and they ought to be savored. They need to be saved. I don't care if stories are, as Prof. Robert Ramsay used to say, "too good to be true." They are good; that's true.

Prof. George R. Stewart in his classic *Names on the Land* (first published in 1945, later revised) set up nine categories of placenames, viz:

> Descriptives
> Possesives
> Incidents
> Commemoratives
> Euphemisms
> Shifts
> Manufactured Names
> Folk Etymologies
> Mistakes

Of these, folk etymologies may hold the most appeal for the casual name-watchers, the people who like "funny names" such as Truth or Consequences, Fake Creek, Texarkana, Knockemstiff, and Pond Pond (for a Mr. Pond) and Surfing (the original name of Atlantic City—the one in New Jersey, not the one in the Far West). There are some people who are always a little sad when some spoilsport scholar—the kind who would "botanize on his mother's grave"—comes along and puts flat factual prose in the place of the poetry of the people.

The people like Borg as a verb (from the *Star Trek* character who simply absorbed his enemies) and Bork as another (from a judge whom they think was badly treated) and they love jokey characters in comedy (like Dr. Sang-Freud) and puns and Pig Latin and all sorts of play with language. They like funny names, fun with names. They like to make up funny explanations for names. Hooray for them! More power to them!

Leonard R. N. Ashley

HOME SWEET HOME:
HOUSE NAMES

A house is not a home.

—Sally Stanford

We cannot omit some mention of the small names (micronyms). A tremendous interest has been taken by names scholars in the names of post offices (many of which did not survive the nineteenth century), and I must admit that in books such as Robert M. Rennick's studies of the astounding placenames of Kentucky there are hours of delight. But for small names I choose to discuss some names less often noted, names such as Sagamore, Boscobel, Sunnyside and (in literature) Hill House in the US and Howards End in the UK, house names.

To bring house names to your attention here, I want to mention Leslie A. Dunkling's *English House Names* (1971), which I reviewed in *Names* 20:4 (1972). As I write, Joyce C. Miles has recently published a charming book on house names which has in its title one of the oddest house names, *Owl's Hoot*, but with this book by Dunkling, author of the famous *Guinness Book of Names* (in which house names are also covered), you have a starting point and a treat, and those in connection with Britain, where house names have always been much more popular than in the US. It has been said that no Englishman is content until he has explained America; here I cannot undertake to repay the favor and explain Britain but I do want to suggest that in the naming of their homes the British reveal something, if not all, of their national character.

Published by the Names Society in the UK, *English House Names*, the author says, has "a touch of Tristram Shandyish light-heartedness, if that means anything to you," and this is both entertaining and appropriate, because Britons like wordplay and humor and even discursive discussion of names. Along with The Grange, The Old Vicarage, and The Elms, the British also have the likes of Dunrovin ("done rovin'," an apt name for a retirement cottage).

Dunkling's book sprang from students collecting house names as a field project in onomastics. The project grew with a feature in the *Times*, a segment on the BBC's "Today" show, and the founding of an Enconymical [House Name] Society.

Students of literature and history will recall a number of house names. These include Thomas Hardy's Max Gate, Sir Walter Scott's Abbotsford, Alexander Woolcott's Wit's End (imitating UK house names such as the real Audley's End—that was an inspiration of E. M. Forster's fictional Howards End), Wisteria Lodge in the Sherlock Holmes stories, Daphne Du Maurier's Manderley in

145

Rebecca, Hawthorne's The House of Seven Gables, Dickens' Bleak House, Gillie Potter's Hognsnorten Towers, Frederick the Great's *Sans Souci*, Washington's Mount Vernon, Jefferson's Monticello, as well as Nightmare Abbey, Castle Dracula, Ashland, Middleton Place, and Tara (in *Gone with the Wind*). Sometimes, in satire, placenames (I thought up Mughattan for Manhattan, Nerdistan, and some others) and funny house names are created. In US fact and fiction, house names are rarer than among our British cousins, partly because we adopted street addresses very early and very widely.

House names persisted even after street addresses (10 Downing Street, 1600 Pennsylvania Avenue, the fictional 221B Baker Street—Sherlock Holmes again) were standard. In addition, joking names have always appeared: Havachat, Costa Plenty, Bedside Manor (for a physician), *Maison Blanche* for the Whites, The Vatican for the Pope family, even (says Dunkling) *Chez Soi* (chosen only to discover that the mail arriving was addressed to Chop Suey).

Dunkling's survey did not discover most of the house names of the West Country (where names in Welsh and even Cornish are popular) but it did establish the greatest number of joke names was to be found on the summer cottages in Kent and along the South Coast of England. A house in Crawley (Sussex) was named Creepy. One in Looe (Cornwall) was Hullaba (and it could have been Water). A couple in Hop Garden Road called their place Boozer's Gloom. There was not only Chez Nous but also Chez When. One man who already had the letters for Number Three simply added a letter, rearranged, and had Remember. A retired Army sergeant from World War II recalled an old song, *Bless 'em All,* spelled the title backwards, and achieved the Welsh-looking Llamesselb. Placenames such as Mile End and Potter's End inspired Tether's End. A house numbered 2B suggests Or Not. ODTAA is One Damn Thing after Another. Retirees refer to former occupations in canting constructions: a baker chose Dunbakin, a cricketer Dunbolyn, a yachtsman Duncruin, a student Dunroomin, a Scottish teacher Dunstrappin, a vicar Dunravin, and many people selected Dunmoven or Donlukin. The Celtic *dun* (dark), found in placenames, works well as the English *done*. You will note that real placename elements are approved in joking names; such names, for a moment, may look authentic.

A house may be named for location: Cornercroft or, with a slang reference to "daft," Round the Bend. Appearance may be noted: Chimneys (Dame Agatha Christie uses this one), Thatchwick, Blue Windows, Gwyndy (Welsh for "White House"), like our White House (synonymous with the US presidency). Our southern plantation names often referred to trees: Oak Alley, The Oaks, The Laurels, etc. The view may be noticed: Tombstone View (Cemetery Road), Broadview, Longleat, Bellavista, Moovista (a Berkshire house overlooking a cow pasture). The environs may be noticed: Forest Edge, Brambleside, Water House, By the Way. There may be mention of some features of the British garden (Rose Cottage, The Lilacs, The Fuschias, Rhododendrons) or the British weather

(Hurricane House, Fog Cottage, Thundry). There is a lot of play, as we have in the US with business names such as Dew Drop Inn and New York's fish & chips place called A Salt and Battery.

We all like to put our names on the things we own. Combined elements of parents' names account for odd forenames such as Leneen or Artwina, and owners' names can be and are combined to make house names such as Don and Ann's Donann or anagramatized for Fred and Ann's Ferndean. A name can be recalled from reading: Mazo de la Roche's Jalna, or Wuthering Heights. Or from travel: Bellevue, Aventine from a Roman hill, Versailles. The coziness of the place may suggest Chosenholme, Home Sweet Home, Omagin. As with pleasure boats, where expense is often joked about in the names, we find All Our Lolly (*lolly* is UK slang for "money"), Kostleigh, Setubac, Stony Broke, Nomoni. I have a friend, carrying a heavy mortgage, who calls her English place The Banks.

Sports, animals, personal names, backspellings (Deriter), family references (Hersanmyne, Uani, Uanme), all score. Environmental influences are reflected: a Dickens Avenue in Middlesex produced Dombey Lodge, Doughty House, Pickwickians, Dorrit's Nest, Dingley Dell, and Chuzzlewit—just as a US housing development called something like Santa Claus Land could have streets named for Donner, Blitzen, and so on. The time of purchase may be noted (Christmas House, March House, Ide House). Almost anything can give rise to a house name, and there are nicknames, too: Buck's House for Buckingham Palace. A public convenience (toilet) in a street named for Shakeapeare in Newcastle-upon-Tyne was always referred to as Anne Hathaway's Cottage.

The TV popularity of John Galsworthy's *The Forsyte Saga* led to more than Joylon. Madame D'Arblay (Fanny Burney) called her house Camilla Lacey after the novel whose profits paid for it. Sir Yehudi Menuhin got the name of his Swiss cottage from a nonsense poem by Edward Lear: the house is Chalet Chankley Bore. (Had he not been a virtuoso of the violin, I think he might have called it Villa Nessplain). Dunkling says Flora Thompson's 1939 novel is responsible for Lark Rise. John Macadam lives at Temperance Steps—in Hangover Cottage. Charles Schulz of *Peanuts* fame lived in Coffee Grounds, in Coffee Lane. If you complain of "being taken" and you call your house Ibindun, your neighbor may respond with Sovi. Idunno may elicit Nordowe.

I have mentioned names from the Welsh (Affalon is for an apple orchard, our Avalon) and Cornish (Tremaine). We could add the Irish (one translates A Hundred Thousand Welcomes) and Scots (The Neuk for "the nook" and Naelumm "no chimney"), the Anglo-Indian (that's where Jalna came from), Australian aborigines (Amaroo is "beautiful place," Carinya is "happy home," Wahroonga is "our house"), even Greek (Kedros "the cedars," Thalassa "the sea") and Latin (often bits of mottos such as the RAF's *Per ardua ad astra*). French provides *Nid d'Amour* (Love Nest) and, mangled, Sam Sufy (*ça m'suffit*, "that's enough for me"). Aarhus is Danish "our house." The local Somerset dialect provides Zummerzett. Dunkling and his researchers collected a rich trove. In those names (as in boat names mentioned, which run to Her Fur Coat, X-pense, and Costa Mucho) we see evidence of the attitude of the namers to the properties named. Names are always more or less indicative of people's thinking.

In Dickens' *David Copperfield,* Betsey Trotwood complained of a house named The Rookery "when there's not a rook near it." In the same way, however, we name everything from malls to housing developments with equal disdain for reality. There may be no deer and no water at Deer Run. The name hopes to create a "feel," that's all.

In the Victorian period in Britain, street names did not prevent people from giving nice names to their proud Italian villas or comfy cottages. Between the two great wars of the twentieth century, the British had a kind of revival of house naming. The trend still continues, but much diminished. What does this tell you about daily life in England as well as at Chequers, Cliveden, Borely Rectory, and Castle Howard? There is plenty of information in carefully chosen names.

In the US, Frank Lloyd Wright named Falling Waters and twice, you know, used the Welsh Taliesen, proud of his ancestry (which is why he put Lloyd in there when his parents neglected to do so). We do not usually name our US houses, though in a campy part of Fire Island, along with signs that read "Tresspassers Will Be Violated," someone came up with the very vulgar White Swallow.

There are house names everywhere in the US (Morven in New Jersey, Olana in New York, and so on) but the most notable are the names of owners. These are given to historic houses, sometimes hyphenating the names of a couple of owners: Horry-Guinard House, Hampton-Preston House, and Caldwell-Hampton-Boylston House are all in Richmond Co., South Carolina. The names range from the ante-bellum plantations of the Deep South to the ranches of the West. Prof. George R. Stewart also found the extraordinarily attractive names of Gold Rush mining camps and claims.

In the South, one might take a plantation name from the Old Country (Frogmore was one), or from a novel by Sir Walter Scott, or from trees or bushes or natural features, or from a sonorous Amerindian name, or one might call one's place a Mount or a Castle or even Midway (between two towns). Fictional Tara refers to the O'Haras' pride in the ancient high kings of Ireland. Sometimes great houses took their names from the towns, but towns could be named for great houses that dominated the landscape, too. Houses with names did not have to stand at the end of long avenues on vast plantations. In one South Carolina town, a house called The Oaks is right beside the courthouse.

I once reported at a meeting of the Modern Language Association on the names of great houses and plantations in South Carolina, much relying on the 30 issues of Prof. Claude Henry Neuffer's *Names in South Carolina* (selections may be published soon). I did not then mention my favorite South Carolinian plantation name, putting more stress on the likes of The Glebe (on the Cooper River on land given to support Biggon Church in 1710), The Pines, Halcyon Grove, a house called Wyoming from *Gertrude of Wyoming* (a poem by Thomas Campbell), Waverley or Waverly from Scott's novel, and so on. Orlando C. Scarborough's plantation's name was The Stockade. There was a penitentiary nearby, and Scarborough contrived to get cheap labor from the chaingang. At night prisoners had to be confined by a stockade. He himself lived farther away in a more elegantly named house, Summerton. But the plantation was called The Stockade. Scarborough's Landing was at Lake Marion, near Wyboo, so you see the unusual name fitted right in there.

A NOTE ON MONTREAL

**Beauty crieth in an attic and no man regardeth.
O God! O Montreal!**

—Samuel Butler, *A Psalm of Montreal*

Serious treatment of the placenames of Canada, in the two major languages and the languages of the First Nations, belongs elsewhere. That must be the work of one of the many Canadian experts on placenames such as Prof. André Lapierre or Alan Rayburn or Helen Kerfoot, government experts—there are a great many who could be mentioned, and, in connection with Montreal (not spelled with a French accent in English) there is a battery of important French-Canadian experts. Forgive the personal as I write a note on a place where I was a child. I want to emphasize that we hold dear the names of the place or places where we grew up.

I went through some elementary, private secondary, and university (McGill) education in Montreal, so I select it just to make a few remarks and to give something Canadian a place in this volume. Moreover, some weird things are going on with placenames in Quebec (not correctly spelled with an accent even in French, because it is an Amerindian and not a French word).

The island on which Montreal stands was once called Tiotika by the aborigines. That, typically, was more of a descriptor than a name, and it indicated an island between two big rapids. When Jacques Cartier arrived in the sixteenth century, on the island there was a collection of huts—that's what *Canada* appears to mean, a collection of huts—called Hochelaga. Cartier immediately climbed the hill that dominated the landscape and called it the royal mountain, so that is where *Montreal*, with or without an accent on the *e*, got its name. In 1642 a town was created by Paul de Chomédy, Sieur de Maisoneuve, that would be called Montreal (for the most prominent place on the island). It was to be one of the major centers in New France. At first it was called Ville Marie (Mary's Town). The *Marie* is the Blessed Virgin, and *Place Ville Marie* is at *rue de Nôtre Dame* (Street of Our Lady) in Montreal, where Maisoneuve's statue stands.

Many street names reflect the Roman Catholic Church's influence on Quebec over the centuries. That began with the first missionaries (and Jesuit martyrs) and teaching nuns and later included the village priests and the schools, seminaries, basilicas (churches built to resemble palaces), cathedrals (churches where bishops have their thrones), and the rest. Quite a bit away from Montreal we see Bourget (the surname of an archbishop of Montreal) and to the west of that Vars (the name of a place in France that was the birthplace of some parish priest in

Quebec whose personal name has been practically forgotten). To the east of Bourget there is a St.-Eugène (and that was the forename of another archbishop of Montreal). Some places named for saints are actually named for historical personages who bore the names and were thus put under the protection of those saints. If you see an *Île Ste.-Héléne* it is not for Helen, discoverer of the True Cross, mother of the Emperor Constantine. It is for another Helen, wife of that founder of Ville Marie, the Sieur de Maisoneuve. A street or a village with a saint's name may or may not be named for the saint. There are anomalies: St.-Bruno near Montreal is named for the Bruneau family.

In addition, by attaching to a saint's name in French an English name from another source, you get a lot of non-existent saints (St.-Isidore-de-Prescott, St.-Isidore-Dorchester) because the English name may look like a surname, and that is not how it functions in the compound name. I expect that English elements will be chopped off such placenames in the same spirit in which a long-established Montreal street name, Dorchester, was replaced to honor recent French-Canadian politician. McGill (Scottish philanthropist) and Craig (governor-general) are still holding their own with Papineau, Viger, and so on, but for how long no one knows. There was a major attempt to Frenchify (or Quebecify) Amerindian names in the province. In the unlikely case of the province breaking off from the rest of Canada, Labrador (Golden Arm) will not automatically be included in the new nation, and many placenames will have to be debated, among other things.

Mayor Camillien Houde is remembered in a street name now. In World War II he advised Montrealers not to sign up for King George's War and he was sent to jail, but he ran for re-election and was successful and had to be released to take office. M. Houde was a character quite as colorful as Huey Long or any other US stump speechifier. Mayor Houde was a dedicated champion of French-Canadian rights. The story is told that he was unable to get the statue of Edward VII removed from Phillips Square—perhaps he never wanted to do that, but let us not spoil the story—so he undermined its dignity by having a public toilet, named in French for the Roman emperor Vespasian (who supported such public conveniences) installed under the statue. When it came time for the mayor to cut the ribbon, he is said to have told the crowd in his carefully broken English that he was asked to "open a urinal" but had not been quite sure what that was. Now that he understood, he said, it was his firm opinion that French-Canadians "ought to have *arsenals*, too."

They may be getting weapons ready now. The battles between the French- and the English-Canadians have long raged. At the moment, Quebec no more wants to break away from Canada and have to cope on its own than Puerto Rico wants independence from the United States; there are too many advantages now enjoyed, too many handouts, to make going it on one's own look really attractive. But in Quebec politics anything can happen. It is reported that in the early nineteen-thirties a candidate for the provincial legislature polled more votes than there were registered voters—and came in second.

There is always a struggle: in the winter of 1999-2000 it was over French-language Pokémon cards and French-language Nintendo instructions for the children. "In North America, we are only 2 percent," French-language minister Louise Beaudoin was quoted in the press as saying, but in Quebec the French-Canadians are powerful, and they got their way. By mid-March 2000 a judge declared that the law against English on public signs was not needed: French-Canadian was no longer a dying language in Quebec.

What is the names fallout of all this? The old cry of the streetcar conductor of days gone by, "Gee-Guy-*la rue Guy*" now probably would ignore the English name if there still were a streetcar on Guy Street, *la rue Guy*. Outremont and Hampstead and Westmount are still Montreal areas, but the name of Outremont (The Other Mountain) is probably correctly pronounced today. Anglophone children used to joke about a boulevard they called "Pie Nine." It was *Pie Neuf*, for Pope Pius IX. Also, they never put what they thought were totally unnecessary hyphens in street names such as *Jeanne-Mance* and *Jean-Talon*.

Today a version of French is pushed in Quebec the way Irish has been in Ireland, Welsh in Wales, Hebrew in Israel, and Catalan in Catalonia ("a country in Spain" as the tourist posters say). The placenames have been much affected along with many other things. If you can manage to get your child into a school conducted in English, the tot is encouraged to start learning French in kindergarten, while students in French-speaking schools begin English, rather reluctantly, in the fourth grade. (This shows.)

The French-Canadians have not only *rue St.-Pierre* but also *rue du Parc-Marguerite-Bourgeois.* She was the founder of the *Congregation de Nôtre-Dame* which educated Amerindians in early Canada. There is a shrine in downtown Montreal and a stone tower which housed the classroom still stands elsewhere.

At McGill University in the forties, right around the corner from The Union, the student hangout where some of us spent most of our time getting out the daily newspaper, attending meetings of various clubs, and playing hearts, was a tavern we called The Shrine, or Brother André's. This was a reference to *Frère André* (he has a street named for him now), a miracle-working brother to whose memory (as well as to the glory of God) *l'Oratoire St.-Joseph* was erected in Outremont. It is a most impressive church. It was said that the pious approached the Oratory on their knees and that the impious left Brother André's, or The Shrine, in a similar fashion.

When I lived in Montreal, fewer people put an accent on the *e*. At one point provincialism—we cannot at least at this stage call it nationalism, though the provincial legislature now calls itself *l'assemblée nationale*—the *québecois* undertook to change as many of the English placenames and the Amerindian placenames into French ones as possible. There was an outcry that forced them to change a lot of the Amerindian names back. Note, however, that Mountain Street (named for Bishop Jehosophat Mountain, one of the early principals of McGill University) still is *rue de la Montaigne,* which erases Bishop Mountain's history. That is outrageous. *Baie de Thompsons Bay* is ridiculous, but *rue de la Montaigne* is offensive. Still, one can see what the francophones are after.

One must be fair and admit that after the Treaty of Paris gave French Canada to the British, the anglophones (as English speakers are now called in Montreal) were pretty quick to start translating *rue de St.-Paul* into St. Paul Street. There was an area, rather far from the English bastion of Westmount, the English speakers called Point St. Charles, which tells you that it originally was French. In 2000, the street signs in Pte.-St.-Charles had to be changed: *avenue* must come first on them, as in French.

Now the process is being reversed. Revolutions do not change much: they put the top at the bottom and the bottom at the top. The French-Canadians were oppressed for centuries. When they became masters in their own house, they undertook to oppress the English-Canadians, a quarter of a million of whom have responded by leaving Quebec in the last quarter of a century. Language was one weapon in the war. Montreal West became *Montréal-Ouest.* French libraries, French universities, French everything—everything French was favored over English. The French-Canadian population is now a lot smaller a percentage of Canada than it was in 1867 but the remnant is fighting much harder not to be obliterated. The anglophones of Montreal were down to 17% last time I checked and declining rapidly. To some English-Canadians, it seems only fair that, outside Quebec, any French-speakers who are 17% or less in their areas should be treated like the English-speakers in Quebec. However, outside Quebec there has been no move (as yet?) to rename all the places with names of French origin and rewrite the early history of North America. That was all part of an era when France was still one of the most important world powers.

A law was passed in Canada early on making it a bilingual country, but a later law was passed in Quebec forbidding public signs in English, and you have heard it was found silly, but it still applies to street signs. *Mount Royal* was different in English than in French-Canadian. English speakers seldom or never noticed that *Lachine* was French for "China." Some French explorer was granted lands in Canada by the French king of the time but all he got was a stretch along the St. Lawrence. He is supposed to have said that they might just as well have given him lands in China. *Lachine* looks and sounds the same as before: but try to find Lake of Two Mountains on the map. Two names for each place on all maps of Canada?

Now Montrealers who learn French use it. The English of Quebec long studied French in both the Catholic (mostly French) and Protestant (mostly English) schools—long with separate school boards—but they just wouldn't use it. The old globe spun on. The movement of English speakers into Quebec

154

slowed; the movement of French speakers west to better farmlands in Ontario stopped. English-speaking United Empire Loyalists (fleeing the US) did not hang around Quebec but moved west or east of it. Immigrants to Canada landing in Quebec from Europe often stopped in Montreal and learned French. Montreal became cosmopolitan and Ontario's Eastern Townships became over 10% francophone.

It is a long time since Beaver Hall on Beaver Hall Hill was the place to trade furs obtained from the trappers. At the top of that hill on Dorchester (for a governor-general when those still came from Britain, his name now replaced) there was the old Fraser Library. That's gone, too. I mentioned in a recent book of mine, *George Alfred Henty and the Victorian Mind*, that as a child I fell in love with Henty's adventure books borrowed from the Fraser Institute, and several oldsters wrote to me after publication to thank me for recalling for them a grand old Montreal institution. Names, naturally, bring back memories.

There are a lot of memories and a lot of possible remarks. I have become personal here just to remind you that names are a considerable part of anyone's past and have sentimental and personal associations dear to us all.

But this is enough to pay a brief respect to the attraction that there is in the names of Montreal. The language wars between the French-Canadians and the English-Canadians have drawn the attention of geolinguists everywhere. Wherever you stand on French-Canadian language policies insofar as they affect names, over time certain French replacements for English names have been much admired: who would prefer Back River to *rivière des Prairies*? You read earlier that *prairie* is just one of many generics that intrepid French explorers and "runners through the woods" put on the maps of what was to be British North America and then became Canada and Nunavut and the United States and may, some day, include a French-ex-Canadian nation as well.

Now here is a list of just some of the pleasant French placenames of Quebec: Ancienne-Lorette, Anjou, Baie-Comeau, Beaupré, Brossard, Cap-Chat, Cap-de-l'Aigle, Cap-de-la-Madeleine, Charlemagne, Châteauguay, Chute-aux-Outards, Contrecoeur, Coreau-du-Lac, Dorval, Ferme-Neuve, Grand-Entrée, Iberville, Jonquière, L'Annonciation, L'Avenire, La Prairie, La Salle, Lac-La-Croix, Mont-Joli, Nôtre-Dame-du-Lac, Papineauville, Pointe-au-Pic, Rivière-du-Loup, Rougemont, Sept-Îles. There are also dozens of saints' names. How about Ste.-Agathe-des-Monts, St.-Boniface-de-Shawinigan, St.-Hyacinthe, St. Léonard-d'Aston, and St.-Louis-de-Ha!Ha! as examples? There are plenty of English names too (from Asbestos and Hull and Thetford Mines to Rock Island and Windsor), and some Amerindian names ([St.Léon-de-Chicoutimi, Magog, Rimouski, Squatec, Tadoussac, and Yamachichi, etc.). In Montreal there is also a mix of names, with thoroughfares called the likes of Boulevard St.-Jean-Baptiste, Boulevard St.-Laurent (St. Lawrence Main), Boulevard Champlain, Boulevard Gouin, Boulevard Henri-Bourassa, Sherbrooke, Bleury, Park Avenue (Avenue du

Parc), McTavish, O'Bryan, and Jean-Talon. The mixed nature of Quebec and its major city are underlined and the dominant French culture shines forth. That culture is what attracts US visitors, especially, to the old-world ambiance of Quebec City and to the more modern but still French metropolis of Montreal.

STREET NAMES OF THE *VIEUX CARRÉ* OF
NEW ORLEANS

The Café des Améliorations was frequented (early 19th Century) principally by elderly, unreconstructed Creoles who refused to admit that American possession of Louisiana was final. For years they met daily at the café, where they concocted fantastic schemes for the capture of the state government, the expulsion of the American barbarians, and the restoration of the territory to France.

—Herbert Asbury, *The French Quarter*

Asbury (1936) is one of many writers about the most colorful section of New Orleans and René Coulet du Gard and others have devoted much research to the US placenames of French origin. Indeed the French presence in North America and the significant roles played by French explorers, missionaries, and settlers from the earliest eras of the white man are all well documented in American placenames. The first international congress on the 450-year panorama of French placenames in North America had a vast corpus to which to do justice, and my small contribution was a paper on the placenames of the famous French Quarter of NOLA (New Orleans, Lousiana). Among papers on hydronyms (for the waterways were the highways of the early days) and names on the land (in Vermont and the valley of the Mississippi) and names that recalled the hunters and trappers and explorers of the early days of what was New France and then British North America and then the United States and Canada, I offered something like the following information as a way of connecting the early French settlement with the continuance of French culture in the modern US.

With only 15 minutes allowed for the oral presentation, I had to select a limited topic and I thought the French Quarter small enough as well as attractive enough to discuss. In the published proceedings, I had a little more space to talk about the famous street names in a city with French connections in a state with a French name and background. This material is recast for you here.

Leonard R. N. Ashley

So now we move from French names in *Nouvelle France* to some names in *Nouvelle Orléans.*

The names of New Orleans are often remarked upon as being colorful because they abound in references to religion (Assumption, Annunciation, Conception, as in French Canada), classical learning (the names of the muses as well as Elysian Fields, Homer, Olympia, Socrates), omen names of high-minded intention (Humanity, Industry, Virtue), and of course the famous streetcar route mentioned by Tennessee Williams (Desire). Bourbon Street and Stor(e)yville have put Louisiana into the dictionaries. They are at least as interesting as the Amerindian names of Louisiana studied by William A. Read (1927) and this fact is reflected in the publication of a number of somewhat repetitive books on The Quarter printed in the other three quarters of the twentieth century while the Amerindian names have essentially not been gone into thoroughly in all that time. What is equally important, if maybe a bit less often stressed, is that the placenames of New Orleans preserve a distant time, the aspirations and the history of the old city which several centuries ago was founded on land that LaSalle claimed and named for his king (Louisiane). This was a land that two French-Canadian brothers—Iberville and Bienville were the titles these two persons surnamed LeMoyne bore—did much to establish, and this was the land to which the Acadians (Cajuns) moved when they left Canada. Some of the most historic old names are to be found in the streetnames of the *Vieux Carré* (Old Square or Quarter). They help to create its unique character.

Not there, or (in fact) anywhere else in New Orleans is there a street honoring the man John Churchill Chase in *Frenchmen, Desire, Good Children and Other Street Names of New Orleans* (which ran to several editions) called "certainly the first vested authority in the New Orleans area," Jacques Barbazon de Pailloux. However, there are in the old quarter many other names recalling the settlement by the river that Antoine Crozat (a wealthy Parisian who was granted a 15-year charter for Louisiana in 1715) told his engineer, Adrian de Pauger, to plan and to call Nouvelle Orléans. It was named after its patron, the regent of France, the Duc d'Orléans.

Now the French Quarter has a principal street named not for the canal, the ramparts, the esplanade or other borders but for Orleans. Chartres Street was named from the title of the son of the regent. John Law, the Scot whose financial advice was being relied on to straighten out the pressing royal debts, and who also wanted to sell shares in a Mississippi Company, chose both Orleans and Chartres with an eye on backing from the regent. He also hoped by choosing those names to convince speculators that the crown was behind his venture. He added Bourbon and Burgundy for royal dukes, St. Louis for the king of sainted memory, and the names of two current and important royal bastards. They were to have streets named Maine and Toulouse, one on either side of Orleans. The two illegitimate children of these titles were the products of the late, lamented

Sun King, and the administration of the Duc d'Orléans was saddled with them. Here we see the habit of New World speculations being bolstered by naming after European royals who never set foot on the territories named for them.

In Paris, Law lived on a street named for a general (dead since 1712) called Vendôme and so Law put, and we find still, Vendome on the map in New Orleans. From four brothers who were tax-farmers and closely connected with Law's bank in Paris came the street name Dauphiné. At the time there was no Dauphin in France and people sometimes wonder why Dauphine was chosen. These brothers were the reason: they came from the Dauphiné. There was, tactfully, no Law on the map. Later, after Law had died (in Vienna, after bringing chaos to the finances of France), it was still unwise to put his name on the map but it is claimed by some that Bienville may have named a lake near New Orleans after Law's wife, Catherine [Knollys].

Pauger's earliest map of the area (1 September 1723) did not appear until several years after the collapse of Law's financial plans. Nonetheless, the principal names on that map are redolent of Law's patronage and promotional efforts. Maybe, as the Duc d'Orléans said, Law "deserved to be hanged" for quadrupling the immense debt which he had promised he would eliminate, but at least for the names for which he was responsible in the French Quarter we may look on John Law more kindly. Without his influence, the names might well have been not French but Choctaw.

The Choctaw are responsible for placenames in Mississippi and Louisiana. In New Orleans we still have Bayougoulas, Tangipahoa, and Pontchatoula. Small wonder that what English calls Double Dutch and a speaker of French might describe as Chinese we Americans, meaning "it's Greek to me," used to call Choctaw. It was a language that the white man found especially difficult, though he mangled all the Amerindian tongues, as you know.

The names that Law gave for the French Quarter—Conde and Royal were two more—may not have been as imaginative as those bestowed on the nearby Fauburg Marigny (where we find Bagatelle, Bons Enfants, Craps, and d'Amour). Or at least we used to find Bagatelle; it has been changed to Pauger. The history of any area means the history not just of the original naming but of all subsequent naming and renaming. On the streets of the French Quarter there are signs telling you that this or that name used to be there some time in the past under French or Spanish rule. (A major monument retains its Spanish name: The Cabildo, once the seat of Spanish government under a governor with an Irish name.) To this day, Law does not have his name on the quarter's streets. The Fleuve St. Louis (as Law called it) has reverted to the Amerindian name for a big river, Mississippi. The company that Law set up to exploit the position on the Mississippi had to return its charter to the French crown in 1731. But some of Law's names remain.

Bayou, a Choctaw word, is often seen in the names of Louisiana. When New Orleans was first laid out between the Bayou St. John (once St.-Jean) and the Mississippi the settlement was to be 4000 feet along the river and 1800 feet in depth, divided into 300-foot squares. The settlement was to be on the site previously occupied by Amerindians called the Chapitoulas (Those Who Live Beside the River). The bayou was given the name of Jean-Baptiste LeMoyne, Sieur de Bienville's patron saint, St. John. As you heard in connection with French-Canada, places were often named not technically for the person but for the person's patron saint. In a sense, one must say in this case that the bayou was named for St. John the Baptist, not for Bienville.

On the riverfront, two squares were set aside for the church (the cathedral stands there still) and the military (it was common to have a *Place d'Armes*). The military space where soldiers drilled has since 1856 been called Jackson Square. It honors Gen. Andrew Jackson, who won the Battle of New Orleans on 8 January 1815 (after the war was over, by the way, but information had not reached these combatants).

The earliest explorers brought the cross as well as the sword and missionaries attempted to bring the natives to Christ. In 1726 monks arrived in New Orleans and in 1727 nuns came, so we have streets called Capuchines and Ursulines. The French colony was transferred to the Spanish secretly by the Treaty of Fontainbleau (1762) and then openly by the Treaty of Paris (1763). It was under Spanish rule for some time and had in its day both *calles* and *rues*. It briefly reverted to the French before the US purchased Louisiana territories from France in 1803.

The state of Louisiana uniquely has not counties but parishes. The parish and city of New Orleans are coextensive, almost 200 square miles. The boundaries have mostly French names or (*lake* coming first) a French feel: the boundaries are Lake Ponchartrain, Lake Borgne, Rigolets channel, St. Bernard parish, Jefferson parish, and of course the river. New Orleans (N'OR-lins, New Or-LEANS, however you wish to say it) of today is a far cry from the time in 1722 when it was the capital of the colony and consisted of about 100 rude houses and some 500 adventurous—some of them transported—inhabitants. Now it has slums but also the elegant Garden District, and, of course, the touristy French Quarter, Audubon Park (did you know that Audubon the painter of birds was one of the several persons who falsely claimed to be the lost Dauphin, Louis XVII?) and many amenities.

Many of the English names of New Orleans are simple ones: Canal, Basin, Common, Magazine (for a storehouse of tobacco, not guns), Camp (for a slave camp near Poydras, named for a local merchant, like Gravier). Felicity was the boundary of the Jesuit holdings when legacies added to what Bienville had granted them. (The Jesuits were driven out by the Spanish in 1763 not to return until 1837 and today they have a tight grip on some aspects of local education.)

German names do not get on the map of the French Quarter. The Germans that Bienville persuaded to stay in New Orleans inhabited the so-called German Coast up river from New Orleans. By the time later settlers arrived in what became a thriving and cosmopolitan seaport, French names had permanently given a special air to the French Quarter and indeed to the whole city.

These French connections were principally French-Canadian ones. Charles LeMoyne, Sieur de Longueuil had 11 sons active as explorers and colonizers of whom Iberville and Bienville, already mentioned, were but two. When Bienville was recalled after 17 years in charge of *Nouvelle-Orléans*—the date of the foundation is much disputed but I accept that established in March 1918 by The Lousiana Historical Society and they voted that the colony was established between 9 and 11 February 1718—the French appointed a new governor who also had French-Canadian connections. He was Pierre François de Rigaud, Marquis de Vaudreuil (de Cavagnal); he was born in Quebec in 1698 and was the son of another marquis of the same title who served as governor of all *Nouvelle-France*. It was he who hampered the efforts of the Marquis de Montcalm to protect the French interests and he who had to turn it all over to the British when Montcalm was defeated on the Plains of Abraham in 1760 by Gen. James Wolfe. During the administration of Vaudreuil in both New Orleans and in Canada, he especially favored those who, like himself, had been born in French Canada.

Today all the significant buildings in what is called the French Quarter are really from the Spanish administrative period. The Spanish regime began on 18 August 1769 when an Irish soldier of fortune, Alexander O'Reilly, arrived with 3000 soldiers, 24 warships, and sufficient persuasion to convince the Superior Council of the city to submit to His Most Catholic Majesty of Spain. The names in the quarter, however, are predominately French, although the post-1803 era is recalled in a street name Decatur, which must be regarded as an American name (though of distant French provenance). The first theater was established in 1792 by French and French-Canadian actors and named for the street in which it stood, *Le Théâtre de St.-Pierre*. The first newspaper there was French, *Le Moniteur de la Louisiane* (1794). The first local poet was French: Julien Poydras has a street named for him (but outside the Quarter). And of course the Cajuns and the culture of the Creoles (people of French extraction but born in the colonies, such as the West Indies or Louisiana—not of mixed blood, as some people think) were French in origin. It is even alleged that *Dixie* derives from the French *dix* (ten) on banknotes, the word mispronounced by ignorant Kentucky boatmen.

Many French placenames imported to New Orleans were modified by the local pronunciation. Today *Chartres* is pronounced "Charters" and the stress on *Burgundy* locally falls on the second syllable, not the first. The local accent is known from movies—The Quarter is useful as a louche location for murder mysteries, etc.—and from a pop musician whose father was a local political figure. Some people say (erroneously) that New Orleans speech sounds like a

Brooklyn accent. Not really. The traditional Brooklyn accent made famous in the movies by William Bendix and others is gone with the Dutch and Irish influences, for Brooklyn has now one of the largest black populations of any city in the world. If you want to see evidence of New Orleans talking, in print, you could not do better than to read John Kennedy Toole's riotous novel *A Confederacy of Dunces*. Some people put the accent on the first syllable of Royal, some on the second, and, with the streets named for the nine muses (outside the quarter) nobody seems to know what to do: Terpsichore is "Terp-sick-CO-ah" or "Terp-see-CORE." In the suburb of Algiers, across the river from The Crescent City (where the Mississippi bends) you will find the name of Socrates Street is pronounced something like "SOCK-rats STRAY-ut." Everyone, local and visitor, however, can pronounce the name of Bourbon Street, where merrymakers with go-cups (plastic cups offered by bars so you can carry drinks in the street, where glasses and bottles are banned for safety's sake—and drink, usually on the way to another bar), whether you saunter or stagger. At Mardi Gras (Fat Tuesday before Ash Wednesday, the carnival or farewell to meat for Lent) the Bourbon Street revelry reaches a high pitch as parades of the "crewes" and costumed revelers pack the area. There is a riotous Decadence celebration at another time.

A street in the contiguous neighborhood of Marigny was named for the Duc d'Enghein (executed in 1804 by Napoleon when accused of an assassination plot actually involving the Comte d'Artois, later Charles X). The locals said "EN-jine" (which is also how they pronounced *engine*). Then the name was changed to Lafayette, then Almonaster. Almonaster is the closest the locals could get to the surname of Don Andrés Almonester y Roxas, a grandee who started out penniless in New Orleans in 1769 and became a millionaire. He owned the land next to the *Place d'Armes* (Jackson Square, as you know) on which his daughter Micaela, the Baroness Pontalba, built the still famous Pontalba apartments. He himself caused to be erected a number of other important buildings, both civic and philanthropic.

The Louisiana Purchase of 1803 laid out 15 million US dollars for 551,538,560 acres. Now each one of the 90 blocks of the *Vieux Carré* is worth a huge number of dollars—and each block was once worth more until it was discovered that many hundreds of buildings in the area were being inexorably destroyed by a terrific termite that came to the port of New Orleans years ago on ships from the orient and since has been gobbling up anything wooden.

New Orleans has been destroyed before this: the Ursuline Convent on Chartres Street (the nuns' second lodging in the city, this one built 1749) is an old building still standing that was in Bienville's village. New Orleans had terrible fires in 1788 and 1794. On Dumaine Street there is a house called Madame John's Legacy. It is a planter's-style cottage of the West Indian design and was built in 1726 for Jean Pascal, a sea captain. He was killed by Natchez

Indians in the 1729 massacre and by 1770 the house was in the hands of another sea captain, René Beluche, master of *The Spy,* a smuggler. George Washington Cable named the house Madame John's Legacy in one of his New Orleans tales. The story tells of a Creole named John who on his deathbed gives the house to Zalli, a quadroon, and her baby, 'Tite Poulet (Little Chicken). Zalli is called "Madame John." She sells the house and puts the money in the bank for herself and her child's future—and the bank fails.

Whatever the value of the wrought-iron balconies and quaint cottages and tourist establishments, etc., the French Quarter has a heritage that is priceless. The street names express some facets of that, in English, Spanish, and French names. The streets designated North seem to run East. Most people do not know or much care what the placenames of New Orleans mean. Baronne, for instance, few could tell you was named for the wife of the Baron de Carondelet. Desire was named for Desirée, daughter of Robert Gauthier Montreuil, and nobody at all is quite sure what Conti or Conde is honored in the streetname Conde. Decatur used to be Levee (where Bill Swann's Fire-Proof Coffee House once stood) and Nicholls used to be Hospital and New Levee became North Peter and South Peter, etc.

The Quarter has only a fraction of the striking names to be found in and around New Orleans, once called "The Wickedest City in the World" (a slogan featured on the cover of Asbury's Pocket Book paperback edition). There are streets called Abundance and Carol Sue, Colapissa and Wide Water, Race and Poets, Piety and Religious, Tchoupitoulas and Zimpel (or Zimple), Mystery and Metairie (Farm Worked on Shares), Pleasure and Patterson (once The Public Road), Dryads and Ptolemy, Governor Nicholls (formerly Arsenal and then Hospital) and one called the French equivalent of Our Lady of Prompt Succor (now Notre Dame). New Orleans in the early nineteenth century was known as "The Wet Grave," and worse. There was the notorious Swamp and there was Congo Square, where black slaves danced. There was the candy shop on Chartres run by "The Chevalier" (who dressed in outdated French wig and knee breeches and introduced the praline). There were Henry Samba (a native of Guinea, who had the first business on what was to be Canal Street—grazing 60 head of cattle) and Annie Christmas (who stood 6'8" and wore a little moustache) and Lafitte the Pirate (there is a Pirate Alley by the Presbytere and a Lafitte's Blacksmith Shop and more), and Marie Laveau (a mulatto born about 1796 who was thought to have had an extremely long reign as the voodoo queen but her daughter really took her place after the mother's death) and a Dr. John of the mid-nineteenth century and a Dr. John of the mid-twentieth century, one a root doctor and one a pop musician—and there were many other colorful characters whose names became famous. There was Storeyville, where the "Scarlet World" or "Tenderloin" was. There was "Bison" Williams, who kept a rowdy Buffalo Bill House saloon, one of countless barrelhouses. Prostitution flourished until the military authorities closed it down to protect the health of servicemen serviced there. A large directory of the whorehouses listed all the names of the establishments, one of which was The Firm, where you had to be of "some importance" or else there was "no admission," and the madams had names like Countess Willie V. Piazza and Olga Lodi, The Italian Queen. They say that the Americans called the French Johnny Crapaud and that from that came craps, with dice introduced by Bernard Marigny, a millionaire at 15, much poorer after playing. Asbury says that Marigny not only named a street Frenchmen after Lafrennière and his friends who "died there for liberty in 1768" bur Asbury adds the fact that

> in 1808, when he was twenty, he [Bernard Marigny] applied to the city council for permission to subdivide part of his plantation nearest the city into lots. In the Faubourg Marigny, which resulted, Bernard named the streets. And of one them, on which he is said to have lost numerous lots playing his beloved game, he impishly labeled Craps!

If you go outside New Orleans, the names of the rest of Louisiana are striking, too, but they are not my subject here. Just permit me one story of names interest about one of those. Off Route 61, some miles outside New Orleans on the way to Laplace, is one of the loveliest of the old plantation houses. About 1856 the house was built for Edmond Marmillion and it is called San Francisco. It is said that it was first called St. Frusquin, a joke on slangy *sans frusçins*, meaning that it cost so much that the builder was left without what we might call a pot to pee in.

Today the odonymy—that is the fancy word for the streetname cover — preserves a great deal of the past, whether locals and visitors take much notice or not. The names contribute to the individuality which stimulates local pride and draws all those tourists, supporting the local economy as the port once used to do. The names are wonderful. Tennessee Williams (who lived at various times on Toulouse and Dumaine and St. Peter and in a number of bars in the Quarter) famously has a character say: "They told me to take a streetcar named Desire, transfer to one called Cemetery, and ride six blocks and get off at Elysian Fields."

Of the French Quarter, Honey Naylor wrote for the Tourist & Convention Commission:

> The French Quarter is a quieter pastel-colored Mediterranean fishing village, and a blaring garish sex shop. It's honky-tonks and haute cuisine, haunted houses and world-class hotels. It's the clip-clop of hooves on the pavement, and a fringed surrey full of sightseers. It's sedate French restaurants, and fast-food chains. The French Quarter combines the earthy and the ethereal, the chi-chi and the downright cheap, the old and the new.

The French Quarter is one of the leading destinations or tourist draws in the US. Louisiana's past may have closely connected it to French Canada (with whom it shared the unit of land measurement called the *arpent*) but we may say that in the French Quarter you can see the "French foot" in a very American way as it trod where others did not venture and where French speakers created a city still vibrant with life, still full of French culture, food, and frolic.

MESTIZISMO: THE ONOMASTICS OF CULTURES IN CONTACT IN MEXICO AND MESO-AMERICA

Great cultures and empires, among them the Aztec and the Maya, flourished here [Mexico] centuries ago. Their direct descendants—over 50 distinct Indian peoples, each with their own language—remain culturally isolated among the country's *mestizo* (mixed-blood) majority, and maintain diverse ancient traditions despite the country's ongoing modernization.

—John Noble *et al.*, *Lonely Planet: Mexico*

The Lonely Planet guidebook begins with the remark that Mexico is indeed a land of mixtures and contrasts, principally due to history and geography. When asked to describe the topography of Mexico, Cortés simply crumbled a piece of paper in his hand and threw it on the table. That has not stood in the way of border crossings. Mexico (once lamented as "so far from God, so close to the United States") is right next to us and Mexican-Americans have (legally) increased 53% in the last decade (as I write) to well over 20 million: they are a third of our legal immigration and, we must not forget, there are millions of illegal ("undocumented") Mexicans in the US as well. Mexican-Americans are a larger minority here than African-Americans. On top of that, US visitors to Mexico increase every year. So it is good for us to understand each other's cultures, and names is one way we can get some idea of Mexico's cultures (plural).

Mexican cultures in contact are well illustrated in the Plaza de las Tres Culturas in Mexico City. There one can see the remains of the principal Aztec market (Tlateloco), a restored Franciscan church of the colonial period, and ultramodern towers of urban housing.

At that place stood the largest market in the world of its time and there Cuautemoc, the last emperor (or speaker) of the Aztecs, was captured by Hernán Cortés. Cortés and his 11 ships landed at what is now Veracruz in Easter week of 1519. With the help of enemies of the Aztecs, he reached the Aztec capital, set in Lake Texcoco, described as "the most beautiful city in the world." The city was taken by the *conquistadores*, its leader Moctezuma killed. Moctezuma's brother Cuitahuac died of fever a few months later, and so the capture of Moctezuma's

167

Leonard R. N. Ashley

22-year-old nephew (and son-in-law) Cuautemoc represented the end of the Aztec power.

At that place the Franciscans, soon to be followed by Dominicans, Jesuits, Augustinians, and other missionaries, established one of their first churches. Their missions, beginning in earnest as early as 1524, imposed the Roman Catholic religion and put an indelible stamp on Mexico, which, despite anticlericalism, the rise of evangelical Protestantism throughout Latin America, and the survival of various Amerindian religions or adaptations of them, still looks very Catholic. Mexico's history importantly involves such churchmen as Pedro de Gante, the marvelous Vasco de Quiroga (who taught various Amerindian tribes trades and crafts which they practice to this day), Toribio de Benavente (Motolina), Bartolomé de las Casas ("Protector of the Indians"), Bernardino de Sahagún (a converted Jew who witnessed and recorded for posterity the last days of Moctezuma's capital at Tenochtitlan), Father Junípero Serra (who founded many missions in California), and many more ecclesiastics, priests, nuns, and the laity who carried the banner of the Virgin of Guadalupe into battle and Catholicism into every corner of Central and South American life.

At that place, finally, is evidence of the modern bustle of one of the largest cities of the modern world, capital of one of the Top 10 nations in size, a thriving and recovering economy despite recent setbacks and the fact that only some 15 percent of its mountainous land is arable.

That Plaza of the Three Cultures struck me as a prime example of the rich history of onomastic interaction, so when I attended the twelfth International Congress of Onomastic Sciences (Berne, Switzerland, 1975) I spoke about Mexico because it fitted so well the conference theme of cultures in closeness and contest. Mexico and Central America are fine examples of the mingling and merging of placenames and in fact all sorts of names, displaying a remarkable *mestizismo*. I expanded the paper for an article in *Names* 24: 3 (1976) and I redact it here, eliminating the many footnotes and correcting the accents on Spanish words which the printers atrociously mangled in 1976. This time I have checked them carefully with the expert help of Prof. Wayne H. Finke. In a detail-packed book such as this one there are, unfortunately, sure to be some typographical, maybe even other, errors, but I trust they are a small percentage of the whole!

The Spanish names naturally abound in the areas of their New World conquest. We see Fresnillo (Little Ash Tree), El Álamo (The Cottonwood), Minas Viejas (Old Mines), Capulines (Grasshoppers), Puerto Lengua de Vaca (Port Cow's Tongue), Mil Cumbres (Thousand Peaks), La Guitarrera (The Girl Guitar Seller), and Poza Rica (Rich Hole, an oil well). Some look like placenames of California (which the Spanish named for a legendary island in an old romance). We find similar names in Colorado (Red), etc. More typically Mexican names include Alazán (Sorrel Horse), Gaviotas (Seagulls), Mt. Pájaro

Azul (Mt. Bluebird), La Rata (The Rat), Bajío (Lowlands), La Noria (The Waterwheel), El Faro (The Lighthouse), El Naranjo (The Orange Tree), El Porvenir (The Future, as French Canada had L'Avenir), La Única (The Unique One), Río Boca de Ovejas (Sheep-Mouth River), named on Spanish principles but reflecting Mexican life.

Mexican placenames can be as unusual as Los Anteojos (Eyeglasses) or as simple as Los Pinos (The Pines, the Mexican equivalent of our White House). Mexicans named their estates as well as geographical features (the Spanish renaming most that already had Amerindian names) and missions, towns, and cities. Some ruined *haciendas* that stand as reminders of the wealth of Jaliscans in the nineteenth century are called La Troje (The Barn), La Esperanza (The Hope), or simply Estancia Grande (Big Estate).

Most of the placenames are in Spanish, even in areas where the *indios* are prominent and may speak no Spanish at all. The news comes in Spanish, whether from television or in print in the tradition of (for example) the opposition papers of the reign of the tyrannical Porfirio Díaz (1896 – 1911) called *La Libertad* (begun 1896), *El Silbato de Tlaxcala* (begun 1898), and *Regeneración* (begun 1900) and opposing the organs of *porfirismo* called *El Partido Liberal* and the partial *El Imparcial.* There is a lively press in Mexico, full of names, even name-calling.

Other names that do not fit are, for example, *Progreso* (a port city of Mérida which Diana Vinding & Kess Scherer in their *Mexico* guidebook of 1968 say "belies its name") and the names that the Spanish gave to the ruins whose original names or purposes they did not know. Thus we have Palenque (Palisades) as well as Chichén Itzá and Uxmal and the impressive ruins the Spanish thought looked like The House of the Governor, The Palace, The Nunnery, The Temple of the Sun, The Temple of the Inscriptions, and so on. This is in addition to the mangling of actual Amerindian names in the same way that we in the US produced Cheesequake in New Jersey or the French-Canadians produced St.-Machoine (out of Acwapmuswan). Still, a mixture of old and new is very Mexican. Mexicans themselves are mostly of mixed blood, and corn deities are venerated with The Blessed Virgin all around the country. The Mexicans in California have brought us similarly mixed placenames and Chicano diversity.

The Spanish conquest of Mexico may be said to have been achieved with the fall of those we call the Aztecs (because they came originally from some legendary Atxlan), who called themselves Tenochas (hence the name of their capital, Tenochtitlán, founded on the Anhuac lakes in the year *One Acatl* (2 Reed, AD 1168). Victor Wolfgang von Hagen's *The Aztec: Man and Tribe* (1961) begins thus:

The Aztecs, of course, did not call themselves "Aztecs." And very definitely they were not an empire. Moreover they arrived so late on the Mexican scene and were so unimportant when they did come to the lakes, which was Mexico, that not a single tribe recorded their arrival. Their "kings" were in reality elected "speakers" and there were no "halls of Montezuma" (except in song), so that the misconception of there being an "Aztec Empire" is actually a non sequitur [*sic*] of history just as was in fact the Holy Roman Empire which [Voltaire remarked] was neither holy, Roman, nor an empire.

These Tenochas or Aztecs settled on lakes named for the Chalcas tribe of Nahoas (Chalco), Xochimilco (Place of Flowers), Texcoco, Xaltocán, and Zumpango, some 32 miles from the Toltec city of Teotichuacán (Place of the Gods). That had flourished as a temple center from 200 BC to about AD 900. These Aztecs copied the Toltec 52-year cycle of *tonaalpohuali* (numeration of fate) and the basic Toltec social structure, even the Toltec *huipilli* (skirts), *temascal* (steam baths), *pulque* (drunk in rites of the goddess Xochitl) and especially the worship of Quetzalcoatl Ce Acatl Topiltzin (which means Feathered Serpent [born on the day numbered] 1 Reed, Our Worshipped Lord). This cult the Toltecs had brought from Tula, in the north. It was because AD 1519 was the year 1 Reed that Moctezuma and his Aztecs believed that the invading Cortés might be the Feathered Serpent himself, who had promised to return in a year numbered 1 Reed.

Well, Cortés was not Quetzalcoatl and the Aztec "chief speaker" was not Montezuma but Moctezuma II (1503 – 1520), the first such ruler having been Acamapitchtli (1375 – 1395) and the fifth Moctezuma I (1440 – 1469). Aztec names are in Nahuatl. That is a Uto-Aztecan language now used by various tribes from Utah to Nicaragua and, experts say to be helpful, it "belongs to one of the five large phyla of Macro-Penutian speech." It looks strange to us and sounds stranger—Xoxtla is pronounced "Soaks-la" and Chiugue is "Chee-wee"—but it is terse and poetic. The placename Tajín means Place where there is Smoke, Fire, and Light, which is to say a necropolis. Natives of Mexico's Michoacán (Place of the Fisherfolk) were called Tarascans by the Spanish. Mazatlán (Place of the Deer) is now an international resort. Tennessee Williams in *The Glass Menagerie* cites it as an escaper's paradise. Coyocán (Place of the Coyotes) is where Cuahtemoc, successor to the Moctezuma whom the Spanish murdered, is supposed to have been tortured in a vain attempt to learn from him the whereabouts of a great treasure. A symbol of resistance, Cuahtemoc's statue stands in Mexico City in the Plaza de la Reforma. There is a Cuidad Chuahtemoc in Chiapas but no city named for Moctezuma. There is none for Cortés, who became a marquis of the Valley of Mexico, received 22 cities and some 25,000 vassals, and yet was ruined. Finally Antonio de Mendoza arrived as viceroy (1535) and Cortés had to go back to Spain, unappreciated, angry and powerless.

At Tonalá (Place where the Sun is Found) superb pottery is still made (despite regrettable influences from Americans and from Mexicans who studied in Japan). The place was once the center of Chimalhuacán nobility and had a temple to the sun. Zihuatanejo (Dark Woman) as a port once vied with Acapulco for the orient trade. Querétero (Ball Court) was where the unfortunate Emperor Maximillian was shot.

The Aztecs picked up the *tlachtli* ball game from the Olmec, the oldest culture of which we know and which gave us the giant heads from La Venta (Wind). Tenancingo (Place of Wells) was founded in 1425. Taxco used to be Talacho, the Aztec *tiaquiz* or market. Some mountains in this area (22 peaks over 10,000 feet) have beautiful if difficult names: Popocatepetl (Smoking Mountain—it has not smoked since 1802) and its companion Ixtaccihuatl (Sleeping Woman) are names you probably have heard. The last settlement on the way up Popo (as it is sometimes called) is Ozumba (Summit of the High Road). Mexico's highest mountain is Orizaba and its peak, Pico de Citaltepetl, is "Peak of the Star." Some places had symbols to denote them in the pictorial writing: Iztepec's was an obsidian dagger over a mountain. This was a kind of heraldry or shorthand.

Much information was lost when a friar destroyed what he called the "royal library" of Texcoco as heathen documents; only 14 "books" survive. The forever to be deplored Bishop Diego de Landa burned most of the *amatal* (paper) codices of the Mayas; only three survive and you may have to go far from Mexico to see them. It was a very long time before the many inscriptions on surviving buildings could be read. Then we learned something of the society of warriors and farmers, merchants and peasants, and of their oddly named divinities.

The fire god was Huehueteotl (Old God), later called Xiuhtecuhtli (Lord of the Year) and Ixcozauhqui (Yellow Face). The cleric and historian Bernardino de Sahagún (who recorded the last days of Moctezuma's capital, which the Spaniards found more beautiful than any city in Spain, and ransacked) described this god as "Turquoise Lord, the yellow-faced one, the holy flame...fire, the old god, our father."(That yellow face— could it be a clue to Asian pre-history of the *indios,* who so treasured jade? Were advanced ancient humans from Asia made into Mexican gods and goddesses, as Feathered Serpent was? Can a mere name start us off on such a train of thought?)

Teteoinnan (Grandmother of the Baths) was the mother of the gods, Iztaccihuatl the mother goddess, and Tocititlán (Place of Toci) was sacred to her. Xochiquetzal, in whose name the familiar words for flower and a brilliantly plumed bird are seen, was the goddess of pregnancy and childbirth. Chalciuhtlicue (She of the Jade Skirt) was the goddess of water. Tlaloc (He who Makes Things Sprout) was the very important rain god; the Mayans called him

Chac and the Zapotecs called him Cocijo. The serpent referred to in the name of Quetzalcoatl occurs again in the names of the deities Chihuacoatl (Woman Serpent) and Coatlicue (Skirt of Serpents). There were gods for the Milky Way (Mixcoatl), the weavers of rush mats (Napatechli) and indeed a whole pantheon, all under the supreme Huitzilpichtli, and different tribes had different names for them all: Mixcoatl was, for example, Camaxtli among the Tlaxcatecas. You will note something striking about these gods and goddesses other than the names, and that is that these difficult names (I choose from various spellings) are not personal names at all but descriptions of appearance or function. It is not given to mankind to know the names of power. The natives must have been interested when Christian missionaries told them of our God, Who would not give His Name, and of our Devil, a fallen archangel who appeared to the first people as a serpent.

But we are straying from placenames, our subject, into personal names, which are relevant only insofar as they enter placenaming. We know the names of some Aztecs and Mayan and other individuals. Among the Aztecs, for instance, there were men called Itzcoatl (Obsidian Serpent) and Quauhtlatoa (Speaking Eagle), strong names, perhaps with clan totem elements, and women such as Matlaxochitl (Green Flower) and Quiauhxochitl (Rain Flower), pretty names—a tradition you will find in Chinese names and our own western names. A few personal names may have been among the aboriginal names (mostly placenames) combined with saints' names when the Spaniards renamed places. Besides the likes of San Isidro de Arriba, San Luis de la Loma, and San Antonio de la Punta we find the same kind of mixture of languages that amuses us in the placenames of French Canada (Ste.-Susanne-de-Boundary-Line, Nôtre-Dame-de-Lourdes-de-Ham, St.Bruno-de-Kamaraska). I realize that the oddity of mixed-language names of Quebec has more than once been noted in these pages. We can buy our serapes in San Miguel Texmulcán and Teotitlán del Valle and travel to Santiago Acatlán, Santiago Tangamandapio, or Santa Rosa Tlahuapán. There are purely Spanish and purely Aztec placenames, of course. One favorite Aztec placename is attached to a small village with a ruined temple (its *yacata* or giant platform bearing five connected ceremonial structures dating from before AD 800) near San Pablo and not far from a place that used to be called Santa Clara del Cobre (because the saintly Bishop Vasco de Quiroga taught the natives trades and Santa Clara always has worked copper). The village is Tzintzuntzán. The name imitates the sound of the hummingbird, the Aztecs thought.

Long before the Aztecs rose to their few hundred years of eminence, other civilizations flourished in what is now Mexico. The Olmecs of Tabasco—a word that got into our dictionaries along with words from placenames such as sisal and other words such as the words for tobacco and chocolate—and southern Vera Cruz (Cortés arrived there on a Good Friday) were the People of the Jaguar, we say, but Olmec means "People of Rubber," for they had learned to tap "weeping trees." You may have seen photographs or, in museums, the giant baby-faced heads they carved. The Olmecs influenced the people at Teotihuacán (who erected magnificent temples to the sun and the moon) and their neighbors the Mixtecas and the Zapotecas.

The first Zapotec city of any size was Xaguixe (now Teotitlán del Valle) but more famous still is the ceremonial site near Oaxaca that the Spaniards called Monte Albán (White Mountain). When the Spaniards came it was being used chiefly as a burial site—it had been in existence since 500 BC—and it was then in Aztec hands, having been captured in 1469 under Moctezuma I ("The Wrathful") and held to protect trade routes to Central and South America.

The Mixtec were at a place the Spaniards called Monte Negro (Black Mountain) and most notably at Cholula and at Mitla. At Cholula (Place of Flight) the Mixtec erected the largest structure known in the history of the world, the huge pyramid or *tlachihuatepetl* (man-made mountain) with tunnels inside (which you can still traverse), though the outside has been much plundered to build churches (there is now one on top). Mitla's Zapotec name was Yupa (Place of the Dead); it was a necropolis. The names can tell us something about the use of these places to add to what we learn from inscriptions, architecture, pottery and other artifacts. The Olmec called the Huastec people Toneyo (Our Neighbors). The *Itz* in the name of Chichén Itzá means rain. It was Well Opening of the Rain People. They threw human sacrifices into *cenotes* (wells) to propitiate the rain god on whom their lives depended. It may have been lack of water that drove peoples to abandon great cities of the past, leaving them to the re-encroaching jungles.

Far from The Yucatán (Place of the Yucca Fruit, which the followers of the Plumed Serpent enjoyed there when they were driven from Tula by the Toltecs and went south), up north in Jalisco, there is a Ixtlahuacán de los Membrillos referring to quinces and an Ixtlahuacán del Río emphasizing the importance of water. Guyamas is on the west coast, due south in the state of Sonora of the border town that both Mexico and the US call Nogales (one of a great many placenames derived from the names of trees and bushes). Guyamas is named for the Guyamenas who once lived there, a small tribe, not like the Maya, but one remembered because of a placename. Aborigines did not name places after their tribes or even their tribal leaders, though now we find in Mexico, Central and South America some places named for leading figures of the earlier cultures. Those were so named by Spanish conquerors that replaced those chieftains.

The Maya spread over what are now the states of Tabasco, Campeche, The Yucatán, Chiapas, and (named for a Spaniard's surnames) Quintana Roo, as well as into what are today parts of Guatemala, Honduras, and Belize (formerly British Honduras). The vast Mayan temples include impressive complexes at Chichén Itzá, Uxmal, Tulúm, Jaina, Chetumal, Uaxactún, Tuxtla, Bonampak, Yaxchilán, Tikal, Quiriga, Copán, and elsewhere. The Spaniards found these structures puzzling. They gave their own names to El Castillo (The Castle) at Chichén Itzá—it was not a castle but a temple to the Plumed Serpent—and for no good reason El Adivino (The Magician) at Uxmal. Later ages have found more information on the likes of stele (as at Copán) or murals (as at Bonampak), and learned to read inscriptions on buildings, etc. There is something to be learned from the few *hunn* (paper codices) that have survived. Such records existed 1000 years before Christ but in the name of Christ were mostly destroyed. They have gone with the Toltec *teoamextli* (records of the gods, *c.* AD 660) and other valuable documents. The *conquistador* Díaz saw piles of Totonac books at Cempoala. All gone. Pious priests and bigoted bishops burned a lot of pre-Conquest history, for which history must damn them forever.

In the absence of more usual records, every shred of placename evidence takes on more significance. It is clear that Nueva Italia was founded by Italian immigrants (1873) but what is involved in the name of Río Cupatizo (Singing River) in the Parque Eduardo Ruiz in Uruapán? The waterfalls "sing", Eduardo Ruiz was a hero, and Uruapán means "Where Flowers Grow" (the Uruapán orchid is purple). Ten miles downstream is the cascade of Tzaracua (from the Tarascan for "sieve"). Names can be as informative as the stone at the first great Mayan pyramid (Uaxactún, with a date equivalent to AD 328). That was found by Sylvanus G. Morley (1916). Mixtec tombs at Monte Albán were excavated by Alfonso Caso (1932). Sculptures of La Venta were unearthed by Matthew Sterling in 1940. (There are some important US names in the archeological records.) The treasures of Palenque (Palisades) were first unearthed by Alberto Ruiz L'Huillier in 1953. All these speak of the past, of men and migrations, of ways of life and thought. "There is," said Bernal Díaz del Castillo very early, "so much to think over."

Bolonchén (Nine Wells) is Mayan. La Gruta de Xtacumbril-Xunán (Cave of the Hidden Women) combines languages in its name as does Alvarado's Leap. The earliest "American" date was found by Matthew Sterling at Tres Zapotes: it is equivalent to 31 BC. There is a lot of information. But details require organization. In Peru, where the Incas could not write, knotted cords conveyed information—but you had to have a stick of a certain size to wrap the cord around. Archeological and onomastic details often require such a core to make sense of the various details in artifacts and Amerindian languages. Given outside information, you see that Chimahuacán, now called Jalisco, once Nueva Galicia, was invaded by people from a bleak province of Spain. In Guadalajara you see the influence of Moorish Spain. In that large city, the Mercado Libertad is also San Juan de Díos and Avenida Hidalgo Poniente (Hidalgo Avenue West) is Antigua Calle 3 (and you have to know the street by number because that's the way the telephone book names it). Avenida Juárez Sur (South Juárez) used to be Antigua Calle de los Cinco Señores (Old Street of the Five Gentlemen, whereby hangs a tale). Such alternate names remind us of change and locals' use of alternate names and also of cities such as New Orleans where signs may occasionally tell you not only the present name but the former one.

Mexico is rich in alternate names. We in the US got Rio Grande from the language of the area when Texas was part of Mexico but the Mexican part is now called Río Bravo. Similarly, the Rio Grijalva is in Mexico the Río Chiapas. In the year 1517 when Francisco Hernández de Córdoba arrived in The Yucatán, Juan de Grijalva landed on the island of Cozumel and called the country Nueva España (New Spain). Officially the Plaza de Mariachis (those strolling musicians who, Tom Lehrer said, will "not go away 'til they are paid"), a people-watching square in Guad (as the Americans there call it), is the place of the small umbrellas (there is a sidewalk café called Las Sombrillas). That café is on the corner of Juárez and Colón, but Juárez later changes its name to Avenida Vallarta as it passes the university. The flea market of Guadalajara is El Baratillo (Little Cheap Place).

Coatzacoalcos (Veracruz state) American residents like to call Coca-Cola. Another place is called Thomas & Charlie. In Durango (founded by Francisco de Ibarra in 1568 on the site of a Tepehuac settlement) they celebrate each year the world's largest mountain of iron ore, called locally Cerro de Mercado (Market Hill). The south beach at Puerto Vallarta on the west coast the natives call Los Muertos (The Dead) though the tourist business likes to put more attractive names on the area's features. When I first wrote about Acapulco in the seventies, the "in" place was Las Hadas (Fairyland), and the beaches are still Hornos (for the morning), Caleta (for the afternoon), and Condesa (no special time, from the Hotel Condesa del Mar opened in 1971). Some unofficial names are eventually adopted officially; others disappear or are used without official sanction. Today, Richard Burton and Elizabeth Taylor and Tennessee Williams having created an international resort, businesses in Puerto Vallarta tend to have foreign names.

The government changed Xicotepec to Villa Juárez but the natives take little notice. Anti-clericalism changed Santa Clara del Cobre (for the associate of St. Francis of Assisi) to Villa Escalante, but few people pay much attention. Río Nautla is also called Río Bobos and few are sure which is official, let alone which Fools it was named for. The Cuyutlán lagoon at Manzanillo on the west coast is locally the Laguna de los Caimanes (Cayman or Alligator Lagoon). The Zona Rosa (Pink Zone), Mexico City's fashionable shopping quarter, gets its name at least on tourist maps. Zempoala or Cempoala, take your choice. El Huizachi junction is also called San Juan sin Agua (St. John with No Water). Ixtapán de la Sal is nicknamed "the Jewish Cuernavaca." Cuernavaca might well be the non-Jewish Miami—or is Miami the non-Cuban Havana by now?

There is a lot to be learned from placename nicknames, but you may have to know dialect or slang as well as a foreign language accent, and Spanish teachers abroad never taught you any of those useful words. You may even have learned to speak Spanish with a kind of speech impediment, but Castilian will only make you a laughingstock in Mexico. You must try to fit in with the place.

This name collecting has to be done on the spot, not by reading atlases in your easy chair at home (as too much placename study is done). Picking up insider material is one of the pleasures of getting out and about in the unfamiliar culture, whether it be discovering that London's Sloane Square (of the Sloane Rangers) is The Spinney (for a clump of trees), Piccadilly Circus is The Dilly, and Manhattan's 42nd Street area is The Deuce (Forty-Deuce). Deucedly interesting.

Back to Mexico. Let's glance at a little town near where the Americans have retired (to Ajijic on Lake Chapala in Jalisco) that's really Mexican. Its dusty plaza last time I saw it was more Graham Greene than green. Its neighbors at the western end of the lake call it El Pueblo (The City, or The Town) but it is not much (except for the white serapes woven there, collected by tourists). It had one hotel when last I looked, but La Quinta has been there nearly 200 years. Protracted road repairs once earned Jocotopec—or Xocotepec, because Mexico, you know, uses the old Spanish substitution of *x* or *j* sometimes, but that does not affect pronunciation—the nickname Pozotepec. Allegedly, the potholes were like *pozos* (wells). This is light years from fancier settlements nearby such as Ajijic (with Montecarlo, a faded luxury hotel, once a place where Porfirio Díaz was said to keep a mistress, now a club), La Floresta and Chula Vista (fancy names for tourists), Roca Azul, etc. Ajijic keeps up with the American theme. It once had a Pink Panther disco. What is has now or will have tomorrow, no one can say.

Names can not only designate places but also come to be equated with the cultures there, and these can differ much in a few years or in a few miles (or kilometers). They constantly change their content. The complete study of placenames involves a continual and historical approach, in Mexico or anywhere else. In Mexico the past is forever involved in the present and future. In addition to correct interpretations we must likewise study incorrect ones: Tijuana, for instance, is wrongly but frequently said to be from some Aunt Jane, while the fact is that it comes from *teehuana* (city of the sea). Cuernavaca is not from Cow Horn; it is a corruption of an Amerindian name. Moreover, Mexican spelling can often mislead us: *papalla* for *papaya*, *bugambillia* for *bougainvillia*, and so on. Some of this creeps inevitably into placenames, naturally in names derived from less familiar Amerindian languages, of which there are many in use in Mexico and some extinct ones. Names from well-established languages such as Mayan, however, tend to be correct, if often combined with Spanish elements. When we say *Spanish* we should say *Mexican*, because Mexican is a separate language with some vocabulary and other features distinct from Spanish. Indeed, most of the Spaniards in the early history of the country did not speak Castilian but some other Spanish dialects, not being generally from the upper class so comfortably situated at home that they would not want to venture off to the New World's challenges.

Just one Mexican habit will be sufficient to distinguish the language, and Mexican placenames in some particular cases, from Spanish. It is the Mexican love of the diminutive. *Momentito* is a *rato* (moment, in Mexican sometimes *ratito*) a little shorter, as in the US we might say a second. Paco is short for Francisco and Paquito is more affectionate. Mamacita is a loving way to say Mama, Jesusito for Jesús. The equestrian statue of Charles IV (at Juárez and Paseo de la Reforma in Mexico City) is El Caballito (Little Horseman). Nuestra Señora de Zapotán is affectionately La Generalita; it is a corn-paste figurine of the Virgin said to have been brought from Spain by Fray Antonio de Segovia and much-revered in Mexico. Placenames include San Jeronimito, El Limoncito, and Palmarito (Palmar de Bravo). There are diminutives in placenames everywhere, Spain included, but Mexico has an unusual number of them.

The Mexicans are mostly a mixture of races and their language is also a mixture. Placenames, as you have seen, may marry languages. Here, more or less at random, are some peculiarly Mexican words: *malateros* (tramps, but meaning people who steer tourists to hotels), *chihuahua* (a hairless dog, whose name is taken from a presumed state of origin—like Weimaraners, Dalmatians, Pomeranians, Afghans, Skye terriers, Kerry blues and so on elsewhere), *guacamole* (a paste with avocado as the principal ingredient), *tortilla* (flat corn bread in Mexico but in Spain an omelette), *semáforo* (traffic signal, recalling the days when these were moving arms, not lights), *peso* (money, from weight of a coin of the MN or *moneda nacional*). The coin was originally a *columnaria* bearing the two Pillars of Hercules from the Spanish *Plus Ultra* symbol, so that the peso, like the US dollar, has the $ sign—one stroke through the *S* in this font but originally two). Other old-fashioned words are *calandria* (horsedrawn vehicle), *diligencia* (stagecoach, which gave its name to inns, the hotel *La Diligencia* on a major plaza in Veracruz, the third hotel on an old site and with the original name), and *zócalo* (*plaza mayor*, central square), etc. In addition, Mexican is alive with colorful idioms. *A carta cabal* = thoroughly, *ir al grano* = get to the point, *poner el grito en el cielo* (put the cry in the sky) = shout angrily, and *calentarse los cascos* (heat up the skulls) = rack brains. This is not to mention the no less vivid but less printable idioms, of which there is an abundance. You do not learn these in formal classrooms, even in Advanced ones.

The names of food are often puzzling even to those who know Spanish: *pan frío* (cold bread) = stale bread or day-old baked goods such as you can find at the *expendio* of the Bimbo bakery. In the US, *bimbo* is a cheap "broad," nothing to do with bread unless you have to spend your bread (money) on her. *Medias noches* (middle of the nights) are small rolls—a midnight snack?—and *bolillos* (bullets) are somewhat larger rolls. Because these are baked to a pale color, the term also serves for *gringos* (white Americans, whom the Mexicans call *norteamericanos* unless they are deprecating, in which case *americanos* will do). I cannot accept the argument that US people went to Mexico singing *Green Grow the Lilacs* explains the origin of *gringo*. *Mocha* is slang for "very religious" and a *comeda corrida* (quick lunch) is not a *corrida* (half a dozen bulls at the bullfight).

The Danes have no Danish pastry (they call it the equivalent of Vienna bread). In Bologna, bologna is said to be Parisian sausage. Similarly, the Mexicans attribute some things to unusual foreign places and we Americans have Mexican tea (made of small pine twigs on the frontier, and also called Squaw tea and Mormon tea), of which the Mexicans have never heard. In fact, the word *Mexican* appears in a derogatory way in a lot of US slang (Mexican promotion, Mexican breakfast, Mexican standoff) that one hopes Mexicans do not hear from us.

Mexicans have many dishes—I mention food because it is of such interest to foreigners—though they no longer eat *xoloitzcuintli* (hairless dogs). They do make *mole* and *guacamole* (no *mole* in it), and *mole negro de guajolote* (turkey in a spicy chocolate sauce). Puebla (People), in full Puebla de Nuestra Señora de los Ángeles—our US Los Angeles also originally bore a long name—cherishes a story about the origin of *mole*. It is said that a bishop (or a vice-regent, or some other official) unexpectedly arrived and a special dish had to be put together on the spur of the moment (think of Chicken Marengo). The nuns threw together chocolate, chiles, and other ingredients for a sauce. Actually, the Aztecs were noted for serving chocolate "with great ceremony" and this sauce was probably an old Aztec recipe or an adaptation of one. Now *mole* comes in various colors, with or without chocolate. It is becoming as well known in the US as *jalapeños* and other chiles, *tacos* and *tamales, tomatillos* and *hitomates, frijoles* and *arroz con pollo*. Less known outside the Mexican and Chicano areas are candies (such as *ate, cajeta, queso de tuna* which is "cheese" from the prickly pear) and some other treats. The *jipis* (hippies) and others long ago made us familiar with *marijuana* (with nicknames such as Acapulco Gold) and *peyotl* (peyote). These have not been as good for us as the development of a wild grass (*teocintle*), which became corn (in British English maize or Indian corn).

An old word is *tezontle* (a volcanic stone used in some pre-Hispanic buildings). In addition to the words derived from a variety of pre-Conquest languages, we have words not only from Spanish (standardized by Alfonso X in 1253 and based on the dialect of Toledo, though the *conquistadores* almost all came from other dialect areas) but also from the eight centuries of Moorish domination of Spain (including the name Matamoros). And there are the US influences, reversing the process that gave us *buckaroos, chaps, hoosegow* and *vamoose* and added *bracero* (more vulgarly, *wetback*), *chili con carne* (which can be "meatless" and with or without beans here), *burrito*, etc. US retirees in Guad call the Minerva Circle, Manoeuvre Circle or Nervous Circle, because of the traffic. Melaque (near Bara del Navidad—joked about as "condom") is to them Malarkey. I have written elsewhere about Mexicans giving "American" names to pets (Dido for a dog that was *perdido*, lost and found), and faddish US names for certain commercial establishments (hairdressers especially), rock 'n roll bands (Los Boys) and discos (Iguana Wanna), etc. Tourists will find El Shrimp Bucket (Cancún), El Bistrot (*sic*, Guadalajara), Patycake (Chapala), and so on. However, in the decades I have been making regular visits to Mexico I have noticed not only the Americanization to be found all over the world these days but also a growing recognition on the part of Mexicans that most tourists, even *americanos*, go to Mexico for a Mexican experience, not to feel that they are at home. They want to see Mexican culture, with Mexican names. Increasingly, tourists are lunching not only in McDonald's but native eateries and the carefully archeologized *ruinas* are being more and more developed for visitors. The end of the petroleum boom of "Pemexico"—*Pemex* is *Petroleos Mexicanos*—has left Mexico with tourism as its principal industry. The government has built vast tourist complexes from scratch at Cancún and elsewhere and has plans for more. Tourists want some comfort, and a small percentage want international luxury, but the *auténtico* or *típico* is the biggest draw. The names help make that.

The *indio* element remains, but the overall effect is Spanish. On the Feast of St. Hippolytus, Tuesday, 23 August 1521, the Aztec "empire" fell. "Let us leave the city," said the inhabitants of Tenochtitlán; "let us live on weeds." The golden spoils of Mexico were melted down, 132,000 castellanos. Each horseman among the conquerors was offered 80 pesos. "Not a single soldier was willing to accept his share," wrote a chronicler, for the sum was "hardly enough to buy a sword." Over the succeeding centuries, tons of gold were shipped out of the New World to be largely wasted by Spain in the Old. The native population was subjected to Spanish brutality ("The Black History of Spain") and some one million *indios* enslaved and reduced to about 70,000. Today the *indios* are more numerous than they were at the time of the Conquest and are gaining more rights, not without fighting, in various areas where they predominate. The last time I was in Chiapas, there was revolution. The last time I was in Oaxaca there were protest parades. The tyranny has partly vanished and, as I write, the rule of a single party in Mexico, which pretty much covers my long lifetime, is possibly about to end. This time political change will come without major revolutions, which are a large part of the history of Mexico, each with its heroes, its names, its placenames. Father Hidalgo and the *indio* Juárez are the most honored revolutionaries recalled in Mexican placenames.

The Spanish names are everywhere: Alamo, Barranca Serra, Casa, Dinamita ("dynamite," from mining), Ensenada, Frontera, Guadalupe, Hidalgo, Isla, Jiménez, Loreto, Mérida, Nuevo León, Ojo Caliente (an "eye" of hot water), Puerto Escondido, Quila, Ríoverde (though names with *río* usually separate the word for "river"), San Cristóbal de las Casas (not for houses but for a much loved missionary with that surname), Torreón, Unión Hidalgo, Valladolid, Zaragoza. Some are beautiful or curious. Venta Prieta (Blackish Sail) is the name of a place near Pachuca where there is still a colony of Jewish Indians, with a synagogue. (Even Protestants may worship publicly in Mexico now. Anti-Catholicism also changed many names in Mexico.) Jardines de Pedregal (Lava Gardens), near the university city, not too far from the *zócalo* where the cathedral of the capital was built on and in some part with the stones of the greatest pagan temple, is a lavish modern housing development on the site where, 2500 years ago, the volcano Xitle (now extinct) buried the civilization of the builders of the great pyramid of Cuilcuilo. There are spas at Aguascalientes and Agua Caliente and Agua Hedionda (Stinking Water). There are Agua Blanca, Agua Negra, Agua Prieta. At the Vista Hermosa (Pretty View) ranch near Monterrey (Royal Mountain) there is a Cola de Caballo (Horsetail) falls. The once-abandoned mining town of Reál de Catorce (said to be named for 14 bandits) is coming back to life. The Casa Villanueva in Taxco is now the Casa Humboldt, having been that explorer's house, then a pension. It is now a tourist agency and shop. The home of the Conde de Cárdena was made into a studio by Fidel Figueroa and is now called the Casa Figueroa but it was once La Casa de las Lágrimas (House of Tears) because the count made the *indios* he judged guilty of crimes work on it to pay the fines he exacted. Near the "Very Noble and Loyal City of Our Lady of Zacatecas," the Spanish thought that the mountain looked like a wineskin, Cerro de la Bufa they called it, and all across Mexico similar imaginative descriptions of natural features occur in Spanish and, less transparently, in aboriginal languages. At El Sumidero, Tuxtla Gutiérrez, *indios* leaped to their deaths rather than submit to the Spanish. Puebla was built (by 8000 *indígenas*) and settled by 40 Spanish families after a Dominican monk had a dream in which he saw two angels laying out a city. Earthquakes have altered it since. Thirty knights and their families settled the Mexican Córdoba; there the last of Spain's 62 viceroys surrendered to Augustín Iturbide, a Spanish soldier who made himself Emperor of Mexico as Augustín I. (Maximillian I was also emperor briefly, as you know). Córdoba bears the nickname "The City of the Thirty Knights" and was not renamed for the emperor, although many Mexican cities were renamed for various political figures, even in recent times.

Valladolid (after the city in Spain) was changed to Morelos. Tuxtla became Tuxtla Gutiérrez. Cuidad Victoria is named for a president, Guadalupe Victoria, Mexico's first, and the only one for half a century thereafter to finish a term in office. That was something of a victory. Dolores Hidalgo combines the original honor of the Virgin and the name of the parish priest who in 1810 raised the *grito* (cry) for Mexican independence, which is repeated every year on the anniversary throughout the country. It made the village of Nuestra Señora Madre de Dolores (Our Lady Mother of Sorrows) the *cuna de independencia* (cradle of liberty) of

Mexico. In that case the Blessed Virgin's name or title is combined with a priest's name. Elsewhere we have the familiar saint + politician combination: San Miguel de Allende.

We have no space to go into all the colorful figures who made a name for themselves in Mexican history, from the evil viceroy Don Diego López Pacheco Cabrera y Bobadilla (Conde de Xiquena, Marqués de Villena, Duque de Escalona). He was appointed viceroy in 1640 by Felipe IV and guilty of selling high-priced licenses to deal in slaves, freedoms for some mulattos and blacks, and water from the public fountains for 3 reales, about 40 cents American, a load. The oddly-named last viceroy (Juan O'Donojú) had a name that reminds us of the many men of Irish origin who fought in Central and South America, some of whom were governors of Spanish possessions such as Mexico and even New Orleans.

Placenames likewise recall such good ecclesiastics as previously mentioned as Quiroga of Pátzcuaro and Casas ("The Protector of the Indians" of San Cristóbal de las Casas) and also the bandit Pancho Villa and the extraordinary Benito Juárez (whom Henry Bamford Parkes in his *History of Mexico* says displayed a moral grandeur unequalled in the whole eventful history of Mexico). More attention ought to have been paid to intrepid explorers such as Guzmán and De Soto. There is no reminder of Francisco Primo de Verdad Ramos, eighteenth-century precursor of *independistas* who do get recalled. I have heard it said, but I cannot establish it as a fact, that it is illegal to erect a statue to Cortés in Mexico—certainly no one has named a place for him—and the statue to Emperor Augustín I (Iturbide) is now under water and none exists for Huerta (who replaced Pres. Madero in a rebellion of the palace guard). There is no placename recalling the *soladeras,* brave women who fought beside their men in the Revolution of 1910.

Politicians are much more likely to be remembered officially than painters and print-makers such as Diego Rivera, José Clemente Orozco, David Alfaro Siqueiros, Rufino Tamayo, and Guadalupe Posada, though they live in museums. Not much notice is taken of writers and poets such as Armando Nervo, Ramón López Velarde, Alfonso Reyes, Octavio Paz, Carlos Fuentes, and Torres Bodet. Or composers such as Carlos Chávez, and Julián Carrillo. Or, naturally, "good" Americans such as Ken Edwards, John Wilmot, Juan O'Gorman, and William Spratling or "bad" ones such as Gen. Zachary Taylor, Col. Philip Kearney, Ambassador Henry Lane Wilson, and the Gen. Scott who trounced Santa Anna on Cerro Gordo (Fat Hill) on 18 April 1847.

You cannot expect them to be on the map with Salinas, Durango, Hermosillio, and León. Francisco García Salinas, nicknamed Tata Panchito, was the proponent of compulsory free education. Jeréz de García Salinas (Zacatecas) is named for the place in Spain where sherry comes from and for him. Durango was founded by Don Francisco de Ibarra in 1553 and named by him for his birthplace in Spain. Hermosillo is for José María González Hermosillo of the War of Independence. Huajuapán de León is not for León in Spain (as Nuevo León is) but for Gen. Antonio de León, hero of the battle of Los Molinos (Windmills, but with no reference to *Don Quixote*) during the US invasion of Mexico in 1847.

But let us pause to say just a little about Padre Hidalgo. Here's color for you. Miguel Hidalgo is claimed as native son by both Abasola (where he was baptized) and by Penjamo. He was born at Rancho Corralejo, near Penjamo. He was ordained a priest, although he did not have all the necessary training in theology—having lost the fees for some of his education, at the gaming tables— and served the parish of Dolores. He had two children (Micaela and María Josefa) by the actress Josefa Quintana. He brought them up in Dolores, where he also said Mass, supervised elementary education, raised bulls for the ring, ran a mine, and started a revolution which ranks him with Washington and Bolívar, among other greats of history. He came to a gruesome end but is revered now as the father of his country.

The great Tarascan center of Tajimora (in Michoacán) is also Hidalgo, now. The town named for Melchor Ocampo (lawyer and scientist, a man associated with the Ayutla Plan which expelled Santa Anna from the country for good) has been renamed for Pres. Lázaro Cárdenas. Cárdenas became a hero by seizing US petroleum interests in Mexico in 1938 (when *americanos* would not support his welfare program) and his son has also been prominent in politics. Chicontepec (the –*tepec* always means "place") is now Tejada (after Brig.-Gen. Adalberto Tejada, 1883 – 1960. Twice governor (1920 – 1924 and 1928 – 1932), he was the first Communist governor of the state of Veracruz. The city of Veracruz was founded on Good Friday of 1519, just as Florida was named for Easter week's flowers. San Benito is usually called Puerto Madero (Chiapas) after Pres. Madero and San Juan de la Punta is now Cuitlahuac, and Santa María de las Parras (1598, where some who forget the Vikings and Vinland say winemaking in the Americas began in 1626) is now Parras de la Fuente.

So not only politicians are involved in name changes, though politicians had a lot to do with dumping religious names by passing the Ley Lerdo (1856) and the Ley Calles (1926) among other measures which struck at the heart of the domination in Mexico by the Roman Catholic Church. Pope Pius IX excommunicared the entire Mexican government because the constitution they adopted established the precedence of the government over the church. Graham Greene and others have written about Mexican anti-clericalism, seen even in placename change. For instance, Tres Marías (near Cuernavaca), referring to the three Marys who found the empty tomb of the crucified Christ, was renamed Tres Cumbres (Three Peaks). Tres Marías now refers only to three scoops of ice cream (like our Neapolitan brick: chocolate, vanilla, and strawberry) on a cone.

That church, however, was long a potent force in Mexican placenaming. It was much more common to give a religious name than, say, Nuevas Casas Grandes (New Big Houses), the name of an extraordinary pueblo culture in Chihuahua, or Cerro de Cubilete (Cakepan Hill) in Guanajuato (said to be the geographical center of the country) or even Saltillo (Waterfall) or El Sesto de las Aves (Perch of the Birds). Places might be named for the saint's day or religious festival (say, Asunción) on which they were founded. Or they might be named for the favorite saints of missionaries (the Franciscans especially liked St. Francis and St. Clare, while Dominicans, Augustians, Jesuits, and other orders all had their favorite saints) or of important personages (who often celebrated the days of the saints for whom they were named). Los Remedios is a sanctuary built (1629) to house a statue of La Virgen de los Remedios brought from Spain. The Desierto de los Leones recalls the Carmelite monastery built in the wilderness in 1606. Valles was once Valle de Santiago de los Valles de Oxitipa (perhaps the earliest settlement in the state of San Luis Potosí, which produced millions of dollars worth of silver annually at the height of its mining operations).

The Trigarantes (1821)—not to be confused with Tresguerras, the architect (1765 – 1833, from Celaya)—were three guarantees of Iturbide drafted in Iguala (where the Mexican flag first flew over a government building, 24 February 1821). Religion was part of that. The guarantees were (1) Mexico will be free and independent, (2) all Mexicans are to be equal under law, and (3) Roman Catholicism will be the official religion of Mexico. The Virgin of Guadalupe, who is said to have been painted when she appeared to a peasant boy, is the patroness of Mexico but, in fact, the power of the Roman Catholic Church has declined, evangelical sects are becoming more and more important, and many Mexicans do not subscribe to Christianity at all, let alone heed the dictates of the papacy. To some extent, Mexico may be said to have eventually triumphed over oppression by an ecclesiastical hierarchy in cahoots first with Spanish oppressors and later corrupt Mexican dictatorships. In recent times, more in South America than in Mexico, granted, priests and nuns have been progressive and led campaigns for social justice. But they must be careful. The Jesuits got far too political in the eighteenth century and were thrown out.

The placename El Triunfo is not religious. It bespeaks the pride of the miners who made the great Baja (Lower) gold strike of the nineteenth century; today it is, like many old mining towns, a ghost town. There is Baja California and Baja California Sur (farther south). San Luis Potosí (formerly Tagamanga, Place of Water and Gold) was San Luis Mina de Potosí when the Spanish struck gold there (1592) and hoped to equal the rich Potosí mines of Peru, the name combining thus Spanish and Quechuan. Today San Luis Potosí is all Spanish, the name of a whole state and of its capital. Made a city by the Duque de Albuquerque (a name familiar to Americans) in 1665, San Luis Potosí was confirmed as such by Felipe IV (1735) and became the principal city of a territory that once stretched to the borders of the French possessions in Lousiana (another royal Louis). The mine has gone with the Mina part of the name. However, not all changes are reflected in placenames: Plaza de la Universidad in Guadalajara remains although the university has moved to another location in the city.

As in some cities in Spain (and the US, too), inhabitants gave themselves names such as Oaxaqueños (Oaxaca), Poblanos (Puebla), Jarochos (Veracruz, from the *jarocha* or peasant dance), Tapatíos (in Jalisco they recall the old coin *tapatía*), but most inhabitant names follow usual Spanish practice. Some cities have special names for districts, of which the residents are proud. Some of these have nicknames as well as names, as does "Pancho" (nickname for Francisco) Villa, "Pipila" (the young miner José Barajas who burned down the front door of the old Alhóndiga de Granaditas in Guanajato during an uprising), "La Corregidora" (a mayor's wife significant in an uprising), "Lagunilla" (Little Lake, the flea market of Mexico City), and Maniche or Marina (a chief's daughter named Malintzin) who was the mistress of Cortés and who gave to the vocabulary the term *malintzinismo,* which refers to any unpleasant attraction to all things foreign. Luis Buñuel called the poor *Los Olivados* (The Forgotten Ones). There are some nicknames of current and recent politicians that I shall consider unprintable. They may be out of office by the time you read this anyway. All history involves incredible numbers of names that are famous and then forgotten.

The history of Mexico offers many name examples and some name problems. The Battle of Buenavista is also called the Battle of Angostura. Mexico gained independence (1821) by The Pact of Córdoba but also in 1821 was Iguala's Plan of Independence. There have been several Revolutions: the Madero Revolution (1909) was one. The Act of Chapultepec was a security arrangement (1945) adopted by the Inter-American Conference on Problems of War and Peace. There have been various *reformas*. Most important were the *Leyes de Reforma* by which Juárez established his *República Federal Laïca.* There have been numerous rebellions, an early one of which was the Miston Rebellion of the *indios* (1540). There have been two emperors, as you have heard. After Augustín Iturbide was elected emperor (19 May 1822) by the new National Congress, the United Provinces of Central America seceded (1823). Borders have had a chequered history. There have been various wars. The most notable onomastically if not otherwise was the Pastry War (1838 – 1839), with France. It involved, among other causes, the losses of a Mexico City baker attributable to rioters. It is a name worth recording beside the likes of the British War of Jenkins' Ear.

The Sad Night was 1 July 1520, when Spaniards were driven from the Aztec capital with the loss of 450 of Cortés' men, 4000 *indios* allied with them, 46 horses, and "I believe," wrote the chronicler, "all the prisoners." But the

Spaniards returned and destroyed the city and left the Azetcs with nothing but "flowers and songs." It all began with the most striking letter ever written in the western hemisphere, which was just this: "Oh great Huetlatoani, great houses float softly on the sea and from their interior rise white and bearded men who pass the time fishing." This letter, from a scout at Veracruz was painted and delivered 300 kilometers away in Tenochtitlán the same day! Just about as unusual was the first letter ever sent to the Americas. It was from Their Most Catholic Majesties Ferdinand and Isabella and was addressed to the Great Khan of India. Dated 3 April 1492, it never reached the addressee.

There was a time when Mexico extended south to the Isthmus of Panama and north to a line running from San Francisco (California) to St. Augustine (Florida), by way of Santa Fe (New Mexico), St. Louis (Missouri), etc. As early as the sixteenth century, Spanish adventurers, seeking fabled cities of gold, came up from Mexico into the heartland of what is now the US. Large parts of the present US used to be Mexican (as you see from names such as Canaveral, Colorado, Calaveras Co., even Silverado) and, at the current rate of change, will be more or less Mexican again soon. What Alfonso de Rosenweig Díaz, Mexican ambassador to the Court of St. James in World War II, called *la mexicanidad* is greatly affecting the modern USA through legal and illegal immigration from south of the border and from the demographic changes among US citizens already here. In addition to the 20+ millions I mentioned earlier, there are four or five millions illegally here from Mexico. Most of them send money home that is sorely needed, and so, quite apart from NAFTA, etc., Mexican and US economies are linked. Mexico is actually encouraging workers to go to the US.

Once the Spaniards of Mexico extended south as well as north and before their arrival the *sacbes* or highway system of the Mayas extended far into Central America. It seems that people from Guatemala went north into the Valley of Oaxaca (of which Cortés later became *marqués*) to build, on the site of a great lake that had dried up, Monte Albán. Mitla, Yagul, Cuilapán, Xoxo, Etla, Noriega, Loma Larga, Xaagea, Dainzu, Labityeco, Zaachilá—all these show signs of being constructed by or under the influence of tribes from the south as well as from the east (Olmec, dating from 800 BC). The Aztec-Totonac culture of the Valley of Mexico and the Mixtec-Zapotec culture of the Valley of Oaxaca are paralleled by connections with the Maya of Chichén-Itzá (Tutui Xius) and those of Mayapán (Cocoms). The Maya who erected Chichén-Itzá fled the Spaniards who came into The Yucatán (1627) and those Maya survived in the jungles of Petén (Guatemala) at Tayasal. That became their new capital and the Spanish did not conquer it for some 150 years.

Mayan history is long. They calculated their Year Zero, which seems to have been 3373 BC, in their *tzolkin* (calendar). Their history is intertwined with that of other Mexican cultures north and south of them, but not with the culture of the Incas of Peru. The Maya resembled the Incas, however, in that they spread their culture by trade rather than by conquest. The Maya, like the Incas, were great traders. Mayan roads extended far and all their roads met at what the Spaniards called the Laguna de Terminos. There the trading center of Xicalango stood.

This all adds up to the fact that the onomastics of Mexico are intimately connected to those of the present United States to the north and to Central America to the south. Therefore, we need to give just a few pages to the neighboring countries which link the two oceans and the two continents of North and South America and form Meso-America to the south of the present Mexican republic. Recall that a great part of the Spanish possessions far to the north once had their Spanish government centered in the old city of Antigua in Guatemala, the Mayans in effect having erased borders between Mexico and Guatemala and the *gebeloc* (Mayan for "idyllic") area we call Guatemala was a *tierra espléndida* where the Spanish governors of the vast new holdings liked to have their seat. Pedro de Alvarado had a capital briefly at Iximiche, principal city of the Cechichel people, but the hostility of those natives compelled Alvarado's brother Jorge (who had been installed as governor) to flee in the same year (1524) to the Valley of the Almolonga. There he founded the city of Santiago de los Caballeros de Guatemala, later called "old," that is Antigua. There a palace was built for the captain-general and to it Pedro de Alvarado returned with his bride, Doña Beatriz de la Cueva. Hers is a name you probably have never heard, but Doña Beatriz ought to be remembered as the first female head of state in the Americas! Here briefly is her dramatic story.

In 1541 her husband was ordered to the Spice Islands, but, in what is now Mexico, Pedro de Alvarado was killed while assisting Diego López de Zúñiga to put down one of the frequent rebellions of the *indígenas*. In August of that year the news reached Antigua. Doña Beatriz ordered the palace to be painted black, for mourning, but she did not allow herself to mope. On 9 September she herself became governor. The very next day, the violent storm that had been raging for three days brought destruction and death. Water had collected in the crater of an extinct volcano (Volcán de Agua) and was released when new tremors shook the mountain. Doña Beatriz and 11 attendants fled her private apartments and sought refuge in the chapel. It collapsed, burying them all. Had she remained in her apartments, she would have been safe; they emerged from the earthquake unscathed. In all, 700 Spaniards and 600 *indios* were killed by "the eruption of the lake." The ruins were abandoned. They became Vieja Antigua.

A Nueva Antigua, oxymoronic as that may sound, was built in the Valley of Panchoy, not far from the first. The government moved there in 1543. Major earthquakes shook the city in 1565, 1689, 1717, and in the early months of 1773. Then came St. Martha's Earthquake on her day, 29 June 1773. A minor tremor was "a divine mercy of a warning of a ruin to come." (Why a merciful God did not stop trouble from coming at all we shall not stop to consider.) The warning got people out of their houses. A great shock ten minutes later then shook the city and reduced much of it to rubble in two terrible minutes. The mountains that figure so prominently in the Most Noble and Loyal City of Antigua, Guatemala, brought down the capital that had ruled the territories from the (now Mexican) provinces of Tabasco and Chiapas to Panama. Antigua, you could say, was destroyed first by water, then long after by fire. Seeing that, the pope forbade the city to be rebuilt. The inhabitants defied his orders; so now you can see, more or less, where Doña Beatriz de la Cueva de Alvarado so very briefly reigned.

You can also see the cracked cathedral, the "Royal and Pontifical" Universidad de San Carlos Borromeo (Central America's first university, 1676), the house of the great soldier-historian Bernal Díaz del Castillo, the first hospital in Guatemala, and old buildings connected with art (the house of the poet Rafael Landivar), commerce (Casa de Popenoes, built by Luis de las Infantas, 1639), and religion (a church with the tomb of Fray Pedro de Bentancourt, "The St. Francis of America," founder of the Belemite Order). Many great names are connected with Antigua. They are part of its ancient heritage and modern charm.

Remember also the rich galley-loads taken from the New World and that Acapulco was one of the most important ports of the New World, and that when men of the cloth such as Fra Junípero Serra ventured north to found missions in California he was traveling very far from what was then regarded by Mexicans and Spaniards in general as civilization. Everywhere the civilization spread, names were put on the land and the names of those who made history were known.

Explorers named geographical features as they went along. Settlements had street-name patterns: sometimes they were named for saints (Santa Catarina) or other people (Hermano Pedro) or for important edifices they passed, sometimes they were numbered, sometimes they had descriptive names (Calle Ancha = Narrow Street, Calle Vieja = Old Street, which presumably had another name at first), infrequently they bore names in the native languages, the whole adding up to a capsule history. The ruins of Yaxha reveal a modern street plan; it was devised between 600 BC and AD 900. Then the city was abandoned—and the names of the streets lost. At Topxte, built between AD 1200 and AD 1400 by the descendants of Maya, and at Quiriga, a colony of the Capán people in what has been called the Old Empire, some onomastic evidence has come to light. Modern names of foreign origin such as Stann Creek, Livingston, Berlin and Genova exist beside Huehuetenango and Chichicastenango and the excavated Kaminalyuyu. There is a Chicimula and a Chicimulila, Quetzaltenango and Quetzaltepeque, San Antonio Sachit and San Antonio Nuevo, three San Cristobal's and three San Pedro's, six San José's, San Rafael Petzal and San Rafael de la Independencia. La Liberdad and La Democracia reflect political factors. There is an El Progreso and a Nuevo Progreso. Travelers may be confused by Santa Cruz and Santa Cruz del Quiche, San Juan Chimalco and San Juan Ixcoy, San Luis and San Luis Jilotepeque, especially when locals and neighbors use only part of the name, as they usually do with (Santiago) Atitlán. The locals may change old names or resist using new official names. "Where am I?" can get an unexpected response.

Expectably, some names have changed. Tayasal is now Flores (Flowers). Some old names remain from the Coztumalhuapa (who spoke Nahuatl as did the Mexicans who built in the Mayan style) and the possibly Olmec builders of Monte Alto (High Mountain, which flourished 100 BC to AD 400). You hear of Mataquesquintal, Tontonicapán, Solola, Poptún, Zunil, Xicacaco, Zacualpa, but Spanish has replaced many native names and we have Río Dulce (Sweet River), Fuentes (Fountains) Georginas, Agua Caliente (Hot Water), Cerritos (Little Hills), and so on. Frequently, American influences are felt. It is years since I first heard *kuqui* (kooky) in Guatemala or read in a newspaper in Esqintla that someone wished to sell a *frenspud* (French poodle). Daily the language feels the push of international English—but most of the placenames are set and unchanging.

Inevitably, there are placename oddities. Guatemala has a Gracias a Díos (Thanks be to God). In Guatemala, 12 villages around scenic Lake Atitlán are supposed to be named for the 12 apostles (but I couldn't find one for Judas Iscariot, whose name as a placename must be extraordinarily rare considering what an important role he played in Christianity). Guatemala's second city is Quetzaltenago, reminding us how loved were that brilliant bird's feathers which have given a name to persons and to currency. The quetzal is a symbol of freedom because it dies in captivity; so it appears on the flag. The eagle seizing a serpent, perched on a cactus, is the center of the flag of Mexico. That recalls the prophecy that led the Aztecs to build their capital where they came upon this sign.

I reported in 1976 that I was told in Guatemala, "Some places nobody ever goes to, so it doesn't matter if they have names, like places people do go to, does it?" As roads have improved—at least until certain areas of Central and South America became too dangerous for American tourists to visit—more places were "gone to." The largest problem arises when something other than the map name is used by locals and neighbors. These people may have names of their own and know or care nothing of maps and guidebooks. However, Lonely Planet and Rough Guides (more likely to take the adventurous off the beaten track than Fromer and more formal Baedeckers) direct tourists to out-of-the-way sites (and sights). Today adventurous tourists go to rural Mexico and farther south.

Moving farther from Mexico, we come to El Salvador (Our Savior) of which the capital is just Salvador (Savior). The names recall the usual saints and such. There is La Unión and similar political placenames, and the native Coatepeque, Quetzaltepeque, Sensuntepeque (the *–tepec* slightly altered), etc. There are placename reminders of cultures farther north and aboriginal names still clinging to both *ruinas* and inhabited places.

Honduras (Depths) is a word from a psalm. The religious note is struck, as in all the countries mentioned here, in many of the placenames. (Jesús María sticks in the mind). This is not unusual. In the US there are numerous biblical, Mormon, and other religious placenames. In far-off Ghana you will find Hail Mary Plumbing, I Love Jesus Dry Cleaner, and a God Is Great gas station. In Latin American countries, religious names were put on the land everywhere as the cross went along with the sword of conquest. This is as true in Nicaragua, Costa Rica, and Panama as elsewhere. The placenames of Central and South America will be the subject of a book by Prof. Wayne H. Finke, and so I do not go into them here except to make that point about religious names and to add that everywhere in that area, as in Mexico, religious names are accompanied by descriptive names in both Spanish and *indio* languages and the usual commemorative and other standard varieties of placenames. Belize was once British Honduras and so there we find English-language names such as Monkey River, Roaring Creek, and Middlesex (the county of London in England), but the occasional non-Spanish and non-*indio* name turns up in other countries.

It is because Mexican placenames, in particular, are echoed in some parts of the US that once were part of Mexico that we in the US are perhaps most interested in them. We have taken on many of them as well as names for various things such as farms and estates: *rancho, estancia, quinta, granja, hacienda,* but not the *ejido* of the "Land for the Landless" Mexican revolutionaries. We may not know as much of the history of Mexico as we should. What "American" can explain the significance of the *escoseses* and *yorkistas,* conservative and liberal Freemasons in one political movement in Mexico? We may not be able to distinguish modern political parties (PRI, PAN, PRM, PRN) or know the real name of Subcomandante Marcos, but we can see certain major trends. We know as much about Mexico as we do about Canada, our other neighbor. With us or in spite of US policies, in Hispanic America *tamanes* (beasts of burden), whom the Spanish conquerors took some years to decide were actually human beings, have improved their lot and other major changes have taken place in modern Mexico, but in the placenames the whole story is enshrined, along with the defeats and despairs, the trials and triumphs, the faith and the struggles, the folklore and the *mexicanidad* of the people. The placenames truly are the key to appreciating the cultures in contact and in conflict that we see so neatly summed up in the Plaza de las Tres Culturas. The background of the minority that will soon, because of great numbers here, have an immense impact on US life in the twenty-first century is worth knowing, for, with Canada too, all North Americans are drawing closer in this century.

Now we turn to the Spanish placenames of our own state of California, which used to be part of Mexico and which is these days becoming more and more Hispanic as the Chicanos increase in numbers and in political and cultural visibility.

In the case of California we shall be concerned not so much with the names of historical persons and historical events as with the fact that a significant number of the Spanish placenames contain spelling or other errors. With Mexican names we have not gone into how well or how badly, for instance, the aboriginal names were recorded by the Spanish and we have seen spellings which are not always standardized, but in the case of California we shall sidestep the issue of the accuracy or inaccuracy in recording and current use of aboriginal names. We can easily look at the way that the Anglos of California have treated the Spanish, or Mexican, placenames.

By the way, in the US we not only have the state of New Mexico but also various places with variations of *México* (here as with all such foreign words without accents): there are Mexican Bends, Camps, Canyons, Cemeteries, Dams, Ditches, Flats, Gulches, Hills, Hollows, and so on down the alphabet. We have populated places—don't call cemeteries populated—named Mexican Colony (CA), Mexican Hat (UT), Mexican Springs (NM), Mexican Town (Arizona), and places named Mexico in Florida, Maine, and New York, etc. Also New Mexico (GA) and Old Mexican Ditch (WY). Moreover, the presence of Mexicans both legal and illegal has contributed a great deal to the national mix and soon will contribute mightily to Hispanics being politically far more significant than they have been heretofore. At that time the following errors in Californian placenames may be of greater significance, but in any case and right now they can serve to show how names get mangled by people who may or may not know the languages from which the names come.

I considered addressing the topic of surnames derived from foreign placenames that have taken a beating in the US (where other surnames, for instance, such as McGwire, McEntire, and O'Bryon are regarded as not terribly unusual, along with LeVine, Booze, and Peabody) but I hope you will find something further on Spanish (of which only a small number of countries have as many speakers as we do in the US) of interest. Then this book ends with an exotic language to show that placenames can be learned in extremely foreign tongues and greatly enrich our experiences and understanding.

THE SPANISH PLACENAMES OF CALIFORNIA

Coming in solemn beauty like slow old tunes of Spain.

—John Masefield, "Beauty"

A number of Mexican placenames in the previous essay may appear here in forms you may think incorrect, for there is often a difference between what appears in an atlas and what I have found in the place involved. Sometimes I have had to choose among variants, and I may not have chosen the one you or even the Mexican government may prefer, whether the placename be in an *indio* language or in Mexican.

When we come to California, the names are more settled, as far as the US government is concerned, but, from the point of view of Spanish, errors appear in current California placenames. There are errors in every state, but in California there are remarkable mistakes attributable to the fact that both Spanish and English have long been spoken in the area. In December 1994 I addressed an annual convention of the American Dialect Society on this subject and subsequently my remarks were expanded for publication in *Names* 44: 1 (1996), 3 – 40. That article is here revised and, with gratefully acknowledged help from Prof. William Bright, expert on California placenames (and editor of the latest edition of the standard book on the subject by Prof. Edwin Gudde), corrected. Any errors that may remain are to be attributed to my editors or damned as my fault, not his. Any errors at all, of course, would be particularly embarrassing in a discussion of errors.

California has a name taken from a Spanish romance. It is a state that has a population, an area, and an economy larger than some Spanish-speaking nations and within it there are many Spanish speakers. It boasts a wealth of Spanish placenames. It has cities such as San Diego, Sacramento, and San Francisco, Carmenita, Sausalito (Little Willow Grove), and Los Angeles. It has counties named Alameda, Amador, Calaveras, Contra Costa, Del Norte (which was nearly named Del Merritt), and these are more colorful than, for example, those named King, Lake, and Orange. It has plain names such as Mountain Top and Turn and Corte Madera (for a place to cut wood). It has embarrassing names (Pecho Rock, Two Tits, Raggedyass Gulch) from rough pioneer days. It has amusing names (Will Thrall and Wimp) and foolish names (Dirty Sock). Mariposa for a county name is nice; Bloody Canyon is not so nice. It has Poso, a non-standard spelling of Spanish *pozo* (well, watering place), and La Brea Tar Pits, which shows ignorance of what *la brea* means (*la brea* has the same meaning in Spanish as does the Amerindian word that gave us Pismo: tar). An informative article could

191

be devoted entirely to wrongheaded California placenames which often are explained by iognorance of languages, Spanish as well as, for instance, Amerindian. In Wintu, *bulli* is "peak" so Bully Peak is completely wrong and Buli Mountain is somewhat confused. La Cumbre Peak is redundant: Peak Peak. So is Pichaco Peak. Cerro Gordo Peak is Big Peak Peak. Lomita Mountain is Little Hill Mountain. Laguna Lake is Lake Lake and Lagunita Lake is Little Lake Lake. Officially there is one valley named Vallecitos (Little Valleys) but colloquially it is often Vallecitos Valley (Little Valley Valley).

Can California's placenames that are Spanish-derived or resemble Spanish-derived placenames be put into more correct form? In the words of one California placename from the early days, You Bet. Will such change take place? Probably not. This is because the United States Board on Geographical Names has taken the practical position that it will not change placenames without application from and attention to the local inhabitants, and the local inhabitants do not seem to know or care about whether the Spanish placenames are correct. The local inhabitants may even be Anglos or Asians. California is no longer regarded as the Wild West, if it ever was. California is now part of what is called the Pacific Rim. It is now more than half non-white in population and, formerly part of Mexico, is not only Hispanic in heritage but, because of immigration, it is also becoming more Hispanic every day.

The placenames derived from Spanish, then, gain in importance all the time. Perhaps when the Hispanic presence is a great deal greater some of the mangled Spanish placenames will be corrected, but changing a placename is expensive and many people think that the name of the place where they live or work is somewhat arbitrary, somewhat unimportant, just a convenient designation. This is especially true of those who have no history to connect with names of Spanish origin. There are a great many Anglos, Asians, and others in California.

In addition to names put on the land by speakers of Spanish (or Mexican, which you know ought to be regarded as a language of its own) there are some apparently Spanish placenames in California that are merely Anglo attempts at local color. A few examples of those will suffice. La Crescenta (The Crescent) was invented by Dr. Benjamin B. Briggs in 1888 for some odd geological formations; it was not applied by any Spanish speaker. Covelo looks Spanish but it was an error. Charles H. Eberle intended "a fortress in Switzerland" but most probably was thinking of a Tyrolian fort (rather near Switzerland) actually called Covolo (by the Venetians). Mount Lola commemorates someone who pretended to be a Spanish dancer (calling herself Lola Montez) but she was actually an Irish adventuress. She was the mistress of the king of Bavaria, among many others, and later she sold her favors at lesser rates in the Wild West. Though buried in Brooklyn's Greenwood (sometimes Green Wood) Cemetery, she remains a California legend.

Placenames in California may recall Anglos with Anglo names (Yankee John for one) and there are English-language names such as Spanish Bay, Spanish Camp, several examples of Spanish Canyon, more of Spanish Creek and Spanish Flat and Spanish Ranch, Ridge, and Spring, and so on. Some mines have names in Spanish (Madre de Oro for what we might call the mother of all gold) and some features are bilingually named: Gobernador Creek, Manuel Peak, Maria Ygnacio Creek, while others are all Spanish, such as Guadalupe y Llanitos de Los Correos and the historical La Casa Primera de Rancho de San Jose.

You will note that the USBGN has removed the accents from Hispanic-American placenames (though an accent sometimes appears over an *n* to distinguish a canyon from Canada) as it has also ignored apostrophes in names— but inconsistently. Earlier I mentioned Martha's Vineyard in Massachusetts. In California we have the Maidens Grave, recalling the fact that Rachel Melton went west from Ohio but did not last long. Throughout this piece I shall ignore Spanish accents and I predict that American Spanish in time will move far in the direction of doing the same, and not only in placenames.

It is not unknown for *el* (the) to be tacked onto non-Spanish names. Definitely Spanish, however, are these: El Adobe de los Robles, El Arco, El Bulto, El Caballete, El Cajon, El Camino, El Campo, El Conejo, El Dorado and so on, as well as La Arena, La Bajada, La Ballona, La Bolsa Chica, La Canada, La Casita del Arroyo, La Cienega (the standard *cienaga* being less frequent in California), La Clavija, Laguna, Las Juntas, Las Lomas, Las Palmas, Los Altos, Los Angeles, Los Lobos, Los Plutos, Los Serranos, and Los Tablas (or Las Tablas). Grenada looks like a frontier spelling of the name of a great Spanish city but it was actually transferred from a Mississippi county as an improvement over the pioneers' pessimistic placename Starve Out. Some Spanish names, as well as some non-Spanish ones, are transfers to California, of course.

Indigenous Spanish names in California go back to the sixteenth century. Early patterns were established by the likes of San Martin (1542) and San Francisco (1595), by Cabo de Fortunas (1543) and Bahia de los Fumos (or perhaps Fuegos, 1542, now San Pedro Bay), by Carmel (1603) and other names associated with the Blessed Virgin about the time that religion also named the likes of Santa Catalina, San Nicolas, and San Diego. Gaspar de Portolá's expedition in January 1770 named three islands: Falsa Vela (False Sail, for one first taken to be a distant ship) and two Las Mesitas (Little Table Hills). These were renamed Isoltes de Santo Tomas by Juan Pérez only four years later and then named Eneeapah (from the aboriginal Anyapah) by Capt. Vancouver in 1792.

A great deal of renaming has taken place over the centuries in California. This was in some part to reduce the impact of the Spanish presence, but that is basically another matter to be discussed in some other place, except that we should note in passing that the USBGN effort and other efforts to record all the

Leonard R. N. Ashley

names on the maps need to be expanded in time, insofar as possible, to include all the names that ever were used in the long history. That is a huge task and becomes historical rather than the practical business of the Department of the Interior and its Geolological Survey of which USBGN is a part. It has nothing to do with postoffice or military defense matters. For the historical names we have to go beyond cartographers to read the memoirs of explorers and early settlers and to include literature and folklore in our considerations of the placename cover.

There is still a longer list of California placenames, both Spanish and non-Spanish in origin, than is available to us now, despite the fact that Prof. Edwin Gudde was one of the earliest and best collectors of state placenames, issued revised work himself and has been expertly revised, corrected, and expanded by Prof. William Bright. Thanks to him the placenames of California are as well studied as those of Alaska (by Donald Orth) or Oregon (by Lewis L. McArthur).

The Spanish placenames of California go back before the founding of the United States. In the late eighteenth century new names included Santa Cruz (1769), San Luis Obispo (1772), Palo Alto and Santa Rosa (1774), Paso Robles and Escondido (1776), and San Luis Rey (1789). The nineteenth-century names began about the time of Contra Costa (1800) and were not as frequently coined as the century wore on. One thinks of San Bernardino and San Simeon (1819), Marin (1834), Las Cruces (1836), Chico (1850), Fresno (1851), Modesto (1870). Do notice such strange hybrids as Altadena (from the heights above Pasadena, itself a name from Ojibway, 1875) and Vacaville (widely known for its prison, the name half Spanish and half French). The –ville is, you might say, early American. Today we hardly notice that a name Walt Disney made nationally known, Anaheim, is from Santa Anna + German Heim (home). In fact, many early California names reflect multicultural factors and were more inventive than erudite. Some were rough and ready. (There used to be a Rough and Ready; it is now Etna, and it ought to be Aetna.)

Some California placenames were not very well constructed or have suffered at the hands of Anglos. What speakers of other non-Spanish languages have done to misshape placenames does not get recorded. Some errors brought to the attention of the USBGN have officially been corrected. El Jarro (The Jar) was once El Yarro. Belota has been corrected to Bellota (Acorn), La Pansa to La Panza. (Paunch—remember roly-poly Sancho Panza?) Some non-Spanish placenames have been replaced by Spanish ones: Alta Loma used to be the weird Iowamosa (Iowa + hermosa "beautiful"). Even though people may struggle with Spanish placenames they like their colorfulness, but that doesn't prevent people from getting names wrong. In San Diego people say Desh-ah for Dehesa (Pasture Land) and in Los Angeles in my lifetime the common pronunciation has shifted between hard and soft g. Californians may fake Spanish names or choose them just because they like the sound. Ortigalito (Little Nettle) is one of the latter. In

194

another tongue they may try Vidette (they needed French *vedette*) or name Livingston for African explorer David Livingstone. Names have sounds as well as spellings and people may get things wrong. Philologists tend to think more of documentation than of living language in the mouths of the public. That needs correction, especially in the study of names.

Anglos of the YMCA concocted Asilomar ("Refuge by the Sea"). Others reached for Avisadero, a word that you will not find in Spanish dictionaries but, for "place of warning," was constructed on sound Spanish principles when the area was still part of a Spanish empire (1844 or so). Californians created Calpine with *alpine* in mind and chose Escalon (Stair Step) and Armada (Armed Force) just because they found the words euphonious. Some Californians who know no Spanish still think they see Spanish in toponyms with completely different origins: Absco (American Beet Sugar Co.), Biola (Bible Institute of Los Angeles), Copco (California-Oregon Power Co.), Esmeralda (she's the heroine of Victor Hugo's *The Hunchback of Notre Dame*), Herpeco (Hercules Power Co.), Irmulco (Irving & Muir Lumber Co.), Mopeco (Mohawk Petroleum Co.), Tumco (The United Mines Co.). You know about Azusa alleged to be from "A to Z in the USA." That's wrong. Nonetheless, I find folk etymologies as engaging as any learned word origins. They show names at work, too. Did you know Nurse Slough goes back to a doctor surnamed Nurse? Did you ever wonder why so many California places are named in memory of San Francisco and Santa Clara? (The Franciscans remembered their founder and the saintly woman from the same Italian town who founded an order of nuns.) You can see why Dog Town wanted to become Magalia (Cottages, with a distinction lent by Latin) and why the straightforward and sometimes bawdy name choices of rough prospectors were changed as civilization set in. You have heard that pioneers were prone to call a boomtown City; they hoped these settlements would grow into cities, though they seldom did. In these and indeed in all placenames we see the mind of the people at work. There is much we can learn about human nature in general and about the particulars of the American Experiment in the lore and folklore of names. That is another good reason for investigating names and getting them right, in any language.

Among folklore aspects of California placenames I like the likely and sometimes unlikely stories connected with the likes of Likely and Jenny Lind. In fact, the singer never went to the state and the California place was ironically named for the braying jackass of Dr. J. T. Lind. There is many a (fake) Amerindian tale connected with Lovers Leap and such. I like the old mining names such as Angel's Roost and I wonder what the explanation was of Jelly Camp. I disbelieve the folktale connected with Igo and Ono in San Bernardino Co. It seems as phony as the story I retell in *What's in a Name?* about Oronogo ("ore or no go") in another state. I am entertained by Garrote (another Hangtown, where someone was hanged); it became First Garrotte when a Second Garrotte inexplicably turned up. Now First Garrotte is more respectable named Groveland. I would like to believe that Modesto comes from William C. Ralston being too modest to have a place named for him, but I doubt the explanation. I am sad that Copperopolis, which has a good rattle to it, is gone as a name from railroad days and that Coalinga seems to have been a name for a simple coaling stop, Coaling [Stop] A. And I have been using *I* again, but all the reactions are personal, and that needs to be underlined. What do *you* think of these examples?

The folklore aspect of toponymy is too neglected; it will reward more research. We should look into Shirttale Creek, Tantrum Glade, and Tin Cup Gulch. There's a story in each one, and in Timbuctoo (a black miner's nickname put on a place he worked). Tie Canyon is for railroad ties. Traer Agua (Bring Water) Canyon and Thing Valley are curious names. One recalls a Mr. Damon Thing. California promises many delights to the student of names and even the "funny name" amateur approach is far from exhausted. There is J. A. Tinker's nose recalled in Tinker's Knob. There was an old prospector nicknamed Texas in the days when you were more likely to reveal where you came from that what your real name had been "back in the states." That was the source of Texas Springs. Taralin Doty (named Tara, like the plantation house in *Gone with the Wind*— and more, as if Tara were not enough, by her doting if not dotty parents) accounts for Tara Brook. There's gold in folklore, though no melon seeds (such as gave us Cerros de los Melones). Modern folklorists should pan for folklore gold.

Also significant and neglected is the fact that California was by no means at the center of the Spanish vice-regency in the New World. Therefore it did not attract as its early explorers or settlers or even officials the people who spoke Spanish (or Mexican) the best. That needs to be constantly repeated. Inevitably that resulted in dialectical or simply incorrect Spanish placenames in a number of cases, and I do not mean Blanco after Thomas White or Moreno after F. E. Brown. (Largo was for a Mr. Long.) After the teaching of Spanish in California improved—it was introduced into the state's public school system as late as 1915—there was some interest in correcting mangled Spanish placenames as well as in improving the standards of Spanish spoken in California. Of course speakers from Spain would look down upon Spanish as spoken in California or, indeed, almost everywhere but Spain. It must not be forgotten that the Spanish of the Americas is different from and (dare we say it?) more important in terms of numbers than the various dialects of Spanish spoken in Spain.

Here come some of the Spanish placenames of California, without (I regret) the Spanish accents that are (I think) useful indeed, especially in surnames we render as Viscaino and Zuniga, and so on. Officialdom finds it convenient to omit them. You know that now. Excuse, please, the frequent "you know that" accompanying certain ideas that have to be repeated; take it as congratulations for having picked up a lot of knowledge by working your way through this book.

The following 150 or so selected Spanish placenames present problems which I wish could be corrected at this time—unless you think a patina of age excuses defects in linguistics and that tradition outweighs accuracy—but do not expect many to rush to improve. You know that, too. In the following list I omit a few names. One is Chowchila, which I used to think came from Chauchiles but have more recently been informed is not Spanish but from the Yokut Indians. That was one of a few names that were incorrectly included in my earlier lists. Live and learn. I am very grateful to Prof. Bright for catching errors. Unfortunately, he was asked after, rather than before, my publishing in *Names*. So editing was not as complete as it might have been when first I addressed this demanding subject. Here I think you can rely on the details:

Arroyo de Matadero (Slaughterhouse Gulch) should replace its replacement Madero (Lumber) Creek.
Batiguitos should be Batquitos (Trenches).
Bean in at least some instances should return to Frijol.
Berryessa is the wrong way to honor the Berreyessa (or Berreyes, or Berrelleza) family.
Borego should be Borrego (Spanish for "lamb" and frequently Mexican for "sheep").
Burro appears in some names where Buro (Mule Deer) may be intended but in California deer is always *venado.*
Cabazon should be Cabezon, the "Big Head" nickname of an Amerindian.
Calabasas should be Calabazas (Gourds, Pumpkins).
Calaboose Creek should be Calabozo (Jail) Creek.
Calero Reservoir should be Calera (Lime Kiln) Reservoir.
Camphora is what Mexicans made of Monterey's Camp Four.
Campito Peak, intended for Little Camp Peak, is fake Spanish.
Camuesa should be Camuza (Chamois).
Canada Verde (Green Canyon—an ñ would be helpful) should be Canada Verruga (accent again—named in honor of an Amerindian chief with a Spanish nickname, "Wart").
Carnandero Creek should be Carneadero (Abbatoir) Creek.
Carquinez hides the fact that Karquin Indians are the source of the name.
Casa Loma is ungrammatical and should be Casa de la Loma.
The Castro (District) by dropping District has become a famous hybrid, but we say Sierra Mountains and admit such hybrids, the question being: why do we approve certain bilingual combinations such as The Castro and reject others? What are the criteria and why are they not strictly applied?
Cavallo Point should be Cavallos Point or even Punta de los Caballos.
Cazadero used for "hunter" is not really Spanish or Mexican. It is "hunting place."

Chaparral might be better, in some cases, as Chamisal.

Chilao is a problem: I think it is from Chileo (Hot Stuff, the nickname of the bandit Jose Gonsales) but Prof. Bright reminds me that it could be from Chileno (native of Chile).

Chupadero (Water Hole). This is a dialect word and the question arises: if the names are to be correct to what extent is dialect permissible?

Coches (Hogs) is Mexican, not Spanish, but surely Mexican names are right for California.

Cordero Canyon, for brothers on the Portolà expedition, was renamed McGonigle Canyon for a settler. Which name when there are more than one should we prefer? Could we have a standard to help us choose in such cases?

Corona del Mar used to be Balboa Palisades. Should it be left as is?

Costa Mesa (Coast, Tableland) consists of two Spanish words but to combine them like this is not Spanish. What to call such a name? Anglo?

Cuata (Twin) is Aztec, from Mexico, but it is not Spanish.

Del Rosa is ungrammatical.

El Capinero is not Spanish but El Sapinero (The Juniper Plain) would be.

El Granada is impossible in Spanish. It belongs to the El Mesa school of American placenaming.

El Mirage is a hybrid, but so are Buena Park, Loma Point, Mount Diablo, etc.

Encina and Encino are both possible in Spanish for Live Oak. Why prefer Encina?

Esperanza (Hope) became Esparto (Feather Grass). Which is right?

Famoso (Famous) used to be Poso, but leave it.

Gabilan should be Gavilan (Sparrowhawk, with the accent on the last syllable in Spanish).

Gardena is English "Garden" gussied up.

Garapatos should be Garrapata (Wood Tick). Do people care what a name translates?

Guadalasca looks Hispanic (the Arabic for "water" is in there, as in Guadalupe) but it is Chumash Indian.

Guejito y Canada de Palomea (Little Pebble Place and Valley of the Dove) needs a diactrical mark and misspells *paloma.*

Hi Vista in Los Angeles Co. is an illiterate combination.

Hornitos (Little Ovens) used to be Hornitas—better now? Remember that the Mexicans like diminutives.

Huerhuero I once thought to be Stinking of Sulfur in Mexican but it is most likely Chumash Indian.

Indio used to be Indian Wells—better now?

Jacalitos (Little Huts) is Mexican but not Spanish.

Javon intended Jabon (Soap).

La Habra (Gorge) is non-standard Spanish and might be altered as Coxo became Cojo.

La Jolla, La Joya, La Hoya—should all these variants exist? The records are full of non- standard variants. Do non-Californians all know how to say La Jolla?

La Laguna should not have been changed to The Lagoon because it isn't one. In California *laguna* is often used to mean "lake."

La Puente in 1770 was correct (the noun was then feminine) and in 1880 was Puente.

Las Choyas should be Las Chollas. Should spellings be changed to suggest pronunciation?

Las Yeguas (Mares) Canyon should be Las Llagas (Stigmata) Canyon.

Lavigia is properly El Cerro de la Vigia (Lookout Hill).

Lechusa should be Lechuza (Owl).

Lerdo may intend the surname Ledro. If a surname is misspelled by its bearer do we correct it in commemorative names, and (if we do not) what happens to commemoration?

Liebre Twins is just one peak that ought to be called Cueva de la Liebre (Hare's Burrow).

Lindo Lake looks as if it might be Lagunda Linda.

El Lobo is not Wolf but Sea Lion. Its present name, Lion Rock, is a little better, but still is misleading.

Llagos River should be Llagas (Stigmata) River or better Rio de las Llagas.

Lomita de las Linares looks wrong but stands here to remind us that looks can be deceiving because it is acceptable as Little Hill of the Linares Family. It was, Prof. Bright says, "the maiden name of someone's grandmother."

Los Banos are Los Banos del Padre Arroyo [de la Cuesta]. Surely full names are not really necessary but (say) King Boulevard instead of Dr. Martin Luther King, Jr., Blvd. does not perform the commemorative task set for it. Large Lake named for Joe Large would be even more confusing. Pond Pond, in the East, is an example of another kind of problem. An outer bridge named for a Mr. Outerbridge in New York has been called a Crossing.

Los Buellis Hills should be Los Bueyes (The Oxen) Hills or even all Spanish.

Los Felis are for a Jose Felix or Feliz.

Madrone should be Madrono (Arbutus).

Mallo Pass Creek should be Arroyo de Mal Paso (Tough Crossing Gulch).

Manzana Creek probably should be Apple Creek.

Marina is Spanish "seashore" but was not used as a placename in Spanish California.

Mar Vista is ludicrous; Vista del Mar seems to be needed.

Medanos (Dunes) Point is good Spanish—in part—but locally pronounced ignorantly. I do not say "pronounced wrong," because all local pronunciations, in my view, are right even if ignorant. The locals are the authorities on pronunciation, however badly they speak. It is they who decide how to say New York, Baltimore, Bogota, Cairo, etc. In Spanish the word *medanos* is accented on the first syllable.

Mesa Peak, Mount Mesa, The Mesa—these are hybrids, but why not?

Mindego Creek and **Mindego Hill** should be corrected to Mendico.

Miramonte in Fresno Co. and **Mira Monte** in Ventura Co. might be standarized but there is nothing you can do with Miramontes Point in San Mateo Co. because it is for a family of that surname.

Molate, for a point and a reef, should be Moleta (Color Grinding-stone).

Mono, often taken for the Spanish for "monkey," is actually from Mono Manache Indians (a tribe of the Shoshone). This is an example of a name that just looks Spanish.

Monserate Mountain uses a Spanish variant of the Catalan Montserrat (the famous place of pilgrimage) and that is acceptable—but what about the name as a hybrid? If you want the Spanish rather than the Catalan, it is Montserrato.

Montara is a misspelling of some Spanish word such as *montaraz*.

Monte Arido gets *arid* right but translates Spanish for "woods" as "mountain."

Montezuma in several names ought to be Moctezuma ("Speaker" of The Aztecs) and the error was first made in Spanish, though it is best known from the US Marines' hymn line, "From the halls of Montezuma to the shores of Tripoli," which also gets the accent wrong on *Tripoli*.

Mortmar is a French/Spanish atrocity, originally French/English Mortmere. That is where English got the surname Mortimer, later also used as a forename.

Muniz is from a Spanish surname but doesn't ring right without the accent *ñ*.

Nevada City is not snowy, in the state of Nevada, or a city, and I do not think it would be much better off with its original name, which was Deer Creek Dry Diggings at the time of the Gold Rush.

Oroville is Spanish + French and was first called, for hoped-for wealth, Ophir.

Palomas (Doves) Canyon was an attempt to improve on Pelones (Bald Hills) Canyon.

Palowalla is carpentered from *palo* (Spanish "tree") and chuck(a)walla (name of a local lizard).

Piedra Gorda is intended as Big Rock but technically *piedra* is "stone," not "rock," and we probably need a distinction between "big" and "fat".

Pinecata is from Aztec *pinacatl* (a kind of black beetle) *via* Mexico but can be regarded as California Spanish.

Point Pinos might be more sensible as Pine(y) Point.

Polita Canyon misrepresents the surname Poleta.

Polvaredo might be Polvareda (Cloud of Dust), but Polvadero might be Mexican for Dusty Place.

Portola really needs the accent on the last syllable to counteract the American tendency to emphasize the penultimate. This is the name of an important explorer.

Positas (Water Holes) is Mexican, not standard Spanish.

Potrero Meadow is a tautology.

Posa (Puddle) and **Pozo** (Well, Water Hole) are used interchangeably in California.

Quito may be for an Amerindian named Tito or (unlikely) for a city elsewhere.

Rancheria is properly used in California only in connection with an Amerindian village.

Rancho Mirage is Mexican + French.

Reliz (Landslide) **Creek** should never be Release Creek.

Rionido should be Rio Nido (Nest River).

Robla should be Roble (Oak) or maybe Roblar (Place of Oaks).

Sacate (Hay) is Mexican, not Spanish.

Salsipuedes (Get Out If You Can) doesn't fit a creek as well as it does a canyon.

San Ardo is truncated San Bernardo.

San Domingo should be Santo Domingo.

San Elijo should be San Elejo (St. Alexius).

San Emigidio should be San Emidio (St. Emidius).

San Luis Gonzaga is named for St. Aloysius Gonzaga of the Society of Jesus.

San Sevaine Flats is not for a saint but for Pierre Sansevaine. There is no way the public will realize it is not named for a saint unless you go to Pierre Sansevaine Flats.

Santa Anita is simply a diminutive for Santa Anna (compare San Francisquito and San Miguelito).

Sierraville is Spanish + French, as typically American as Spillsville or Tompkinsville.

Sierra Nevada Mountains is a tautology, but it is not official.

Silverado was based on El Dorado (The Gilded Man).

Solomar was made of *sol* (sun) + *oro* (gold) + *mar* (sea) by dim locals.

Sunol needs the restoration of the ñ to squelch rumors it is for Sun Oil, one of those ugly California names such as Stoli (Standard Oil), Oleum (Petroleum), Petrolia (Petroleum), Oildale, etc.

False Point Sur, even **Big Sur** are names in which the word for "south" need not be Spanish.

Tambo is local Spanish dialect for *posada* (inn) but should we have a standard word?

Tassajara in local Spanish dialect describes a place where strips of meat are hung up to dry out. The USBGN seems to prefer Tassajato although in another case they chose Trembladera over Trembladero (Quagmire). Do we need consistency?

Tecate looks Mexican but is possibly Diegueno Indian. Name of a popular beer.

Temettati Creek has a word in the hybrid that Mexicans sometimes claim comes from *temetate* (maize mortar) and identify as Aztec in origin but it is likely Chumati Indian. In any case, the double *t* doesn't look like good Spanish.

Tenaja is Spanish *tinaja* and in our southwest used to mean a natural cistern rather than a large jar.

Tepusquet (Copper) is Mexican from the Aztec and suffers here from misspelling, as do even English words in Californian placenames such as Terminous.

Tesquequite (Efflorescent Rock) is Mexican from the Aztec.

Terra Bella seems to be Latin + Spanish.

Thermalito is Greek with a Spanish diminutive suffix.

Tiburon (Shark) **Point** is a hybrid but better than Tiburn Point, also seen.

Trancos in **Los Trancos Creek** ought to be feminine as in *trancas* (bars).

Tulare is properly Tular (Where the Cattail Grows), Mexican from the Aztec.

Urbita is Latin + Spanish. The place has been off and on called Urbita (Little Town) Springs.

Valyermo might well be Val Yermo (Valley Desert).

Vasco (The), a ranch name, is short for Canada de los Vaqueros (Cowboys Canyon) or Buckaroos Canyon if you want it to be more American.

Vasquez Canyon has a notorious outlaw's name and locally is pronounced VES-kez.

Venada should be Venado (Deer).

Ventucopa is a silly parody (by "Dinty" Parady) of Ventura (which is short for San Buenaventura) + Maricopa (an Amerindian name imported from Arizona).

Viejas (Old Women) **Indian Reservation** is a combination of Spanish and English.

Ximeno is for the name Manuel Jimeno Casarin of Jimeno and ought to be Jimeno.The *x* still appears in some Mexican words for the *j* sound, as you know.

Yorba Linda ties the Spanish surname Yorba to the Portuguese Olinda.

In this list, in my opinion, it would be sensible to alter immediately all the incorrect spellings of the names of saints and other people. After all, what good is a commemorative name if the person commemorated is obscured? I also think that in the case of geographical features there is no excuse for retaining errors in Spanish articles, grammar, or spelling, although in the case of inhabited places I can see that the locals might object to the trouble and expense of changing names, if only in connection with changing stationery and signs. Some people would rather look stupid than spend money.

I really have few objections to the combining of Spanish words with words from other languages such as Point (English) and –*ville*. That is very American, as in Pleasantville. To retain errors in Spanish (or Mexican), however, becomes increasingly less defensible as the population more and more knows and uses Spanish (or Mexican). The USBGN policies about local input in placename decisions may in time lead to some changes.

Dr. Roger L. Payne, secretary of the USBGN, has kindly provided me with a report on USBGN decisions regarding items in the list given above and he reiterates the USBGN policy to establish "the local use and acceptance of a name." In private correspondence (23 January 1995) Dr. Payne stressed that the USBGN finds that names are frequently corrupted and altered by users who come from different cultural and linguistic backgrounds. He notes that these corrupted forms are preferred and usually honored by the USBGN. Thus it is not to be expected, even though California has become much more Spanish-speaking since then, that changes will be called for in the future. There seems to be no move now to make geographical names grammatically correct although there has for some time been a move to make placenames politically correct. Of course demographic changes are always occurring. Over time local pressures may alter. More knowledge of foreign languages—and, in a sense, Spanish (or Mexican, or Puerto Rican, or Cuban, or Columbian, etc.) is far less "foreign" in certain parts of this country than other languages may be said to be—may come as the English-speaking population declines and speakers of other languages proliferate.

Among relevant USBGN decisions (dates in parentheses) regarding the Spanish placenames of California are the following. I give more than 40 decision results from the activities of more than a century of the operation of the USBGN.

Arroyo Burro (1961). Adopting local usage (variants Arroyo Burro Creek, Barger Canyon, San Roque Creek also in use locally).

Arroyo Calabasas (1902). Adopting the US Geological Survey, US Census Bureau, and Post Office spelling, variations having been Calabazas and Calabaces.

Bodega Bay (1950). From Bay to agree with local usage.

Berryessa (1897). To select the spelling (not Berreyesa or Beryessa) used in the Postal Guide, etc.

Burro Spring (1959). To reflect local use (though The Troughs was also used locally).

Cabezon Indian Reservation (1903). Made official with the spelling used by the US Bureau of American Ethnology, US Census Bureau, and General Land Office, variations: Cabazon Indian Reservation, Cabezone Indian Reservation, and Cabezons Indian Reservation.

Calabasas Peak (1902). Consonant with Arroyo Calabasas decision.

Calabazes Creek (1901). Adopting the spelling used by Sonoma Co. officially and on the grant of the Rancho Agua Caliente [Hot Water Ranch], variants elsewhere being Calabazas Creek and Calavezas Creek.

Carquines Bay (1905). Making official the local spelling, variants being Carquinas Bay, Karquenas Bay, Karquines Bay, and at the same time adopting for the same reason Point Carquinez and Carquinez Strait (variants similar to the bay name).

Point Cavallo (1895). To make official the name used locally (variants are Caballo Point, Plaza de los Caballos, Punta de los Caballos, Punto Cavallos).

Canada de los Coches (1961). A decision defined its use for federal purposes (variant: Canada Arena).

Coches Prietos Anchorage (1935). The USBGN accepted the Coast Geodetic Survey information on the correct Spanish for "dark barges" or "black barges" (variants Coches Prietos Anchorage, Coche Prietos Anchorage).

Gabilan (Range 1904). USBGN made official the local name and in 1972 defined its federal application (variant Gavilan Range).

Garrapata Creek (1961). USBGN defined its application for federal use under this name.

El Lobo (1932). A name chosen by the USBGN for a previously unnamed feature.

La Jolla Peak (1961). The local name was made official (variant La Joya Peak).

Jacalitos Hills (1908). A decision related to Jacalitos Creek and on the same bases.

Huerhuero (1897). A land grant name was taken from the Land Office Map and a California Mining Bureau Map (variant Huero Huero).

Huerhuero Creek (1897). Decision related to Huerhero on the same bases. (The Huerhuero grant used Huero Huero for the name of the creek).

Los Trancos Creek (1897). Making the local name official (variants Los Stancos Creek, Los Trancos Creek, Stancos Creek).

Tassajara (1957). USBGN adopted the local use though an 1897 decision opted for Tassajaro, then used by the County, the Geological Survey of California, and the State Development Commission.

Tassajara Creek (1967). USBGN adopted the local usage despite the 1897 decision related to Tassajara.

San Emigdio Creek (1903). USBGN adopted the land grant form also used in a California Mining Bureau report and by the County Clerk (variants San Emedio Creek, San Emidio Creek, San Emidion Creek).

San Emigdio Mountain (1903). USBGN adopted the land grant name as with San Emigdio Creek (variants the same as with the creek).

San Emigdio Mountains (1973). USBGN adopted the local name (variant San Emidio Mountains).

Salsipuedes Spring Number One (1968). Two decisions, one to adopt the name in local use and another to define its application for federal use (variants include Number One Salsipuedes Springs).

Salsipuedes Canyon (1978). A spelling conflict between the name on US Geological Survey and US Forest Service maps was settled with the California State Board's agreement (variant Salce Pudes Canyon). In this as in other cases you will notice that a number of authorities are taken into account by the USBGN. The board attempts to please as many as possible on the basis of facts.

Sacate Creek (1978). Officially recognizing the local usage, recommended by the California State Board, decision reconfirmed 1988 (variants Sacata Creek, Secata Creek).

Sacata Ridge (1978). A decision related to the Sacate Creek decision and on the same bases. One decision may affect a number of related placenames.

Polvidero Gap (1908). USBGN adopting officially the name on US Geological Survey maps (variant Poliverda Gap).

Pitas Point (1961). Adopting the local usage (variant Point Las Petes, Point Las Pitas, Point Los Pitas).

Monte Arido (1938). Naming a previously unnamed feature at the request of the US Forest Service (variant Montecito Peak, the triangulation station at the summit being named Montecito). The forest rangers may ask that unmamed features be named for their convenience. What is named and what is not, and why?

Montara Mountain (1895). To go with Montara (variant Point Montoro).

Mono Meadow (1932). Making this local usage official at the request of the National Park Service.

Mono Pass (1932). Related to the Mono Meadow decision.

Mono Jim Peak (1987). On the recommendation of a former naturalist at Inyo National Forest (named for an Amerindian named Mono Jim in the tradition of Paiute Pete and Curley the Crow, who contrived to be "the sole survivor of Custer's Last Stand" by not being at the battle at all).

Los Banos Creek (1962). Local usage (though locally pronounced as if bearing a Spanish accent) with variants Arroyo de los Padres, Garzas Creek, Las Garzas Creek.

Lion Rock (1960). At the request of the National Park Service, USBGN gave this name commemorating the killing nearby of a mountain lion by a sheepman named Brooks.

Zapato Chino Canyon (1964). Making official local usage, USBGN gave this name (variants Zapato Canyon, Zapatos Canyon).

Zapato Chino Creek (1964) with similar reason (and similar variants) to Zapato Chino Canyon.

There have been other USBGN actions of the last half dozen years. This, however, is enough to give you an idea of what the USBGN does and the government agencies with which it deals. It is to be noted that "federal purposes" (not primarily historical or linguistic considerations) lie behind all decisions. The

USBGN is ready to select from what is often a number of expectable variants— there is seldom a surprise—any single name that has local support, because what officialdom wants above all is one name, one place. This, of course, cannot be invariably counted upon. Think about any habits in your own locality giving unofficial placenames locally whatever the official names might be. Sometimes the unofficial names dominate. You will have noted reliance on national, state, and county bureaux (including the census, postal authorities, Indian Affairs, geodetic and coastal surveys, mining bureaux, forest and park services, development commissions, county clerks' offices, etc., and that the USBGN information on names considered everything from mail delivery to Indian management and that documentation ranges from ancient land grants and maps, official and unofficial, to modern surveys. The USBGN also acted on recommendations from individuals as well as government entities. Bill Stone, that former naturalist at a national forest, mentioned above, submitted the information about Mono Jim, the Paiute guide. That guide was killed in 1871 while attempting to recapture six escaped convicts. You see also that, occasionally, the USBGN can be expected to change its decision, although considerable thought goes into its decisions and like any bureaucratic entity it likes to act once, decisively.

If Californians would approach the USBGN with well-founded requests for placename changes based on local usage and Spanish rules, we might see some improvement in the correctness of Spanish placenames in the state. If there is no such pressure from the public there, then the names on the map, however incorrect they may be, will be the sole official and recognized toponyms. As Spanish (or Mexican) is more widely spoken in California, the appropriateness of placenames correct in the language, or even the translation of some existing Anglo placenames into the language of the current inhabitants, may, possibly, be given consideration and action, as I have said. The USBGN policy of respecting local use may make correction of Spanish or even translation into Spanish a social and political concern where Spanish speakers predominate. Already Cubanos are in the majority in some parts of Florida and Chicanos are in the majority in some places out west. In another country with more centralized authority and more of a tradition of language control, placename changes might not happen even when there are major demographic changes, but in multicultural America, where the English Only movement has not had a large impact and there are areas where minority languages predominate (as well as large cities where over 100 languages are spoken—a huge problem for the public schools and all other governmental institutions), minorities often may have major influence and major effects.

The US is settled to such an extent that great numbers of new settlement names are not to be expected, even in a state as rapidly growing as California. There is, however, a constant demand for new micronyms (such as street names) and there is a growing ethnic awareness that may have an impact. Change of existing names will have to be balanced against the usefulness of the retention of names with histories of their own, but the twentieth century in Africa demonstrates the fact that politics often have little respect for the past. Changes in the names of streets, and in the names of whole nations, respond to masses in motion.

Names usually change very slowly and sometimes turn out to be the sole legacy of dead languages, but all languages are constantly in a state of flux and events always alter cases. Bureaucrats, geographers, cartographers, and historians naturally prefer a single and permanent name for each and every toponymic entity, but this cannot always be counted upon. The death of someone like Pres. Kennedy may precipitate a flurry of name changes. It is wise to name only for the dead but that case and other cases suggest that we require not only death but also a little wait to see if destroying old names to erect new memorials is indeed the best idea. No government policy can keep the public from using unofficial names or guarantee that only the "best" (by whose standard?) historic individuals are honored, and this is especially true in democracies where small but vocal minorities are catered to by politicians and where affluence buys influence.

As for famous names on the map of California, we see Martinez (a very common Spanish surname) and Mulligan Hill (for an Irish sailor named Mulligan or Milligan). Near San Diego, there is Perez Cove, elsewhere a couple of Lopez creeks, Lopez valleys, Lopez dams. For which individuals or families of Lopez? Among the the *A*'s we see surnames such as Alvarado, Alviso, Amador, Andrade, Anza, Arana (Gulch), and Arguello. Aumetos Bay's name may come from the surname Armenta, or it may not. Avila can be either a placename or a surname, both from Spain, because in that country as in many others surnames can derive from placenames. Navalencia has sometimes been imagined (when it could not be found in a Spanish atlas) to be a Spanish surname; the fact is that it comes from two varities of oranges, Navel and Valencia. It is neither a personal name nor the name of any other place.

Some placenames derived from surnames are likely to be misinterpreted. Flores Peak is not for flowers but for a Mexican bandit of the name and Murieta was a pseudonym used by several Mexican bandits in California. Families are noted in placenames such as Las Nietos and Las Aguilas. Some Spanish surnames have been wiped away, just as Anglo named Willmore City is now Long Beach. Others may have been twisted out of shape, just as Morris Goldbaum of a century ago is today hidden under Goldtree. There is sociodynamics in a thing like that.

There is psychology in the desire to commemorate important people. In the placenames of California there are many examples of that admirable practice. Some Amerindians are remembered there if only under their baptismal names (Nicasio and Novato) or nicknames (one Barber of Barber Springs or the

207

Panamint recalled in Death Valley at Hungry Bills Ranch). You will recall that Spaniards tended to give Spanish names to Amerindian converts (Geronimo) and this produced some disguised aboriginals among commemorative names. It is always worth repeating that no person would have had a place named for him or her in an aboriginal culture. It was only with the coming of the Europeans that Amerindian persons might get their personal names on the land. That recorded some history, though (as with, say, post offices in early Kansas) maybe only forenames, not surnames. Frontier anonymity and casualness also led to many a creek being named simply or a Jim or a Bill, and we may never discover the identity of the person honored. If a nickname was used instead of a forename, the task is even harder. James "Cussin' Jim" Smith was ironically remembered with Holy Jim Canyon. "Lee" Harl (a fervent admirer of Gen. Robert E. Lee) gave us Leesville, a placename that is commemorative but, extraordinarily, does not include any part of the honoree's official personal name.

California has its Elsie Caves and it named Sister Elsie for a nun and Mount Emma and Polly Dome. It has several places called Jack Canyon or Jack Spring, for various Johns. There is a Jacks Valley in one county for John "Coyote Jack" Wright and Nigger Jack Peak for John "Nigger Jack" Wade in another. (Someone may want that changed. The USBGN has responded to political correctness elsewhere and has moved on from *nigger* to *squaw*. You know they don't dare attack Squaw Valley.) McGill Creek has now been corrected to Miguel Creek (for Miguel D. Errera) but there are may others whom we might describe as buried under misleading tombstones.

When you see a forename, it is more likely to be that of an Anglo than a Chicano. Angelo Creek was for a hotelkeeper. Kingdon was for Kingdon Gould. For Anglos there are Fort Dick, Fredericksburg, and Gustine (for a girl called Augustine). Spanish forenames in placenames are much rarer. Still we see Jose Basin, Jose Creek, Jose Opening, Juan Flat, Juan Spring, Juan y Lolita Ranch in Santa Barbara Co., and Ignacio and more. We find ourselves dealing on a first-name basis with people we shall never know.

The overwhelming use of Spanish forenames in placenaming involves saints' names. The British writer who called himself Saki says in "Reginald at The Carleton" that in England in 1904 saints' names are "associated nowadays chiefly with racehorses and the cheaper clarets," but the Spaniards took their birth days seriously. They prayed to their patron saints. They bestowed saints' names on places everywhere, often because the place was named on the feast day of that saint in the church calendar. Similarly, religious dates account for Animas (souls, Feast of All Souls) and the Nativity is intended by Nacimiento when it doesn't mean "source". In a sense, saints' names function sometimes like streetnames such as Cinquo de Mayo. "Date" names like that are more common South of the Border and in Latin America in general than in the US. In The Yukon there is a Fourth of July Creek and in Quebec a *Lac du 17 décembre.* In

France's Montpellier, the end of World War II was marked by a *Place du 8 Mai [19]45.*

Errors in saints' names do occur but they are rare; these names have always been familiar in Spanish culture. Errors in other words do crop up, despite the straightforwardness of Spanish spelling. You know Spanish spelling is very regular, especially when compared to the orthography of English. Dialect and substandard pronunciation account for oddities in Spanish, as they do in English (in Brooklyn, New York, you hear De-KLAB for DeKalb and in Chicago something like GO-thee for Goethe). Should we preserve the colorful errors of the past such as Picketwire for Purgatoire? Should we correct them? Which policy is better for ethnic pride and Californian dignity in these more sensitive times? Should we do away with misleading names (Lemoore elsewhere commemorates Dr. Lovern Lee Moore) or Gulling (for Charles Gulling, he of the Grizzly Creek Ice Co.) and J. O. Pass (S. L. N. Ellis named that for John W. Warren, who got there but managed to carve only the first two letters of his name on a tree)? Today J.O. is an abbreviation in rude sexual slang.

There is even a California placename derived not from a forename or a surname but a middle name: Benali recalls a San Franciscan lawyer called James ben Ali Haggin. And there is one placename in California that some people have said is Spanish but really is just a Spoonerism. The story is worth telling: In 1859, Sam Brannan wanted to turn the hot springs of Agua Caliente into a popular spa, the "Saratoga of California." They say he stumbled over that and produced the Calistoga of Sarafornia.

Canada de Rodriques (with an *s*) is in Ventura Co., but in San Diego Co. the valley, the mountain, and the trail are all Rodriguez (with a *z*). This kind of thing is found also in the surnames Alonso and Alonzo. Spanish permits the use of the mother's surname rather than the father's when the father's is too common, and thus we have Picasso and Lorca and in California the name Cabrillo for a famous explorer (surnamed Rodríquez Cabrillo). Personal-name variations involve other aspects of linguistics coming to the aid of toponymy, just as in the case of the generic *arroyo*. In Spain, *arroyo* is a stream or brook and when dry is *arroyo seco*, but in the US *arroyo* is a wash or gulch. Also, Spanish dialectal words often are found. In New Mexico, for instance, a place 25 miles SE of Las Vegas—a place, by the way, the natives and some others usually call "Los Vegas"—is Chapalito. In archaic Spanish there was *chapalito* (little hat), comparable to French *chapeau* (hat). As Spanish developed, some words changed meaning: *atarque* started as "division dam" and gradually, as we might say, accumuluated mud until it was any earthern dam that collected silt.

The principal way, however, in which old-fashioned or dialectal Spanish affected the placenaming of California is in the way the explorers and missionaries heard and phonetically wrote down the aboriginal names. Those transcriptions—here is a point you may be bored with by now if you have read this book of mine from the beginning, but some things must be repeated because it is also possible for people to read selected essays in the book on the basis of personal need or interest—were filtered through the dialects of the transcribers. There is a lot of linguistic evidence preserved in placenames that can contribute to dialect studies as well as enlighten sociological research into languages, cultures, and settlement patterns.

As the population of California changed from aboriginal to importantly Hispanic and then to predominately Anglo, some Spanish names appeared and then disappeared or were altered. We may, in the light of demographic changes to which I have referred, expect further change, though it must be said that resistance to placename change is greater now than it used to be. The Guardian Angel has disappeared who was once honored in Punta de Angel Custodio; now the place is Pedro Point. Rio de las Animas is now Mojave River. Nuevo San Francisco is now Solano. One Agua Caliente is now Palm Springs. Agua Dulce is translated; today it is Sweetwater River.

Naming and renaming for conquest or convenience by early people on the ground was followed by naming for other purposes—scholars have taken too little interest, for instance, in personal and political reasons for naming— including nostalgia, commerce, and boosterism. There was even, as you are well aware, a romantic revival of Amerindian names. In the process of placenaming over time some Spanish names were replaced by non-Spanish ones and *vice versa*. Modena is now El Modena, Marion is Reseda, Mud Springs is El Dorado, Apex is Escondido (which the Spanish tended to reserve not for heights like this but for hidden water sources). Today the Amerindian name Auxumne is Spanish Merced, Amerindian Tixinli (or maybe it was Tiximili) is San Luis Obispo, and an English name gave way to Palo Alto, perhaps part of the distinctive pseudo-Spanish colonial coloration of many things Californian from architecture in the great palazzi of Hollywood moguls and the suburban tract developments and the trailer parks. Even non-Hispanics seemed to think that Spanish Colonial was apt for California.

Standard Oil called its second refinery in the state El Segundo. In 1931, La Quinta (Country Estate) was named for a hotel. Lamanda Park was made "more Spanish" as La Manda as early as 1905. That was the year of the big push which altered Lomalinda to Loma Linda, Lahonda to La Honda, Elrio to El Rio, Elmonte to El Monte, and so on. Some time later it was noticed that Lamanda was confected by Leonard J. Rose out of his own first initial and the forename of his wife, Amanda. It never had any Spanish element, and in 1920 it went back to being called Lamanda Park. Some other names which appear to be of Spanish origin may be discovered to be no such thing.

Today opportunities are few for an individual to put a name such as Lamanda Park, or Hollywood, on the map. The urge remains, nonetheless. So does the hope of changing an Incinerator Road to Burnham Road and getting rid of nineteenth-century names now in disfavor such as Nigger, Puke, and Sucker. This may be rewriting history, but many people seem to agree with Henry Ford that "history is bunk" and could care less (which means they could not care less). They will gladly change a Curious Butte into Striped Mountain or Paps into Twin Peaks and they certainly feel uncomfortable with racial epithets and vulgarities of all sorts in placenames if not in popular entertainment (where titles such as *You Don't Know Jack* on television, *The Spy that Shagged Me* on a movie, or *No Bull* on an autobiography get by without cries of "how vulgar!"). If they knew more French, some Americans might object to the Grand Tetons.

The directness of early California pioneers gave us some names we later regretted such as Solomon's Hole, One-Horse Town (changed to Mule, and it may once have been One-Mule Town), and Drunken Indian (changed to plain Indian). Californians dumped Sweet Pizzlewig Creek—but now it is Pizzlewig Creek. They were spared many "ugly" names that disappeared with mining and lumber camps and lack of knowledge of the meaning of some Spanish names (such as Atascadero, Miring-Down Place) saved some others from extinction. The outlook of those who opened the west and rushed there for gold produced appropriate names for those people; later people expressed their way of thinking in removing many such names. Isla de Alcatraces (Penguin Island) became Alcatraz and then that name took on new meaning. Yerba Buena was retained; it sounds nice even if you don't know it is Mint. Canada de la Hambre (Hunger Valley) became Alhambra Valley, moving from hunger to Moorish magnificence. Pioneers chalked up Loafer Creek, Newcastle, If I Can Mine, Italian Swiss Colony, Swedes Creek (once designated Sweede Creek), Norwegian Gulch, Portuguese Sheep Camp, Palermo, and Berlin (later patriotically changed, just as Berlin became Kitchener in Ontario—I mean the Canadian Ontario, because there is an Ontario in California, too). Some of this pioneer history stuck. Some of it did not. We constantly, in fact, are editing the past. Strange, sometimes, what lasts.

At the same time other people turned to history for new names in California as the east coast in the nineteenth century turned to the ancients and had a Classical Revival. Trees are pleasant to find in an arid landscape and both the Spanish and later the Anglos liked the likes of Alameda (Poplars), Alamitos (Little Poplars), Alamo (the Texas one is the most famous, of course), and Aliso (Alder). The speakers of English added Cottonwood, Walnut Grove, a few Poplar places, some Oak places, etc., not to mention Thousand Palms. There is a Poplar-Cotton Center. To match Spanish *acampo* (pasture) there is a Pasture Gulch. To match *algoso* (weedy) there is Weed (but it comes from a surname). There is a Weed Patch in Kern Co. For *aromas* (the stink of sulfur or sulphur in this case) we have Sulphur Creek, Sulphur Spring, Stink Creek and Stinking Creek.

You will notice I have been choosing examples from the first letter of the alphabet. Were I to go through the whole list there would be a book, not a part of a book. Amaragosa (Bitter Water) River is on the US Geological Survey map as Badwater, and in the *Omni Gazetteer of the United States* right after Badlands and Bad Name Spring come Badwater and Badwater Springs. Here is a word many Anglos will know from wine bottles but perhaps could not translate: Almaden is both an obsolete placename in California by itself and still found in half a dozen combinations in Santa Clara Co. It also occurs in San Luis Obispo Co. as, among other combinations, the redundant Almaden Mine, for it means "mine" or "mineral." Californians know to accent Almaden on the last syllable.

As is true elsewhere in the US, some names are spelled according to the local pronunciation and in California some Spanish names are thus distorted, but Spanish on the whole is not one of the tongues that Americans have declared "too furrin to say" and too hard to spell. It is only outside California that Americans have much trouble with La Jolla, San Joaquin, San Jose, San Rafael, Suisun, if not with Yuba. Americans may not pronounce these names as Spaniards might but the local way is always the right way—there. In California pronunciation has transformed personal names, which is bad for history. The French surname Beausore yielded Beasore, German Fierbaugh came out as Firebaugh, and a celebrated Danish name (Lasuen) there occurs in records as Lassin, Lasson, even Lawson. Now the maps have it correct, but less famous Peter Lebeck is recalled as Lebec and used to be mentioned as LeBeck, Lebeque, etc.

Some Spanish names may be hidden under distorted spellings even now. I can understand why some names were not pronounced or spelled correctly, especially when people from all over the world poured into California after James Marshall struck gold at Sutter's Mill (24 January 1848). One might say that the names have been made more American. That is the case with Spanish + English combinations and English translations from the Spanish. Correcting names may come to be regarded as more American as the society increasingly recognizes pluralism.

That name Badwater Springs is on the Pat Keyes Canyon map. That reminds us that Anglo commemorative names are often full names. This signals that the person was recognized as rather obscure even as he (seldom she) was honored and that a full name or even a title was necessary to make the individual noted clear. So we have Judge Davis Canyon in California. This happens all over America: Major Deegan Parkway (New York), Gov. Harvey Canyon (Kansas) and, especially in the Deep South, bridges and highways and such with the long names (sometimes including nicknames and Jr. and titles such as Gov.) of what we may call non-celebrity celebrities. California has Dan Hunt Mountain (Hunt Mountain would be ambiguous), Davy Brown Creek (as Brown Creek it would be open to misunderstanding), but there are also Franklin K. Lane Grove, Mount Ida Coolbrith, Mount Mary Austin, Mary Blaine Mountain, and Jack London Historic State Park (historic?). It also has a few Spanish names such as Jose Serrano Adobe and Father Garces Monument (no accents such as they used).

Capt. Vancouver called one feature simply Lasuen Point that could have been Father Lasuen Point. Elsewhere the famous padre is honored by a forename: Fermin Point.

The USBGN way with apostrophes causes trouble in California as it does everywhere else. Johnsville honors William Johns, Janes Creek is for H. F. Janes, but Janesville is for an obscure blacksmith's wife named Jane Bankhead—or maybe one Jane Hill. Spanish has no apostrophes so it does better in this awkward system. The Spanish problem might be distinguishing which one of a number of persons (say) San Vicente is intended to honor in a placename if indeed any saint was intended. The place might have been named for the saint's day in the calendar, for a particular devotion of the namer without regard to the date or call for intercession, or for a person who had been baptised with the saint's name. Part of the Sierras (Saws) was named for Santa Lucia by Vizcaino around 13 December 1602. That date tells us that St. Lucy of Syracuse and not some other St. Lucy (because there are more than one) was intended. Naming for saints is not as simple a matter as first appears, common as it was in California. You have heard a lot about it in this book because it is a placename feature I have deliberately chosen to be able to offer you some comparisons and contrasts in naming practices. It does express piety. It marks places as Christian, wiping away the aboriginal names the way that the Spaniards built churches on the sites, sometimes with the stones (as you heard) of the temples of heathen gods. Occasionally, though in Mexico and such places and not in California, the Spaniards combined the name of a Christian saint or some other Christian name with a pre-existing pagan name. Mixture may not be kosher but it is very Mexican.

Some Spanish names once or still on the map of California derive from aboriginal languages filtered through Spanish as well as other languages. The Costanoan tribe, for instance, is involved in names such as those of Aptos Creek (which we adapted from the 1807 Spanish land grant named Rancho de Aptos) and it may even come from a personal name (which is very rare). Ausaymas is a placename taken directly from that of a Costanoan village. Algodones looks at first as if it may be from *algodón* (cotton) but it was, in a slightly different form, the name of a Yuman tribe. Aguanga Mountain is from the Picha word *awanga* and seems to be a Shoshone Luiseño placename. As is the case elsewhere, Amerindian names have survived better on geographical features than on owned and inhabited places. Amerindian names have a certain suggestion of the wild about them, of the antique and even the preserved, as in Sequoia and Yosemite parks.

The full discussion of Amerindian names in California is well beyond my competence. The serious scholar will find some books and articles on the subject in the almost 150 items of a select bibliography (pp. 32 – 40) that accompanies my "Spanish Placenames in California: Proposition 1994" in *Names* 44: 1

(March 1996). You do not need all those details here. It is worth noting, nonetheless, how much research is required to produce and back up a discussion of just some of the names of just one state.

It can be said here that Amerindian names are, in fact, the weakest aspect of all the works on county names, city names, steeet names, etc., and have presented the greatest problems to Prof. Edwin Gudde and Prof. William Bright and the other experts who have collected and commented upon California placenames. Distinguished scholars and industrious amateurs have labored over Californian names for over a century and still the placename cover and the history of California before the arrival of the white man remains very imperfectly known. It may be the least understood aspect of California's unusually turbulent and extremely colorful story.

The early Spanish presence can and should be better archeologized and better remembered. California has neglected to honor adequately or at all such big Spanish names of history as Hernando de Alarcón or Nicolas Gutiérrez. Manuel Micheltorena's only monument now is a street in Los Angeles and a school named after it, and sprawling LA has so many streets that it is glad to notice anybody or anything. Every year hundreds more names are needed there.

It is unclear whether any of the Jones placenames honors the extraordinarily named Thomas ap Catesby Jones, whom Californians who are really up on their history will know raised for a single day (and by mistake) the US flag over Monterey on 19 October 1842. Both early Spanish history and early Anglo history of California are very vague in the memories of most people, and, after all, California is a state where most people seem to go, rather than come from. So C. C. Nahl and other Californian artists go unnoticed while national interest puts Richard Nixon Birthplace in the placename list right after Nitwit Camp.

One expects that Hispanics will be providing more and more street names and perhaps even names of malls, towns and other places in California. It would be useful if they remembered the early Spanish and Mexican history. California can do better than Brown Material Road and Superconductor, although its most famous recent placename is the unofficial Silicon Valley. Those who have special reason to be proud of the Spanish presence in the past should express their feelings in names. It is hoped that non-Spanish speakers will not find themselves as ill at ease in California as some do now with the Cuban-Americans (worse: Cuban Exiles) in Florida.

The Hispanicization of California is well on the way even now, as Hispanics are just about to surpass African-Americans as the major minority in the country and, once better organized, will certainly have more political clout than African-Americans or Jews. A while back, I addressed the demographics of the Hispanic birthrate and immigration (legal and illegal) in other forums. As I write now one presidential candidate is promising to make legal all illegal immigrants who crossed our porous border with Mexico before 1986. I have previously noted in articles, in onomastic and geolinguistic journals, that California has altered various policies on immigration. We shall soon see if the public relations flack supporting Proposition 187 to deprive illegals of expensive social services—which passed—was correct when she predicted "Mexicans in California would number 15 to 20 million by 2004."

I do not think that English Only has a chance nationally, as I say in my recent book on *Language in Modern Society*. (The dreaded *I* again, but opinion must be distinguished from undisputed fact.) I certainly do not think that the sovereign state of California will ever establish Spanish as the sole language there. It is possible, however, that the rise in the number of Spanish speakers in California may create at least pockets of Hispanicization so extreme that there will be an Anglo flight comparable to the anglophones (as they are called there) who have fled French-conscious Quebec. If enough Cambodians arrive in California I suppose the state could vote to speak Cambodian! I'm not worried. The English Only movement (which started in California and was strongly championed by my friend and fellow McGill graduate the late Sen. Hayakawa) has not appealed to the vast majority of Americans. Nonetheless, English is *de facto* the national language. This is convenient. Americans and in fact the whole world see English as a lingua franca. Our nation will presumably continue to respect the rights of minorities. Our poll-driven politicians will cater to the most vocal minorities. Hispanics have not yet "got their act together," but they will. They will be, I predict, too wise to insist that Californian placenames be in Spanish to the extent that the people of Quebec want to eliminate English placenames. They will not vote for California to rejoin Mexico. California and Mexico are already quite close enough. The amount of money that flows into Mexico from former Mexicans working in California is so great it might as well be argued that Mexico should join California.

Just before the Civil War, California was considering exercising its option to divide into two states. In the turmoil that followed, the idea was abandoned. Whether the idea is ever brought up again or not, the state is going to become increasingly split or bilingual. The state has changed its demography radically over the centuries. A recent huge influx is now reversing somewhat. But there will always be Anglos seeking sun. New arrivals, especially the notorious "little old ladies in tennis shoes" from the Middle West, did not have much interest in the Spanish and Mexican history and the placenames that recalled it. Today, Anglos are swamped by Mexicans fleeing north. Mexicans have given Southern California such an Hispanic feel that it almost seems wise to think of Southern and Northern (never South and North) California as two different cultures. Los Angeles is no Miami (where what was once thought of as a spinoff of Jewish New York has become a spinoff of Havana), but the Spanish language is heard everywhere in SoCal. Anglos across the country are eating tacos advertised on television by a talking chihuahua.

In this article I do not propose to tackle national language policies or the macrosociolinguistics or the politics. I am talking about placenames and not in the sentimental and inspiring style of Nellie van de Grift Sanchez on *Spanish and Indian Place Names of California* (1914) but, I hope, in the scholarly way of George R. Stewart. Professional scholars and county historians such as Alan K. Brown (San Mateo, 1964), Myra Bedel Cochran (Orange, 1967), Lou Stein (San Diego, 1978), Donald Thomas Clark (Santa Cruz 1980 and 1993, Monterey 1991) and others, and historians of street names such as Rosario Andrea Curletti (Santa Barbara, 1950), Eugene B. Block (San Francisco, 1971) and Louis K. Loewenstein (San Francisco, 1984), and others have published useful books. Studies of placenames in California have been published by major presses and by amateur authors self-publishing, and there have been studies of The Sierras' names, the names of The Cascades, Winslow Anderson on *Mineral Springs and Health Resorts of California* (1890), Jacob Neibert Bowman's *Place Names from Private Land Grant Cases* (1947), and a great deal more. The subject fascinates many Californians, as well it should, and is of interest to us all.

We non-residents of the Golden State take delight in California names. With this section, limited to Spanish names and with a focus on correcting Spanish names that may have gone wrong, professionals and amateurs may be inspired to do more work on the subject. Local names neeed to be more widely appreciated in every community and every state and especially in states such as California where the population is so diverse and could benefit from some understanding of background. Conscientious public-school teachers such as Lou Stein and Tamara Van Etten in their day brought the study of Californian placenames to children. Placenames ought to be a part of the curriculum today. California should guard and cherish the placenames on the land whether they are of Spanish origin or not.

Standard bibliographies by Sealock & Seeley and Carlos Sole, and others, can direct anyone interested to what has been done and what still needs to be researched. From time to time municipal authorities or entertaining journalists bring Californian placenames, especially the colorful Spanish placenames, to readers. One early magazine article, for example, was Nellie van de Grift Sanchez's "Origin of California" in *Motor Land* 33 (1914), 7, 13. The arrival of the automobile gave an impetus to noticing placenames. Editorials such as "Short Names or Long Ones" (*New York Times*, 4 November 1928, sec. 3, p. 4, col. 6) regarding the shortening of Spanish placenames occasionally stir debate. "Funny name" columnists (see "The Spanish Confusion," *Sunset* 157, 1976, 54 – 61 on strange local pronunciations of Californian placenames, of which Jesus Maria as "Sus-MREE-uh" is one) bring placenames to the attention of ordinary people. Scholars contribute to the learned journals, to gazetteers, etc. George R. Stewart, combining a scholar's interest in toponymy with a novelist's writing skills, interested many in geographical names or American history. His work on the names of Gold Rush mining claims still can entertain people who otherwise

216

would have believed that 49ers are only in sports. Charles Matthias Goethe's two books (1949, 1950) on gold mining names are also attractive.

In various ways, on the subject of the placenames of California, especially the colorful Spanish placenames, even the general public can be reached by collections of the 1000 most interesting names, by folklorists (such as in F. W. Hodge's "Early Spanish Bungling of Indian Names," *Western Folklore* 9), local historians performing their labors of love, and academic specialists writing dissertations and publishing university-sponsored research on specific names or clusters of names.

California has a number of social problems of great magnitude and complexity as befit what is essentially a large nation on its own. California is much concerned with flux, as befits an America always becoming, and an era now in which the pace of change is ever faster. Compared to those problems, the questions about Spanish placenames, or any placenames, are trivial. But they are not trivia. In the process of coping with problems, neither the state nor the American nation can afford to lose track of the past, some knowledge of which may help to guide the future. I say now as I said in 1994, when Californians were struggling with balancing the fiscal crisis against the multicultural considerations, that even placenames are part of the Californian heritage worthy of preservation.

The Romans used to say that there was "always something new out of Africa." In the US, there is always something new out of California. One development of the late nineteen-nineties was the early prominence given in California to the question of what part plebiscites may play in the government of the whole country, politics going beyond platforms by polling rather than by principle to legislation by public relations and propositions on the ballots. That stressed public input. It would be good for the public to pay some attention to the minor matter of the placenames of California. They suggest inter-cultural cooperation in the light of a patriotic necessity. The old names contain lessons for a multicultural present that challenges us all to face change with innovation but without losing sight of where we came from.

Leonard R. N. Ashley

THE PLACENAMES OF TURKEY AS A GUIDE TO TOPONYMIC STUDIES

> **For this is to be taken as a granted veritie, that names among all nations and tongues...are significative, and not vaine senseless sounds. Among the Hebrewes it is certain out of sacred Scriptures, Saint *Hierome* and *Philo*, likewise among the Greekes, Romans, Germans, French, &c., yea among the barbarous Turks, for among them *Mohamet* signifieth glorified or laudible, *Homar* lively, *Abdalla* God's servant, *Seliman* peaceable, *Agmad* good, *Haniza* readie, *Neama* pleasant.**

— William Camden, *Remains Concerning Britain* (1623)

The most striking names aspect of Turkey derives from the fact that in the twentieth century, as part of an intensive campaign of modernization and revolution, Turkey swept aside the caliphate and empire of the Ottomans. The old system had existed for many centuries. Gazi Mustafa Kemal's new government suddenly imposed surnames upon the Turks, all at once and for the first time. Up until then Turks used the common Arabic personal name system of *X* son of *Y* (and even "mother of *X*" sometimes in lieu of a personal name). Now, by decree, each adult male Turk had to take a surname for himself and his wife and this surname was to be put on their children and all descendants of them. Brothers often took different surnames, which obscured family relationships. Some men took names derived from their fathers, their own occupations, their original places of residence, and so on; the surnames were in the traditional western mode, for this naming was a westernizing move.

Gazi Mustafa Kemal was the leading spirit in all this. Gazi (Victor, a military title) Mustafa (with the added given name of Kemal, Perfect, which an admiring teacher had bestowed on him when he was young) received by legislative fiat the unique surname of Atatürk (Father of the Turks). He became Kemal Atatürk and, like leaders such as Hitler, Stalin, and Tito, was often known only by new surname. His wife and (adopted) daughters got another surname. Some of his generals took as surnames the names of places where they had triumphed over the forces of the Sultan and brought down the weakened old Ottoman Empire (nicknamed "The Sick Man of Europe" by the foreign powers that hoped to carve it up). Before the collapse of the Ottoman Empire there was plenty of fighting.

Along with name change came other language change: Turkish people henceforth would have to write their language in a new modified Roman alphabet. The Turkish language previously used Arabic script, common throughout Islam because of their holy book, The Koran. In this new Romanized script (with some accents) Turks were to write those new forenames and inheritable surnames that made them look like westerners, although most of their country is not in Europe but in Asia. Will Turkey become a Middle Eastern power or part of the European Union? It seems to want to be part of the EU and to be a model for secular Islamic states also.

Turkey still has on the map of two continents some of the oldest placenames of the world. Because of the focus of this book, it is not personal names but placenames that I shall briefly deal with here. Turkey's history, with the rise and fall of a number of empires in addition to the Ottoman Empire (named for one Osman), is replete with personal names and placenames generated by a surprising number of peoples. Many of the oldest placenames, because of the Turkish revolution of the twentieth century, have been changed. Thus names you may know, such as Antioch, Smyrna, Adrianople, Hallicarnassus, and even Constantinople are no longer on the maps.

The switch from Arabic script to that modified Roman script is now well over half a century old. Western scholars can somewhat more easily cope with the ancient and difficult language. The modern secular republic of Turkey has become increasingly important in world affairs, standing as it does at a kind of world crossroads, but largely because of the reading difficulty there was no adequate study in English of Turkish names. So I wrote *Turkey: Names and Naming Practices* and in a *Festschrift* for a friend, the distinguished names scholar Prof. W. F. H. Nicolaisen, I also authored a brief article (*Names* 47, 1999) on names in Turkey. That article I present in a somewhat altered form here as a way of concluding a book on placenames with a piece on an exotic country's placenames. This article can well illustrate certain useful aspects of the study of placenames. It will point up two facts. One, that politics can wipe long-established placenames right off the map and replace even very famous names with new ones. Two, and this may not have come to your mind, learning how to translate those new placenames and what places used to be called will assist you to understand the people and their history, the classical world and the modern.

This cannot be a full discussion of the large question of Turkish language reform in the twentieth century. It can, nevertheless, do something to make a reader better informed about the names on the land in Turkey which the reader may see on the map or possibly in person in these days when the attractiveness of the country and its people and the affordability of tourism there encourages a great number of foreigners to visit the sights of Turkey. Discussing the placenames of this large country is somewhat simplified by the fact that a very great many of the placenames need no gloss. They are descriptive. Anyone who knows the language, or consults a Turkish dictionary, can make out most of the names now in use, if not those that were famous when Turkey was *Magna Græcia* (Greater Greece) or the Roman province of *Asia Minor* (Lesser Asia).

Atatürk's revolution was designed to make Turkey a more Turkish as well as a more modern country. He determined that Turkish, now spoken from Sinkiang to Skopje, would prevail. Constantinople, named for that Constantine who was emperor of the Byzantines, was renamed İstanbul. Along with this came many other changes. For instance, consider Gordium, famous for the Gordian Knot. (That was a puzzle designed to test the ingenuity of any potential ruler, rather like the sword in the stone of King Arthur's time.) Characteristically, Alexander the Great disdained to fiddle with the knotty problem. He simply cut the Gordian Knot with his sword. Gone! But Gordium is also gone. It is now the (ruined) village of Yassi Hoyük. Caria (known for Carian marble) is buried under the placename Milas. You probably have heard of the king of Caria called Mausolus; he gave us *mausoleum*. (The monument has been almost completely taken away to a foreign museum, as have too many archeological treasures of Turkey.) Byzantium (which gave us *byzantine*) and Pergamon or Pergamum (which gave us *parchment*) are gone. Today you can see Bergama. You have heard of Mt. Ararat (where Noah's ark is still being sought). The name is gone, replaced by Agri Daği. You have heard of The Hellespont (which Lord Byron famously swam in imitation of a classical lover, Leander); today you see Canakkale on the map. The old name is gone. You have heard of Antioch, where St. Peter first used the word equivalent to *Christian.* The place is now Antalyka. Ephesus, where St. Paul of Tarsus walked, is now Efès. Even the name of Troy, of the Trojan war, has disappeared; it is now Truva. There is a (not very large) wooden horse there, if you manage to find the place. There are famous places all around you in Turkey but today you must know their new names if you want to seek them out.

Here I shall in the first part comment on a considerable number of ancient names and discuss the nature and impact of their recent Turkish substitutes. In the second part the examination of Turkish placenames will bring us up to date and, noting that modern commemorative names are comparatively few, will offer a small and select lexicon of Turkish geographical terms that will greatly assist the average person who reads about or travels in modern Turkey. This will enable any person to decode a lot of placenames. With the old and the new placenames of Turkey briefly treated in this way, the toponymy (placename cover) of what at first may seem to be a "barbarous" land, and a baffling names problem, will appear far less inscrutable or forbidding. You will see the Turks "up close and personal," and that adds to international understanding and your personal growth.

Further, this is an examination of a county whose placenames for thousands of years were difficult for westerners. That was because the names were written in a script very few westerners could spell out or pronounce. The new script may encourage the salutary belief that knowing something about the placenames of a country about which you may read, or even visit, is not only useful but not as daunting as might first appear. You need to be made aware that, with a short list of basic words of its placenames (and a few of the old titles of the Ottoman Empire that still appear in commemorative placenames), understanding and getting around that country is both possible and pleasurable.

Let us now turn to names that the educated person might well know from some classical education that, unfortunately, now is not of much use. Reference to the goddess Lekto (who had a shrine there) is now not under Lekto; the place is now called Babakale (Papa's Fortress). Former Daphne is now Harbiye. Our Santa Claus was a St. Nicholas who was, in the fourth century of our era, bishop of Myra. But Myra is now Demre. Hadrian, the Roman emperor, had Hadrianopolis (the Greek for "city" ends the word) named for him. Later the place became Adrianople (Hadrian's city). Now it is the major Turkish city in the European part of the country. All reference to the Emperor Hadrian is gone. The place is now called Edirne. Germaniceia, named in honor of a Roman who triumphed in Germanic lands, is now Marquasi. Theodosiopolis (for the Byzantine Empress Theodosia) is now Ezurum. Pompeiopolis (once also known as Solis) is now Vuran Šehir. Cæsarea is now a little less recognizable as Kayseri, while Cæsarea ad Anazarbus is Anavarza, the *cæsar* gone completely. Neocæsarea is Niksar. Diocæsarea (once also known as Olbia) is Urzuncaburç. There was once a Sebastiopolis, but now it is Sulusaray: a martyred saint has given way to a mere waystation (*serai*, a word that gave us *caravansary*, is the place where caravans paused). The Byzantine Greeks renamed a place Stavropolis (City of The Cross). Gone, along, by the way, with many Greeks who once lived in Turkey. (There were both efforts to drive Greeks out and efforts to exchange populations with Greece. Both movements reduced the Greek element in the Turkish populaton.)

In Turkey there once were many places that one of the generals of Alexander the Great called Antioch, after the general's father. One of these remains but now you know it is no longer called Antioch. The Antioch of Pisidia is now Yalvaç. Another general, Seleucis, created a dynasty. A whole Turkish empire (the Seleucid) was named for him. Today *Seleucid* is a term used only in architecture, describing a beautiful and intricate style of long ago. Seleucia Pera is Čevilik and Seleucia in Isauria is Silifke.

Of the many places named for Alexander the Great, very little is left. Considering his immense impact, the paucity of Alexander names is really amazing. Inhabited places tended to be renamed as different powers took them over. We still have Alexandria Troas in Turkey, in the area called The Troad, (where the various cities built one upon the other at the site of Troy once stood) but it retains this Alexandria name because it is a ruin, uninhabited. Only one great arch still stands, though it is still strong. (I have stood on top of it because there was no keeper or anyone else to tell me not to try that. The ruins are out of the way and visitors are few.) A city called after Alexander was later given the name Alexandretta (Little Alexandria) by Italians, but now the Turks have given it the Turkish version of "Alexander," which is İskanderun. Through trade with the Venetian Republic, and sometimes marriage with Italians (even by sultans), there was an Italian influence in Ottoman times, but it has now been almost completely expunged in the placenames if not in the Turkish vocabulary.

We might note in passing a couple of facts about renaming. First, uninhabited and ruined places tend to keep old names while inhabited places may not. Second, there were all those places in Turkey named for Alexander and his generals but the names often repeated created little or no confusion. This was because in the old days communications between them were poor and there were many warlords, fiefdoms, little kingdoms, empires coming and going (including the Khazar Empire, the Kipchak Empire, the Seljuk Empire, the dominion of the Golden Horde achieved by the Scythian shepherd who rose to become Timur the Lame, whom we call Tamburlaine, and many others), and each poltical unit could have its own names, as we can have a Washington in many different states. If a place with a name that was repeated elsewhere became rather prominent, you could always call it Cæsarea ad Anazarbus to distinguish it from another Cæsarea or (say) call your city Seleucia Pera, indicating the territory where it was. A dozen places named the equivalent of *Antioch* in ancient Turkish lands were possible. In modern Turkey a dozen such cities would not be totally impossible (there could be departments as in France or states as in the US, etc.); but the Turks have now to deal with a single Antioch only. And they want it to be named in Turkish. It is, actually, close to Syria and it is, in fact, the only place in all of Turkey where I noticed any significant Arabic script (other than in religious connections, old inscriptions, and so on) and not much of that. Antalyka is very Turkish, as are all Turkish places. I had to look hard to find a Roman Catholic church in a city where that denomination was once very prominent, not a denomination but *the* Christian church. Such a foreign religion is not regarded as adequately Turkish. Atatürk's slogan was that one ought to be proud to be a Turk. Every Turk is. The renaming of places is part of that. The problems with the Kurds relate to that.

The renaming, however, means that Nicæa, well known in Christianity for the Nicæan Creed, is now İznik. Another great early council of the Christians was held at Chalcedon (AD 431); today the place is called Kadikoy. Teos, Tuspa, and other places long abandoned retain ancient names of no terrific importance while Nicæa and Chalcedon, for example, have lost their names and their Christian connections. Places where St. Peter or St. Paul preached, where the

223

Blessed Virgin is said to have lived, where St. John wrote his gospel, have lost their old names and the Turks therefore tend to forget the Christian heritage and the fact that the Eastern Roman Empire of Byzatium flourished with its capital named for Constantine. It was Constantine who, they said, seeing a cross in the sky converted his empire to Christianity. Justinian ordered built one of the greatest churches of Christendom—later a mosque and more recently a tourist attraction in İstanbul. The Greeks called the great church Hagia Sophia (Holy Wisdom). There is nothing Greek or Christian about it today. The sultans ruled from Topkapi, a palace in what is now İstanbul. The vast palace, with its Sublime Porte and all its treasures, stands by the Bosphorus. It is not like the huge Europeanized palace of the "Sunken Garden" on the other side of the water. Topkapi has a number of small buildings and reminds us that the original emperors ruled from a collection of tents. On the whole, the rooms are not of palatial size, though rich and grand.

The Turkish capital today is not İstanbul but Ankara (where the huge monument to Atatürk is a major feature and whose revolution suggested that city was central). The new name, Ankara, causes us to miss the former connection in English with the fine wool we call angora. (The Turks call angora *tifliz*.)

Other names famous in the classical past but replaced now include the following: Philadelphia (Ataşehir), Sardis (Sart), Hallicarnassus (Bodrum), Harran (Aktinbasak), Metropolis (Ayzazynköyu), Prienne (Gulbache), Nicomedia (Koaeli), Tralles (Aydin), Smyrna (İzmir), and Edessa (Šanliurfa). Şanliurfa is the modern name of a very ancient city that Alexander the Great renamed Edessa. At one point Şanliurfra was simply Urfa (East) but then it received an honorary prefix (Renowned) as a result of its loyalty to the revolution of the nineteen-twenties. Urfa was a name the locals were proud of. Over the centuries they had had so many name changes that they ordinarily, perhaps, would not have wanted another. But—and this is significant— there was something special. The city of Aintab and (later, yielding to local pronunciation, which can also change placenames, you know) Antep had come into national prominence for its brave performance in the overthrow of the Ottomans. For that, Antep became Gaziantep (Victorious Antep). So Urfa wanted its own proud title too. That was rather like the USSR adding a glorious extra to the name of Stalingrad because of its dogged defense, and great sacrifices, in the Great Patriotic War. Of course in time Stalingrad's name changed, for Stalin went and with Stalinism went the name Stalingrad. Today Leningrad is back to being St. Petersburg, and the USSR is no more. Turkic peoples in some of the former autonomous constituent states of the Soviet Union are now pressing for changes, among them placename changes.

All through recorded history changes have swept back and forth across the country of the Turks and the Turkomen and other Turkic peoples. Movement has been constant ever since the original Turks (whose name derives from Chinese and who came into such areas as Anatolia from the Far East) arrived, driven westward by upsets at home, settling in what is now Turkey. With the build-up of the great Ottoman Empire over centuries names changed. With its final collapse in the twentieth century names changed.

We have all through this book seen how placenames were changed to reflect demographic changes and particularly to claim new ownership. Names on the land, encountered by invaders, were often changed, sometimes translated into a new language but perhaps more often replaced with something more expressive of the nostalgia of the new people for where they came from or new plans or hope for where they had arrived. As I said, one empire after another existed up to that of the Ottoman sultans. The long line of sultans began with the warlike Osman, reached its zenith (an Arabic word) in the reign of Suleiman the Magnificent, and declined into office holders who were far less successful and even less secure. One of the late sultans kept pistols handy in every room in which he lived. Another gave lavish banquets but would eat nothing but an egg prepared by his mother and delivered to him with her seal guaranteeing that no one had got to it to poison it. All along, sultans worried about retaining power as Commanders of the Faithful, military as well as religious leaders. Some upon achieving power executed all rivals. The Turk, people used to say, could tolerate "no brother near the throne." Sultans held precarious thrones. Much power, nonetheless, resided in the mother of the sultan and in certain eunuchs of the harem and other court officials. Sometimes a sultan was little more than a prisoner in his palace. But the names of the sultans were put on buildings and cities and the names of women and enuchs were, traditionally, not.

The territory over which the sultans ruled at the height of empire covered a vast area and included peoples of different races and cultures. But the Ottoman Empire, which united them all eventually, like all the other empires, fell.

The history of Turkey goes back way before the Ottomans, way back before recorded history. Some tools of the Neolithic Age have been found in modern Turkey. There are the remains of settlements of later times such as the Bronze Age. There are remnants of once thriving Assyrian trade colonies, great Hittite walled cities, the remains of hegemonies of Phrygian, Lydian, Urartrian, Ionian, Carian, Lycian, Persian, Greek, Roman, Byzantine, Seljuk, crusader and Ottoman and other empires. Each power had its own placenames; each left some marks upon the land. At Çatal Höyuk (the second part of whose name makes it clear it was just a village), southeast of Konya (an ancient capital of Turkey), is a Neolithic site that is claimed to be the oldest human settlement ever found (unless perhaps you want to argue for Jericho, or can locate the Garden of Eden). There once was a flourishing city of Kanesh, but that Hittite stronghold is now aptly called Kultepe (Pile of Ashes). Every place has a name or many names and every name has a story, though sometimes the story is lost.

We miss the least when the placename changes are minor as with these: Sinope (now Sinop), Çeramos (now Keramos), Anamurium (now Anamur), Didyma (which once boasted one of the greatest temples of the ancient world, that to Apollo, now Didim). Miletus was shortened to Milet. Mylassa became Mylas. Milidia became Malatya. Prusa (for the great king Prusias) became Bursa, which rather puts Prusias out of the picture. Taurus became Yorus. Trapezus became Trabzon, though we continue to call it in the English tradition Trebizond (and Sir Winston Churchill refused to stop saying Constantiople even after the name İstanbul was adopted, and common in English without the accent that indicates an "ee" sound at the start, Churchill's argument being that foreigners had no right to tell Englishmen what words to use in their own language). The French put in place certain long-lasting placenames, such as The Dardanelles. A lot of history is involved in the existence of a French-inspired name there.

Some more information, such as that classical cities were turned into Islamic fortresses, is contained in such name changes as that of Thyatira becoming Akhisar (White Fort), Andriace becoming Dalyanagazi (Dalyana the Victorious), Arsamæia of Nymphalos becoming Eskikale (Old Castle), and Cibyria becoming Gölhisar (Lake Fort). Military might was the key to the success of the Ottoman Empire. The way it operated was to advance into a territory, subdue it by arms—the Turks were in the great cavalry tradition of Ghengis Khan and the Mongols—build a big fort or strengthen the walls of the captured city, and defend it. Then the sultan would order that a big mosque be built at the place. Mosques, you must know, are complete community centers, for in addition to a place to pray they usually have a school, some business properties (whose rents pay for the upkeep of the whole complex), a soup kitchen, even a hospital (an Arab invention which armies in the east brought back to Europe after knights hospitallers were created in the crusades). This community center construction brought to the site hordes of workmen, with their families, and many of them stayed on after the construction job was done, forming the nucleus of a new citizenry. In this way strong positions, commanding large areas of country, were established and the power of the sultans and the religion of Islam were spread.

In this security, trade flourished. Trust among followers of Islam facilitated an elaborate banking system that made it unnecessary for actual money to be carried from place to place: you could be given money or goods in one place and a letter to another place would see to it that the appropriate amount would be deducted from your account, or you could deposit money or goods at one place and get credit at home and be able to travel back without cash or fear of being robbed. The Knights of St. John of Jerusalem, starting out as knights hospitaller in the crusades, established a credit something like this between east and west. The knights grew so rich as bankers that they controlled monarchs who had to borrow and were themselves eventually destroyed by the king of France, who envied their wealth and power. (The Knights of St. John of Jerusalem are also often called, from a headquarters they once established, the Knights of Malta.) These knights were accused of heresies (probably because they had picked up some other Islamic ways) and even (falsely, very likely) accused of idol worship (of Baphomet), but it was really their money that enemies were after. The knights had grown immensely rich on east-west trade.

Traders from all over were welcomed to the Ottoman *han* (trading post). Under Islam, all races and peoples were considered equal or at least tolerable and in the Ottoman Empire, for instance, a number of very high positions were held by Jews who had been expelled from the Iberian Peninsula and elsewhere. Under Islam, Christians and Jews got along well together, though the sultan was the caliph (deputy) of God and Mohammed was His Prophet. So strong was the religion that it was said that if you had 100 sons you ought to name all of them Mohammed (presumably with another name as well, for convenience). Many persons' forenames were religious (some derived from the numerous Names of God or the names of relatives and friends of The Prophet) and all Muslims prayed, and pray to this day, five times a day, as you will see all over the so-called secular republic of Turkey. What is not in evidence in Turkey is the rule of mullahs or the imposition of Islamic law. Atatürk saw to that in an early move in the war between Islamic fundamentalism and modernism (which will be a highly disruptive battle for most of the twenty-first century, it seems). Placenames everywhere in Turkey reveal both the religious and the secular interests. Placenames everywhere are affected by the results of religious and religio-political upheavals. The Turks and their mercenaries established and defended the Ottoman Empire by force of arms and went out to spread the faith. At one point they got as far west as Vienna.

In Turkey's secular republic the sultan is gone, the caliphate has moved, and the charge to defend the holy places of Islam (Mecca and Medina) has passed to the government of Saudi Arabia, a fact that is causing a notable amount of political unrest in the region, unrest that is spreading to involve the rest of the world. The very name *Mecca,* the place of pilgrimage, has immense political power, and the faithful who make the pilgrimage (wealthy Saudis have improved facilities to meet the needs of millions) get a name change that marks their fulfillment of that religious duty (once in a lifetime for any Muslim who can possibly afford it).

Placenames also remind us of such classical antiquities as the Chimera (now called Yanartas, Burning Rock) and the great library of Ephesus and much more. Once in a while we come upon a strange name story. One example is the name Kaunos. The Turks invented a god called Kaunos (supposedly a son of Apollo) so that a shrine dedicated to him could be set up in competition with the very successful (commercially as well as culturally, of course) shrines to Apollo such as that at Didyma (Didim) and Delphi. The names of deities, by the way, are often extremely interesting. They may reflect the process of anthropomorphizing certain qualities, deities being very often not personages recognized Out There but projections of things human beings feel inside or comments on natural objects and forces people experience.

Because certain places of pilgrimage and sacrifice to deities were famous so were certain areas known for certain products (which could result in placename transference) and, in the case of Lydia, the Lydian mode in music. Lydia was the kingdom of the rich King Midas (of the Midas Touch). Telemessos in Lydia is now significantly called Fethiye (Conquest). Its ruins are especially sad.

Aegius became Erciyes Daği (the second word meaning "mountain" as you may have noted with the name of Mt. Ararat). Phoenicus became Finike, Therepeia became Tarabya, Magnesia ad Sipylus became Manisa, Attaleia became Antalya, and Iconium became the grand city of Konya, where there are some ancient buildings with striking names and captivating histories.

Antiphellus became Kaš. The new name is pronounced KOSH not KASH, but real change in the Antiphellus of old may be seen in the fact that there is a tourist trap there now called Kas 'n Carry. That names depends on English speakers not saying the name of the town correctly, ignoring, that is, *š* that introduces an "sh" (as the *ç* makes the sound "ch"). Assos became Beyrhamkale (that *kale* always refers to fortifications) and Heiropolis (now a necropolis and ghost town, but much visited because it is right across the road from a livelier tourist attraction) became Pamukkale (Cotton Castle). The reference there is to the billowy white deposits of mineral from the hot waters that flow down the hillside. They look like cotton—or they did, to someone, and in the same way we in the US got unusual placenames such as Monkeys Eyebrow. Canada has Skir Dhu (from Scotland) and Seven Pence Ha'penny Brook (Nova Scotia) so odd names are not a US specialty and, in fact, "poetic" names such as Monkey's Eyebrow are to be found in every country to one extent or another, although Turkish names are "easy" because the Turks tend to be very direct (and easily translatable) in naming, which is principally why I chose Turkey for this particular section, along with its wipe-out of famous classical placenames.

Some of the great cities of the ancient world fell into decline without becoming principally cities of tombs. Simena became simply the village by the Muslim castle, which is what *Kaleköy* means. Pamphilian is mere Perge ruins. Xanthos is a ruin at Kinik. Peristrema has abandoned churches at Ilhara. Sardis, where King Croesus was famous for his wealth, is no longer really on the map. But look for Sart, as I told you. It will not, unfortunately, give you any idea of the glories of ancient Sardis. In Ephesus you can see, as in Italy at Herculaneum and Pompei, etc., a whole city of the ancient world, albeit in ruins. At some of the many classical sites in Turkey there is far less to see, maybe just a few broken columns in a field, stones that you may not even recognize as part of some wonderful old edifice. Some ruins impress mostly by their extent, such as the walls and gates of the largest Hittite city, where there is little else and the names are lost. Yes, there is a Lion Gate (now so named because of the decoration), but no one can say whether anything like Lion Gate was the actual name when the huge city lived within the eight (some say ten) kilometers of walls. Nearby is a little Turkish town of which most of the population is away most of the time, working, for there is little or no work to be had there.

Many Turks, you may know, go abroad to work. When my scant Turkish gave out, I was often able to converse with the locals in my pitiful scraps of German or even French because some family members had been *Gästarbeiten* (guest workers—come, work, and get out) in Germany or elsewhere. Some people I met knew German also because of German archeologists working in Turkey. Various US teams have worked there too, but American (except for *OK* and some teenage slang the disco-goers have picked up) is basically unknown outside the big cities. There the rug dealers especially have learned to do business in American and a surprising number of other languages. There are whole streets in some places where you can speak American in any shop. The English-language spread due to the international youth movements and popular music and films has hit Turkey, of course, but it chiefly affects the young. In time it may change a lot of things.

Inevitably there has been even more alteration in minor names such as the names of streets (and sometimes districts that took their names from streets or notable single buildings or concentrations of shops, etc.). *La Grande Rue de Pera*—French was fashionable in nineteenth-century Constantinople, and one French cutie caught the eye of the sultan—is now İstikal cadessi. Politicians have been honored in various street names and Atatürk may have more than one street named for him in a town, besides the inevitable monument in the central square. That is only to be expected. He is revered in Turkey. It is illegal to defame him.

What is less easily explicable is why, for example, Sepetçi became Beyaz Altin (White Gold). Prostanna became Akrotiti (High Place) then Egridir then Egidir (because *egridir* is "crooked" and *egidir* is "sweet"). The best change of all transformed Çirincke (Ugliness) to Sirince (Pleasantness). To appreciate changes like that one has to know more of the language (but you could always look in a pocket dictionary) than I count on here. And it won't help you to know placenames such as The Bosphorus, The Dardanelles, The Golden Horn, or The Sublime Porte; the Turks do not use those terms, any more than Italians have ever used such placenames as Rome, Leghorn, or Milan. Those are English inventions.

Now here is the little language lesson that will equip you with the key to the majority of Turkish placenames. You need to know these few terms and how to pronounce them. You already know about *c* and *s*. The *c* with no accent is pronounced like English *j* and there are two versions of English *i*. The one with the dot in Turkish sounds like "ee," as you saw with İstanbul. Thus *cami* is "JAM-ee" and blue jeans are called *blucin.* The *ğ* you will surely notice. Between vowels the letter is not pronounced but affects the vowels on either side of it, while at the end of a word such as *dağ* (which you learned means mountain) it is sounded like English *j*. So Nemrut Dağ is Mt. Nimrod. Turkish sprinkles umlauts all over vowels, but you know how they work from other languages. Turkish has vowel harmony and agglutination and a number of other strange features, but you do not have to worry about that. You may even see in the list that follows some cognates with languages you know: notice *plaj* is from French *plage*. (Turkish has a considerable number of words from French, chiefly luxury items and leisure activities.) Soldier on now with the following.

At first this lot may appear not only strange but too difficult to learn, but really that is not the case. You always pick up at least some new words whenever you travel in exotic places and you might as well have a grip on a set of words that will be truly useful to you. Yes, the foreign words for "yes" and "no" and "please" and "thank you" are naturally helpful when you travel, but what I am suggesting here is that the nature of Turkish placenames is such, whether they are used of buildings and streets or villages, towns, cities, or natural, geographical features, are going to rely very heavily on a comparatively simple basic vocabulary and that if and when you master that vocabulary you will greatly improve your ability to appreciate where you are and will get a great deal more information off the maps that, of course, are essential in any tourist's pocket or purse or knapsack

Get the following place-related terms by heart. Other words will crop up that you can find in your pocket dictionary, but these words that follow you will find are so common that you really need to be able to translate them without going to your little dictionary. Some, once you say them aloud, will look more familiar than you think! Throughout this book packed with names I have not asked you to memorize anything, but this once I say: learn these words and go and enjoy the place where they are used in so many placenames. This much palaver has been to build your confidence. Now build your new Turkish vocabulary!

Column 1		Column 2		Column 3	
bahçe	garden	*iskele*	dock	*nev*	new
banyo	swimming place	*kale(si)*	fort, citadel	*ören*	ruin
bedesten	warehouse	*kapi*	gate (of a walled city)	*orman*	forest
bir	one	*hamam(i)*	bath	*ova(si)*	plain

bulvari	boulevard	*hasatanesi*	hospital	*pazzari*	bazaar
cadessi	street	*hisar*	fort	*plaj*	beach
çarši	market	*kaplica*	spa	*saray(i)*	waystation palace
češmi	spring, fountain	*kilise(se)*	church	*šehir*	market, town
chora	rural area	*kiman*	port	*soguk*	street
dağ(i)	mountain	*konaği*	mansion	*sokak*	street
deniz	sea	*köpr*	bridge	*tabhane*	hostel
dödenler	falls	*köy*	village	*tatil köyu sitesi*	holiday village site
eski	old (not used of a person)	*küle*	tower	*tersane*	shipyard
garaji	garage	*kümbet*	tomb (above ground)	*türbe*	tomb
göl(u)	lake	*mağara*	cave	*ulu*	large, great
güzel	beautiful	*mahalle*	neighborhood	*vilayet*	province, department
iki	two	*manasteri*	monastery	*yayla*	nomads' summer village

il(i)	province	medydan(i)	public square	yeni	new
ilica	hot spring	mezarlik	necropolis	yeri	place
imaret	soup kitchen (of a mosque)	nehir	river		

Add useful words such as *büyük* (big, the main branch of the river Meander, which gave us a verb in English—is Büyük Menderes) and *kücük* (small, a palace on the Bosphorus is called Kücük Su, Small [by the] Water). As in any language, the polite words should be in your vocabulary and will help with asking questions about placenames, etc. The names of colors often turn up in descriptive placenames. The Turks tend to stress white, green, black, red, blue, and yellow, mostly in that order of frequency. *Ak* (white) occurs in a lot of placenames. *Yesil* (green, the color associated with The Prophet but also seen in scenery, tiles, etc.) is frequent. Rebellious Kurds call the city of Diyanbakir (which much earlier was known as Amida) Kara (Black), and there is elsewhere a Kara Ada (Black Island) and Kara occurs in a number of nicknames, etc., for the people are dark-haired, dark-eyed. You know there is a famous Blue Mosque (from the color of the decorative tiles) and you may have heard of the Green Mosque of the Sufis, etc. You need to know numbers for such placenames as Dortkilisi (Four Churches). You do not need to know Arabic, though Arabic script is required to read all sorts of old writing from that used in architectural decoration and on tombstones— which used to have turban tops to indicate the rank of the deceased—to embroideries on the palls on the coffins of the celebrated. But you do need to know the modern alphabet. Turkish has 29 letters, some with extra accents, as you have noticed, but no *q,w,* or *x.* Foreign names may be respelled in Turkish placenames to approximate their pronunciation and on occasion can be far enough from the original that you may not be able to determine who is being commemorated, especially if it happens to be some Frenchman or some German of whom you never heard in the first place.

With the admittedly limited and subjective word list I have given you, you can translate literally thousands of Turkish placenames. You will, for instance, see that Uludağ is Big Mountain (even if you do not discover that it used to be Mt. Olympos) and Uludeniz is Big Sea. You will not, of course, recognize Dicle (the Tigris) or Asi (the Euphrates) in their new guises.

It will also be helpful for you to know not simply some common forenames (the only way important people were known up until the twentieth century) but the fact that with those often come, before or after the name of men (there are few women noted, and they tend to have pretty names such as Yildiz, "Star"), a title from the old Ottoman Empire. Many titles, unlike the English custom, followed the name (suggesting that they were added to the person) but exceptions to this rule were important titles such as *Aya, Gazi, Sankta,* and *Sultan,* and, occasionally, *Baba* (though you know Ali Baba of the Forty Thieves). Sometimes in placenames Gazi follows the name but it usually precedes it, as you saw with Gaziantep. Here are Ottoman titles no longer used for persons but remaining on places, streets, etc.:

Aga Sir
Ata Father, also a general term of respect
Aya Saint
Baba Father (Papa, used for saints and others)
Bey Lord (pronounced BY, by the way, not BAY)
Efendi Sir
Emir Governor (often a military title)
Fatih Sultan Commander of the Faithful
Gazi Victor (a title for winners of important battles)
Hatun Lady
Hidiv Khedive (a military leader—the British made Lord Kitchener Khedive of Egypt)
Padašah Great King, Emperor
Paša General (in English we spell it as in Glubb Pasha and in old books Basha)
Šah King, in English Shah
Sankta Saint (there are saints in the Islamic as well as other religions)

With these terms you can make sense of placenames such as Sultanahmet, Osmangazi, and Dr. Emin Paša Sokak. Notice that while Sultanahmet is a single word sometimes the titles are joined to, sometimes separated from, the personal name. All personal names and all surnames, have meanings; they can all be translated because there are no names that are "just names." If you see a placename with or without a title but with the forename given as well as the surname that is because the surname alone would be misleading (as in our Dr. Martin Luther King, Jr., Boulevard rather than King Boulevard, an example cited much earlier in this book). Thus we find Adnan Menderes as a placename to make sure a figure of political life is recognized in the name. Menderes alone would, in fact, refer just to the famous river (from which the statesman took his surname).

As is true everywhere else, history is contained in the commemorative placenames, but the foreigner will probably not have heard of many people the Turks honor by name. The problem is exacerbated when Mezraa became Maruretulaziz (confusingly the two names of that governor were run together for a start) and then the name went to Elaziz and then to Elazig, so that in effect the name of the person commemorated was quite lost. Politics can put some names out of favor as well as in favor. And old names may cling even when officially altered. For example, in İstanbul there is a Kennedy cadessi for our assasinated president (for whom there seems to have been a vigorous campaign to put his name on places all around the world as well as on many US places). But you may find that the locals call it Sahil Yolu because it runs (as in Trabizon or Trabzon, where there is a similar Kennedy road) beside the water. When, as can happen in Turkey, you run into people who cannot read their own or any other language, what you point to on the map makes no sense to them. You must deal in the placenames they may have used from time immemorial whatever officialdom says the placenames ought to be. You may find yourself asking, "Which way to the village that has the museum where the things that were dug up around here are kept?" rather than "Where is such-and-such?"

You will also find that certain long streets change their names several times as they run along even if they go in a straight line. A street in İstanbul, for example, that runs from the palace of Topkapi to the Covered Bazaar, etc., has a number of names, each redolent of history. Leaving the gate of Topkapi you set off toward Aya Sophia (Hagia Sophia) on Millet cadessi, which then becomes Ordu cadessi and then Yaniçeriler cadessi and then the Divan Yolu. That is Divan Road, and the Divan was the high council of the sultan; they sat on a kind of sofa while the sultan sat on a throne, or squatted on a low platform, accompanied by his chief minister, the vizier. The walk along this street (or streets if you think each name change warrants calling it a new street) will bring to mind through the names the governing classes and the Hordes and the New Soldiers, which we call Janissaries. This is just a small part of the 8000-year history of Turkey and along the way you will encounter The Pudding Shop, a bit of history of the hippies of the sixties who paused here on their way even farther east.

Kennedy's name is an example of modern history and of a foreign name that is recognizably rendered. However, you may run into the likes of Sanšo-Panšo (who is our paunchy friend Sancho Panza from *Don Quixote*). He gets his name on at least one restaurant. British and American names turn up often on establishments catering to the tourist trade. In Sultanahmet in İstanbul there is that Pudding Shop (whose Turkish name is translated Tulip), still around from the old days when hippies passed through on The Magic Bus on their way to druggy nirvanas in Katmandu and elsewhere. Nearby is The Vitamin restaurant. In Bodrum you find a disco with the old name of the city but in other places the disco is probably in English or otherwise "cool." In Bodrum a native remarked to me that Hallicarnassus was a strange name for a Bodrum Disco; he did not have any idea that Bodrum was once called Hallicarnasus. He did know the story of a certain princess, however, whose name was on another disco locally.

Americans traditionally say you should never eat in any place called Mom's (or play cards with anyone named Al) and to that I might add that when traveling abroad you should never patronize any place named in any language but the local language, certainly never your own language. You do not go to İstanbul to eat in a Pub; walk a few blocks more to a place named with the Turkish word for Cistern. It is a restaurant the government has established in what used to be the extensive underground water supply the Romans built for the area now called Sultanahmet. It is very elegant and, by US standards, inexpensive. And you can say you had a fancy meal in a cistern; it was for a time also, quite recently, a garage or chop shop, but the government redid it (in its ancient splendor) as a tourist attraction.

I can translate the names of Turkish establishments for you, and you may get some surprises. The dictionary can also help with street names such as Örücüler (Carpet Menders) and Yağçilar (Oil Merchants), etc., so it is useful to add to your vocabulary the Turkish for the likes of *silversmiths, coopers, darners, fruit merchants, confectioners, weavers, barbers,* etc. In the old days, and still, to a lesser extent, businesses of the same type tended to bunch together, which goes beyond lending local color and helpful street naming to providing excellent opportunities for price comparisons and haggling (with soccer, haggling is one of the great Turkish sporting activities). Another hint: any establishment with a view of the monument to Atatürk is located on the main square; prices are cheaper anywhere off that square, and you need not go far from the square to get them.

It is safe to wander anywhere, so take your street map and set off, looking up words in the dictionary, asking the names of things, soaking up the color, getting in touch with the culture, picking up a bit of the history. Atatürk cadessi is always at that *šehir* or principal market square and is always a main drag, though locally it may be called Biriniçi Cordon, First Street, as it were. Atatürk cadessi (and Gazi Mustafa Kemal bulvari, etc.) will have replaced some old name, usually. Nothing will ever have wiped that leader's name off. Turkey loves its hero.

This book has dealt so much with US and other places more or less familiar to you—to write about all the placenames would have been to have written the history of the world—that I decided to conclude with something "far out". I chose Turkey. Any country whose language you regard as forbidding, and whose writing system basically uses the Roman alphabet, would have done just as well. Placenames are not all that hard to understand, wherever you are, as long as you can read the letters. (Some Turkic languages are written in non-Roman scripts, it is true, but the modified Roman alphabet will serve you all over Turkey.)

Naturally not all or maybe not many of my readers will visit Turkey or even Mexico or Montreal, maybe not New Orleans, but if you do go, knowing something about the placenames will be good, and if you are just an armchair traveler, well, that is good, too. The best result of all travel away from home is returning to see where you live in a new and better light, and so even in books you can be stimulated to take an interest in the placenames of your own neighborhood (a fine assignment for school children but fine for adults as well), county, or country.

If and when you do venture abroad, go with a map and a dictionary in hand and you can learn a lot that will enliven your trip anywhere. I trust that if you go to Mexico the section here on the names of that country will clear up a lot of things for you, give you some history while you are getting some sun.

As the languages and toponymic practices of more and more countries are made known to us, names scholars can construct and test and improve theories about how and why placenaming operates. But ordinary people need not go into that. They can just keep their eyes and their guidebooks open. They can learn the names of people, places, and things and discover not only the uniqueness of each culture they encounter but the universals regarding what mankind (personkind, if you insist), the naming animal, chooses to name and how s/he names it.

Remember, as Confucius said, first we have to get the names right. If the names are not right, thinking will not be right, and the right things can never then be accomplished. That done, we can find, as Sir Francis Bacon once said, a wealth of delight in names of all kinds. An interest in personal names bespeaks an interest in people themselves and an interest in placenames can always enrich your experience wherever you live or travel.

And so you have come to the end of this book on placenames in many aspects. There is a piece about the author (with a lot of detail in which you may have no interest, but it does suggest the author's long-time concern with the topic, which is useful to know about in the modern world in which a crime or a catastrophe can cause a contract for a book to be inked the day after a gun goes off or a building falls down) and there is an index. Originally I argued that an index in a book in which names proliferate on almost every page would be ill-advised, raising the price greatly. The publishers saw the value of an index and insisted. These days, they said, people who consult books tend to sample rather than to read. I have tried to make my book readable, even engrossing, and I would like it to be read through—but there is an index. In the index you will find the names of all subjects, persons, periodicals, and books mentioned (which constitutes a kind of bibliography or guide to further investigation) but not all the placenames. There are, at least, all the personal names, and this will enable those who cry loudest for indexed books (that is scholars who hope to find their own names in print) will have to be content. To have included all individual placenames in addition to a detailed placenames entry would have made the index impossibly longer. Find individual placenames under relevant topics, countries, states, and, in some cases, cities. And read.

And consider always the importance of placenames on what a poet has called "significant soil," the particular places that each of us holds especially dear. These are the placenames that anchor your life and are most significant for you. Each of us lives in a personal world and has in her or his head a kind of unique map of what we think the real world to be.

I hope that this survey of various kinds of placenames, any section of which could have its approach applied to other places, cities, states, or countries, features, folklore, and all the rest, will serve the general reader and both amateur and professional readers until, at some very far distant date, the Place Name Survey of the United States will be available as the standard reference and similar references, probably online rather than in printed books, will exist for Canada, Mexico, and everywhere else. Meanwhile, The American Name Society's publications best serve the US scholarly community and I am especially grateful to ANS and its current journal editor (Prof. Edward Callary) for permission to revise my own material which has already appeared in *Names*, material that is the foundation of this present book, which concludes as it began with thanks to many scholars. This book of mine in its turn is if not the cornerstone then at least a brick to suggest the nature of the great unfinished edifice of placename scholarship.

THE END

Leonard R. N. Ashley

INDEX

This index is very detailed and very long: page 138 (for instance) yielded about 30 entries. This book differs from ordinary books on placenames (written chiefly by geographers and local historians) in that its immense erudition (if I may say so as author) ranges over English and world literature, folklore, linguistics in several languages, the history of various US and foreign places, in fact over many of the neglected aspects of toponymy, for a full understanding of placenames demands scope. Toponymy is too important to be left entirely to the geographers, cartographers, and government standardizers, valuable as those experts are. Placename study requires a lot more than a knowledge of official names on maps. It likewise is much more than a fascination with the humor in so-called funny names. Those two approaches have convinced the general public that placename study is either a boring bureaucratic science or a trivial hobby. Of course neither this book nor any other single book can cover all of the subject. I somewhat scant Canada (which has been well addressed by Alan Rayburn's collected articles and books by others, especially in relation to French Canada) and I pay special attention to Mexico, the US's partner in NAFTA and in other ways much connected to the US. But there are whole continents left for others to write about in terms of placenames, especially Europe (which I touch on only in connection with the British Isles) because on The Continent (as if there were but one) philologists have for centuries studied placename evidence. Other scholars can follow my example with other topics, the generics and designations of geographical features, names and naming customs, names official and informal in all languages of places, towns, counties, states, countries, the neglected topic of perception and the psychology of naming (most psychological interest has focused on the naming of persons), and so on. There are millions upon millions of placenames dead and current that could be studied. There are thousands of languages and all of history to consider, from Adam taking dominion over the other animals by naming them to the claiming, naming and renaming of territories and the way that sentiment casts a rosy light on certain loved placenames. Placenames in literature have also been neglected despite the fact that they often demonstrate as much creativity as the author's coining of character names. Prof. W. F. H. Nicolaisen's wise comment that all placenames in fiction are fictional has not yet been taken to heart by most literary onomasts. The London in Dickens or the Deep South of twentieth-century American novelists and short story writers are more or less as fictional as William Faulkner's Yoknapatawpha Co. (a Chickasaw placename). The geographers must learn more about culture as a whole and the literary critics more about geography and history. Their studies can be scientifically rigorous and also, as I demonstrate, presented in a popular, entertaining, memorable style.

239

I have written this and other names books for all readers, especially that general one, and I have here foregone appending a long bibliography. I suggest that serious researchers, who can find in printed sources or online any book or article with simply the author's name or the title, make use of the index provided as a place to start. I trust no one, scholar or not, will damn my book as unscientific or incomplete because it has nothing of what Sir W. S. Gilbert would call "merely corroborative detail added to give artistic verisimilitude to an otherwise bald and unconvincing narrative." It boasts scholarship aplenty. Listing anything beyond authors and titles actually mentioned would be supererogatory, impossible. The fact of the matter is that over several decades it must have taken thousands upon thousands of books and articles to make this book. I am naturally fully grateful to the authors of them all and to the participants of somewhere between a hundred and two hundred scholarly conferences involving placename studies which I have attended in the US and abroad.

❑

241

Leonard R. N. Ashley

Sanchez, Nellie v. d. Grift 216
Sancho Panza 234
Sansevaine, Pierre 201
Santa Anna, Gen. Antonio López de 182
Santa Claus 222
Santa Fe 185
Saudi Arabian holy places 227
Saunders, Ed 107
Savannah 137
Saye and Seal, Lord 13–14
Scarborough, Orlando C. 148
Scherer, Kess 169
Schmidt, Frank (of Frankfort) 79
scholars of California placenames 216, see also Bright, Sanchez, &c.
school curricula, names in 216
school name 214
Schoolcraft, Henry Rowe 30, 32, 139
Schultz, Charles 147
Scilly, Isles of 49
Scotland 138
Scott, Sir Walter 145, 148-149
Screws of the World, The, see *News of the World, The*
Seaport 113
Seattle 34
Seeman, Helene Zucker 99–100
Segovia, Antonio de 177
Sellers, Helen Earle 10, 12
Selling the Lower East Side 106, 112
Selucis and his empire 222
Serra, Junípero 168, 187
Serrano, Jose 212

Shaftesbury, Earl of 98 see Ashley Cooper, Anthony
Sheboygan folk etymology 137
Short Names or Long Ones 216
Shotover Hill origin 59
Sick Man of Europe, The 220
Siegfried, Alanna 99 – 100
significant soil 237, see also Montreal
Silicon Valley 214
Simon, Kate 97
simplicity 20, see also forenames
Sloane Rangers 176
Slyke, D. O. van 138
Smith, James "Cussin' Jim" 208
Smith, Richard "Bull" 138
SoCal 215
Soho (London) 97–98
SoHo (Manhattan) 99–100
SoHo News 102
SoHo Reporter 102
SoHo Weekly News see *SoHo News*
South Carolina 67, 135, 148–149
South Dakota 135
South Street Seaport (NYC) 113
Southey, Robert 45
Spanish 40, 79–81, 83, 126, 135, 159–161, 167–190, 203, 206
Spanish and Indian Place Names of California 216
Spanish in California 191–217
Spanish Placenames of California (Ashley) 191, 197
spelling 176, 201–202, 204–205, 209–210, 212, 214 see also Amerindian names,

256

ABOUT THE AUTHOR

Leonard R. N. Ashley, Ph.D. (Princeton), LHD (Columbia Theological, Hon.), is Professor *Emeritus* of Brooklyn College of the City University of New York, where he taught for nearly 35 years. He was earlier on the faculties of the University of Utah, the University of Rochester, and (part time) the New School for Social Research. He spent several years in the Royal Canadian Air Force where, as second assistant to the Air Historian, he wrote (for NORAD) the top-secret report on *The Air Defence of North America*. He has published extensively on literary onomastics (how names function in imaginative writing and in popular culture). Here he addresses names in their most scientific aspect, names of places, but he relates them to everyday life for the non-specialist reader.

Ashley's published works range from military history (collaboration on *A Military History of Modern China*, authorship of *Ripley's "Believe It Or Not" Book of The Military*) and critical biography *(Colley Cibber* and *George Peele)* to literary history (*Authorship and Evidence in Renaissance Drama* and *Elizabethan Popular Culture*) and linguistics (*What's in a Name?* and co-editorship of the proceedings of half a dozen international conferences he directed for The American Society of Geolinguistics—of which he has been repeatedly elected president since 1991). He is the author of numerous textbooks and anthologies such as *Other People's Lives, Mirrors for Man, Nineteenth-Century British Drama,* and *Tales of Mystery and Melodrama*. Recently he has written a series of ten books on the occult published by Barricade Books (New York) and reprinted by several British publishers and in Dutch and German translations. These books are: *The Complete Book of Superstition, Prophecy, and Luck; The Complete Book of Magic and Witchcraft; The Complete Book of Devils and Demons; The Complete Book of the Devil's Disciples; The Complete Book of Spells, Curses, and Magical Recipes; The Complete Book of Vampires; The Complete Book of Werewolves; The Complete Book of Dreams and What They Mean;* and *The Complete Book of Sex Magic*. He has published poetry in more than 60 "little magazines" and anthologies, more than 150 scholarly articles in journals, especially *Names* (the journal of The American Name Society, to whose executive board he has been continually re-elected for two decades and of which society he has been twice elected president). He refounded the Place Name Survey of the United States (on one of those two occasions he was president of The American Name Society) and contributed to Frank Abate's massive *Omni Gazetteer of the United States*. Ashley's regular *chronique,* reviewing books on The Renaissance, has been for more than 20 years a feature of *Bibliothèque d'Humanisme et Renaissance* (Geneva). His *Dictionary of Sex Slang*, in preparation for more than 20 years, is now in press. He has contributed to a great many standard works on literature such as Freedley & Reeves' *History of the*

Theatre, the series *Great Writers of the English Language, Readers Guide to World Drama, Reference Guide to American Literature, Encyclopedia USA, Encyclopedia of British Humorists, Encyclopedia of British Women Writers, Dictionary of Literary Biography, New Dictionary of National Biography,* and other reference books. He has edited *The Reliques of Irish Poetry, The Ballad Poetry of Ireland, Shakespeare's Jest Book,* and other works and has recently written on topics ranging from the diaries of Anaïs Nin (in *Anaïs: An International Journal*) to Victorian literature for boys (his *George Alfred Henty and the Victorian Mind*). Placenames especially fascinate him and he is able to add to what geographers bring his knowledge of literature and folklore.

Names of Places has companion volumes from this author called *Names in Literature, Art Attack: Essays on Names in Satire,* and *Names in Popular Culture.* As the ten volumes on the occult add up to a kind of encyclopedia of that subject, so the four books on names mentioned here add up to a set on the art and science of onomomastics to go along with Ashley's pioneering general survey of the whole field (*What's in a Name?*, 1989, revised 1995). Ashley has recently edited the previously unpublished placename studies of Prof. Allen Walker Read, the dean of American placename study who began with a study of some names on the land in Iowa as a master's thesis in 1926, in *America: Naming the Country and Its People.* Ashley's latest book is on geolinguistics (of which he is the foremost US scholar), *Language and Modern Society* (published in the UK, the US, and India). Forthcoming soon from Ashley are more on names (specialized books respectively on the placenames of Cornwall, Mexico, and Turkey, designed for travelers in those areas) and a major book on Scandinavian folklore and popular culture (with Ola J. Holten), years in preparation.

This present books also represents many years of research and writing, all of it here revised for the general reader and presented in an amusing, relaxed and personal style.

Printed in the United Kingdom
by Lightning Source UK Ltd.
102214UKS00001B/217